Modern Bride®
Wedding Celebrations

The Complete Wedding Planner
for Today's Bride

CELE GOLDSMITH LALLI

Editor-in-Chief of *Modern Bride*

and **STEPHANIE H. DAHL**

JOHN WILEY & SONS, INC.

NEW YORK · CHICHESTER · BRISBANE · TORONTO · SINGAPORE

Interior Design and Composition : Impressions Publishing Services

Cover Photo: Antoine Verglas/Phillipe Achard

Interior Illustration: Luann Roberts

MODERN BRIDE is a registered trademark of Reed Properties Inc. used under license by Cahners Publishing Company

In recognition of the importance of preserving what has been written, it is a policy of John Wiley & Sons, Inc. to have books of enduring value published in the United States printed on acid-free paper, and we exert our best efforts to that end.

This publication is designed to provide accurate and authoritative information in regard to the subject matter covered. It is sold with the understanding that the publisher is not engaged in rendering professional services in the subject matter discussed.

Library of Congress Cataloging-in-Publication Data

Lalli, Cele Goldsmith, 1933—

    Modern bride wedding celebrations : the complete wedding planner for

    today's bride / by Cele Goldsmith Lalli and Stephanie H. Dahl.

        p. cm.

    Includes index.

    ISBN 0-471-56882-1 (pbk.)

    1. Wedding etiquette. 2. Weddings—Planning. I. Dahl, Stephanie

H. II. Title.

BJ2051.L35 1992

395'.22—dc20   91-45504

Printed in the United States of America

10 9 8 7 6 5 4 3 2 1

Dedicated to
Michael Lalli and Clifford Dahl,
"the wind beneath our wings"

Acknowledgments

We would like to thank the following individuals who, through personal interviews, shared information, or practical assistance, have made this book possible:

Mrs. Rosa Lee Harker, Mr. Aaron Dahl, Miss Elyse Salman, Ms. Mary Ann Cavlin, Ms. Geri Bain, Mrs. Patricia Magloire Wolfe, Mr. & Mrs. Jules Erwin, Mrs. Anne Witkavitch Sagnelli, Ms. Nannette Poillon, Mr. John McCoy, Mr. & Mrs. William Gambino, Ms. Cynthia Lazarin, Ms. Gail Silva, Ms. Alice Cerniglia, Mr. Kaveh Keshvadi, Ms. Marcy L. Blum, Mr. Robbi Ernst III, Mr. Charles White, Mrs. Patricia Brenner, Mr. & Mrs. Jack Schacter, Ms. Verna Huson, Ms. Frances Fox, Miss Anita Gaylor, Mrs. Malinda Gaylor, Mrs. Jacquelynne O'Rourke, Mrs. Lydia Massa, Mr. Bob Moalli, Ms. Michele Piccione, Ms. Donna May Cammarotta, Ms. Eva Hofmann, Ms. Sylvia Weinstock, Mrs. Yvette Walker Hollis, Ms. Laurie Vaughn, Dr. Paul Dasher, Ms. June Becklin, Mrs. Lynn Ann Harvey Blank, Mrs. Betty Martinson, Mr. Andrew Flagg, Mr. Donald Paglia, Ms. Ellen Goldstein, Mr. Marv Tuttle, Mr. Ken Scott, Ms. Tambra Riggs, Mrs. Fran Moavero, Dr. Elizabeth Erwin, Mr. Nick Triffin, Rev. Benedict Tighe, Dr. & Mrs. Jaspal Mayell, Mrs. Bette Katzeff, Mr. Don LeFevre, Rev. Robert Weiss, Rev. Stanley Aronson, Mr. Robert Fickett, Rev. Bartlett Wright Gage, Rev. Matthew Berko, Rev. Dennis Albrecht, Ms. May Chao, Rev. Ronald S. James, Mrs. Meredeth AlMansoori, Dr. & Mrs. Bharat Bhalla, Ms. Rocky Pollitz, Mr. Gordon Truett, Ms. Pamela B. Nelson, Miss Mika Inatome, Ms. Katrina Thomas, Mr. Wayne J. Smith, Mr. Richard Kubinec, Miss Stella Johnson, Miss Jill Lacerenza, Mr. & Mrs. Johnny Orzechowski, Mrs. Gerard Klein, Ms. Yvette Salomon, Mr. Alfred Yazzi, Mr. Ben Silversmith, Mrs. Aurea Elgarico, Mrs. Norma Burnich, Mr. Pulefano Galeai, Mrs. Cahn Tran, Ms. JoAnn Gregoli, Ms. Susan Lane, Mr. Denis Reggie, Mr. David Ziser, Ms. Mary Todoric, Ms. Victoria Mal, Mr. Mark H. Roberts, Mr. Richard Rader, Ms. Pat Gleason, Mrs. James Venglar, and Dr. Deborah Vinnick Tesler.

Preface

The way we live and love is very different today than it was ten years ago, let alone fifty years ago. Nowhere is that more apparent than in the most traditional rite of passage—the wedding celebration. The ritual itself has not changed, nor has all of the excitement and anticipation that surrounds it. But what *has* changed are the participants. Couples are much less likely to meet in their neighborhood, place of worship, or even their hometown. Today, young adults travel to pursue an education or career opportunities. In so doing, they are likely to meet and fall in love with someone who is intellectually, academically, and emotionally compatible, but with whom they have little else in common — someone who comes from a very different religious, cultural, or socioeconomic background and whose family may not even speak the same language.

An event as traditional as a wedding is universally associated with fairly rigid guidelines and expectations based on what has always been done in your family or among your friends. That was fine when the two people marrying each other had common roots. Now, the differences are more the rule than the exception, and these are the challenges couples face as they plan their 1990s wedding. This book focuses on helping you identify your similarities and your differences; then it provides you with constructive ways to plan a deeply meaningful celebration that forms the foundation for a wonderfully happy life together.

In researching this book, we bring advice from couples who have successfully overcome the disparities in their backgrounds, and from clergy and wedding consultants who have helped couples to see how the factors unique to the couple's respective backgrounds can enhance their wedding and their lives. We also bring our combined experience of thirty-seven years in the wedding planning field: I, with *Modern Bride* for twenty-seven years, and Stephanie as a feature writer in the magazine for ten years. Addi-

tionally, our personal lives reflect today's trends. Twenty-eight years ago I became engaged to an Italian Catholic whose immigrant parents arrived in this country just five months before his birth. I was from a Jewish family settled here for four generations. Our intellects, our educations, our cultural interests, and our souls were totally compatible, but our family backgrounds could not have been more different. We bridged the gap with sensitivity, love, and reasonable compromise, and our life together is more fulfilling as the years go by.

Stephanie, a Roman Catholic Texas Democrat, fell in love with a Methodist New Yorker who votes Republican. They came from different directions, but somehow they arrived at the same place. Their long-term, long-distance courtship and their twenty-three year marriage is yet another testimony to accentuating the positive and eliminating the disparities. Now, neither can imagine being married to anyone else.

While we were a bit ahead of the times, young adults in the '90s are used to diversity among their peers and often seek out these characteristics in choosing a lifetime partner. Parents, however, are often not so adaptable and feel threatened at the prospect of the merger of their daughter or son with someone whose traditions are so different from their own. Therefore, the primary concern for many engaged couples is, "How do we make our families understand that we truly are well matched and that, rather than undermining our family ties, our marriage can strengthen them?"

The answers to this and all the other questions involved in wedding planning are in this book. It is a reference/workbook intended to provide you with everything you need to know to plan the wedding, and the marriage, of *your* dreams.

Cele Goldsmith Lalli
Editor in Chief
MODERN BRIDE

Contents

CHAPTER 1
Variations on a Theme

The phone rings with insistence in a Long Island condominium just before 2 A.M. Shirley finally rolls over and picks it up.

"Mom, it's me," comes the voice from the other end. "Now don't get excited, Mom, it's okay. Everything's okay. But I just had to tell you first. Paul asked me to marry him, and I said yes! Can you believe it? I'm getting married, Mom!"

"And this is how I found out that my Jewish daughter was marrying a Polish Catholic from Albany, somebody I had only laid eyes on once, I might add." Shirley shrugs, then laughs, as she tells the story.

Cut to the end, because the story does have a happy ending. In spite of the worry over ethnic and religious differences, in spite of the difficulty of long-distance wedding planning, and in spite of the fact that Shirley and her former husband, the bride's father, were barely on speaking terms, the couple was married as planned and is now living happily in Boston. In fact, they were more married than most people, having had a prewedding celebration in Albany with the groom's family and friends, a formal wedding and reception in Brooklyn hosted by the bride's father and his new wife, and a day-after reception brunch given by the bride's mother on Long Island for friends and relatives on her side of the family.

If this complex state of affairs sounds routine to you, then you are part of mainstream America, a land where the traditional nuclear family is hard to find and where clear-cut ethnic, racial, and religious majorities no longer rule the realm, or write the rules, for weddings and marriage. And even if you don't have a major hurdle like a difference in race, religion, cultural, or regional backgrounds to overcome, you'll still have enough minor hurdles to manage, like asserting your style, maintaining control while trying to please everyone, and finding enough time and money to plan the wedding, and the life, the two of you want. It's all a part of the challenge, and the excitement, of getting married in the nineties.

Like most brides-to-be, you're probably older and more experienced than your mother was when she got married, but your life is also likely to be much more complicated. You may have been raised in one place (or several), gone away to school, established a career in another location, and traveled at home and abroad in between. Your fiancé may have a similar checkerboard history. Perhaps you met at school, or at work, or in the apartment building where you live, far away from your hometowns. Perhaps you've known each other for a while, or perhaps you haven't; perhaps the two of you are just old enough to recognize "the real thing" when you find it.

Regardless of where you come from or how you got to where you are, you have now made a commitment to share a lifetime with a person with whom you have much in common, but who may be very different from the family and friends of your past. The thrill of getting to know each other in a deeper, more intimate way is both romantic and exhilarating, but it can also demand some serious skill in the arts of communication and compromise, especially where friends and relatives are concerned.

Between the time you say "yes" and the day you say "I do," you will experience emotions you never knew you had, ask questions you never thought you'd ask, and find solutions to problems that you never knew existed. You'll reflect, and maybe sometimes you'll doubt. You'll make discoveries about your fiancé, and discoveries about yourself, and each of these discoveries, even the unpleasant ones, should bring you closer together. Nobody is perfect. True and lasting love depends on the mature ability to give and receive love in spite of one another's faults.

For most couples in love, planning a wedding provides the first real-life test of their relationship. The ways you express your feelings, your ability to negotiate a compromise, even how you handle all the additional demands of relatives and friends at this time will indicate how well you'll be able to deal with differences and difficulties in your future married life. If you can't assert yourself as a person and as a couple now, will you be able to do it later on, when the conflicts are likely to be much more seri-

ous? Think about that . . . but you don't have to answer yet.

However, you do have to recognize up front that periods of major life changes are emotionally charged and that mixed feelings of excitement, euphoria, and anxiety are normal. Planning a wedding, with its myriad details, multiple decisions, and millions of things to do, creates stress even under the best circumstances. It is also an occasion that brings out the best and the worst in people, mainly because they care so much. Those who are closest to you feel they have a role to play, and those who aren't always have something to say (and always prefaced with "If you want my objective opinion . . .").

That's why it's so important that you form a shared vision with your fiancé and assume control from the very beginning. This is not selfish, just practical; somebody has to be in charge to orchestrate such a major social event. Yes, weddings are a public celebration of the bonding of two families, and yes, the wishes of those who have loved and nurtured you through the years deserve to be considered and respected, but the wedding itself, regardless of who is paying for it, belongs to the two of you.

To stay in control, you have to learn how to manage the realities of your particular situation without necessarily seeking to change those realities. If you can do that with consistency and consideration, and without creating a bridal "Reign of Terror," then you will actually minimize the stress and increase the enjoyment for everyone involved, especially for you and your fiancé.

The trick is to find that management style, your wedding style, based on your mutual values and priorities within the context of your own family and social circumstances. And that is what this book will help you do.

To begin, let's face some facts: nobody has enough time; hardly anybody has enough money; and, with all due respect to Mr. Tolstoy, not even all happy families are alike. A wedding brings two separate clans together, each with its own values, traditions, and expectations, and causes them to interact with each other. It's quite a challenge, even for happy families, and more of a challenge still when internal relationships are less than ideal.

Talking about ideal, let's also debunk the myth of "the perfect wedding" because there is simply no such thing. Weddings are people, and people aren't perfect. Maybe dad has a fondness for younger women, Aunt Tilly has a fondness for drink, and your future in-laws have a fondness for what you consider the exotic. Whatever it is, it doesn't matter; you've got to deal with it because these are your people, and they aren't "perfect."

If it's any consolation, our experience with engaged *Modern Bride* staffers and our letters and conversations with brides and grooms around the country and in our own families indicate that imperfect people and uncommon circumstances are more widespread than the rumors of "the perfect wedding" would have you believe. Pictures in magazines are, after all, only pictures of models, not of real couples, and newspaper accounts of glorious society weddings rarely, if ever, report the behind-the-scene conflicts.

So take heart. You don't have to race out and have your teeth capped and your hair dyed, mom and pop don't have to sell the heirlooms and mortgage the family farm, and your motley relatives and unruly friends don't have to be banished to the back pew in order to have a wedding that is perfect for you. You just have to identify your biggest challenges as soon as you are engaged, set your priorities before other people try to establish them for you, and keep your sense of humor intact, even when you cry.

How to Use This Book

Whatever your circumstances, you're not alone. *Modern Bride's Wedding Celebrations: The Complete Wedding Planner for Today's Bride* is written for you and your fiancé—not for your mothers, fathers, relatives, or friends, but for you two. Begin by taking the personal inventory, "Your Wedding Profile," in this chapter. These questions cover five key areas of

your personal and family backgrounds, and thinking about them together should help the two of you identify priorities and anticipate difficulties so you can develop a practical, workable wedding plan. There are no right or wrong answers in this profile; there are simply the realities of your situation that must be considered. Scoring at the end of each section indicates your "complication factor" in that area as few, some, or many potential problems.

By completing the profile, you will be able to identify your particular circumstances in this book, thereby learning how to adapt and personalize your wedding planning to fit who you are. The book is organized in wedding-planning sequence with basic, uncomplicated information presented first, along with charts, checklists, and special sections: "To Have or Have Not," "Questions to Ask," and "Terms You Need to Know." When you have high "complication factors" in areas that affect that aspect of wedding planning, you will want to read the "Contemporary Solutions," where topics analyzed in the profile are identified in the margins. Those with low profile topic scores can simply skip the solutions and go on to the next topic.

We recognize the tremendous diversity in backgrounds and situations that exist among couples marrying today, and we've heard the undercurrents of panic and frustration in the questions that are prefaced with, "I've looked in all the books, but I just can't find. . . ." We have written this book to do something about that, something that acknowledges the way America lives and loves today, as opposed to the way it did 50 years ago, something that enables couples from diverse backgrounds and nontraditional families to have a happy engagement experience and a memorable wedding day. Rather than undermine your chances for a wonderful wedding, the richness of diversity can mean a fuller celebration of happiness on the wedding day for those willing to use the guidelines of conventional etiquette as they were intended to be used—not as a sword, but as a tool.

The most beautiful weddings are those that reflect the special love and the special character of the couple being honored. That is what you want, that is what you deserve, and that is what is possible on any budget in any type of ceremony and reception in any locale. You just have to take charge and make it happen.

"I think I can . . . I think I can. . . ."

We think you can, too, and we'll help you do it.

 # YOUR WEDDING PROFILE

Take this inventory together. Within each set of statements, circle the number of the statement that best describes your shared attitude or situation. Then total the numbers to determine your "complication factor" in that area.

PERSONAL BACKGROUND

1. We are about the same age.
2. We are of the same generation, though one of us is a few years older than the other.
3. One of us is 10+ years older than the other.
4. We are of different generations, with more than 15 years difference in age between us.

1. This is a first marriage for both of us.
2. One of us has been married before.
3. Both of us have been married before.
4. One or both of us have minor children from a previous marriage/union.

1. We have the same level of formal education.
2. One of us has slightly more formal education than the other.
3. One or both of us plans to finish an education after marriage.
4. There is a significant difference between our formal educational backgrounds.

1. Both of us are established in the pursuit of our careers.
2. One of us is established in a career, and the other is "just working."
3. One of us is unemployed.

4. Neither of us has a job/career that he or she would want to pursue or that we can count on.

1. We share many long-term goals and short-term interests in life.
2. We share some goals and interests in life, but we feel free to pursue independently those that we don't share.
3. We agree on basic long-term goals, but actually have few day-to-day interests in common.
4. We are as different as night and day. It's a wonder we got together!

1. As singles, we have adopted similar lifestyles.
2. As singles, we have slightly different lifestyles, but they will be compatible.
3. As singles, we have markedly different lifestyles and both of us will have to modify a bit.
4. As singles, we have markedly different lifestyles and one of us will have to adapt.

1. After we marry, we will live near close family and old friends.
2. After we marry, we will stay where we live now, with no family and few friends nearby.
3. After we marry, we will relocate to a new place completely away from family and old friends.
4. After we marry, one of us has to relocate to a new place away from family and friends.

1. We believe that the man and the woman are equal partners in marriage, sharing all responsibilities, all chores, and all decisions.

2. We believe that the man and the woman are equal partners in marriage, but that responsibilities, chores, and decisions should be divided by interest and ability.

3. We believe that men and women are equal in marriage, but we believe in traditional roles in the home.

4. We believe that the partner who generates the greater income has a right to devote more time and energy to work and less time and energy to domestic chores.

Total Personal _____

CULTURAL BACKGROUND

1. Neither of us has a strong ethnic identity.

2. We have the same ethnic identity.

3. One of us has a strong ethnic identity and the other does not.

4. Each of us has a strong, but different, ethnic identity.

1. Both our families have been in America for several generations.

2. One or both of us is a first-generation American.

3. One or both of us is a naturalized American citizen.

4. One of us is a foreign national.

1. We are of the same race and the same national origin.

2. We are of the same race, but different national/ethnic origins.

3. We are of different races, but the same national origin.

4. We are of different races and entirely different national/ethnic origins.

1. We are from the same region of the country where we now live and work.

2. One of us is from the region where we are now, and the other has assimilated by living here.

3. We are from different regions of the country, but we have assimilated here where we live and work.

4. Both of us are from different regions of the country, and one of us will have to relocate to where the other is after marriage.

1. We have the same urban, suburban, or rural background from the same part of the country.

2. We have the same urban, suburban, or rural background, but we come from different parts of the country.

3. One of us is urban/suburban, and one of us is rural/small town, but we come from the same part of the country.

4. One of us is urban/suburban, one of us is rural/small town, and we come from different parts of the country.

1. Both of our families reside in the area where we live now and where the wedding will be held.

2. Both of our families reside in the area where the wedding will be held, but not where we live.

3. One of our families resides in the area where we live now and where the wedding will be held.

4. Although neither of our families resides near where we live now, the wedding will be held here.

1. Generally, we agree in matters of taste: clothes, food, music, furnishings, entertainment, etc.

2. While we don't always agree on individual choices, our tastes could be considered complementary.

3. One of us clearly has "classier" taste than the other, so the other defers.

4. We rarely agree in matters of taste, so we have to learn to compromise.

1. The most important ingredient for a beautiful wedding is a group of loving, convivial family members and friends.

2. The most important ingredient for a beautiful wedding is a nuptial couple in love.

3. The most important ingredients for a beautiful wedding are ritual and tradition.

4. The most important ingredient for a beautiful wedding is money.

Total Cultural _____

SOCIOECONOMIC BACKGROUND

1. We come from similar socioeconomic backgrounds.

2. Although our socioeconomic backgrounds are somewhat different, our attitudes and values seem to be similar.

3. Although our economic backgrounds are similar, one of us has a more "socially conscious" family than the other.

4. There is a wide disparity between our socioeconomic backgrounds.

1. We are both financially solvent and independent.

2. While neither of us has been financially secure before, we expect to be better off when we "pool our resources" as a couple.

3. We will be beginning marriage with outstanding financial obligations (loans, credit card debt, alimony, etc.).

4. As newlyweds, we may have to depend on our families for some financial assistance.

1. We expect to pay for the entire wedding ourselves.

2. We expect to pay for most of the wedding with some contribution from the family(ies).

3. We will contribute to the cost of the wedding, but our family(ies) will pay for most of it.

4. Our family(ies) are paying for the entire wedding.

1. The friends and family whom we would like to participate in our wedding can well afford to do so.

2. The friends and family whom we would like to participate will find some way to do so.

3. Not all the friends and family whom we would like to participate can really afford to do so.

4. Many of our friends and family will find participating in our wedding a financial hardship.

1. We can afford to take a honeymoon anywhere we want to go, and we will make that decision together.

2. We can afford a reasonable honeymoon, and we will plan and budget accordingly.

3. We cannot afford a honeymoon right after the wedding, so we will postpone it to a later date.

4. We cannot really afford a honeymoon, but we're going to take one anyway because you only get married once.

1. We expect to receive a sizable combination of gifts and cash from our wedding and related parties.

2. We expect to receive some gifts and mostly cash from our wedding and related parties.

3. We expect to receive mostly gifts from our wedding.

4. We expect to receive few gifts and little cash from our wedding.

1. We already own a house/condo in which we will live as newlyweds.

2. We already rent a house or apartment in which we will live initially, with hopes of buying our own home sometime soon.

3. We have to find a larger place to rent and can only dream about owning a home one day.

4. We will be living with in-laws as newlyweds.

1. We are better off financially and educationally than our parents were when they got married.

2. We are as well off as our parents were when they got married.

3. We are not as well off as our parents were when they got married, but we'll get there.

4. We will never be as well off as our parents were/are.

Total Socioeconomic _____

RELIGIOUS BACKGROUND

1. We are of the same religious faith.
2. We are of different faiths, but neither of us practices.
3. We are of different faiths, but only one of us practices.
4. We are of different faiths, and each of us—and our families—practices that faith.

1. Our religions are the same, and we will continue to practice our faith together in marriage.
2. We are of different religious backgrounds, but will either compromise or not practice at all.
3. Only one of us practices a faith, and he or she will continue to do so after marriage.
4. We will work to integrate the practice of two religious traditions in our household; perhaps one of us will convert.

1. Religious tolerance and understanding will not be an issue in our marriage.
2. It is not important that our family have a particular religious identity.
3. One of us will have to work to understand and accept the other's practice of a faith.
4. Ours will be a true "interfaith" marriage wherein different religious traditions will have to be respected and understood.

1. We have agreed on a religious ceremony and celebrant.
2. We have agreed on a civil ceremony and celebrant.
3. We want a religious ceremony, but can't decide which faith or clergy to use.
4. We need a concelebrated religious ceremony with the clergy of two faiths represented.

1. Neither of us has any civil or religious impediments to the marriage.
2. One of us has been married before, and that could be an impediment to marriage.

3. One of us has a religious difference (unbaptized, non-Christian, non-Jewish, etc.) that could present an impediment to marriage in a particular faith.
4. One or both of us has impediments to marriage in our separate faiths.

1. We have not been cohabiting before marriage, and our parents and relatives would have expected us not to.
2. We have been cohabiting before marriage, and our parents and relatives have generally accepted that as the modern way.
3. We have been cohabiting before marriage, and that arrangement has been very difficult for some of our parents and relatives to accept.
4. We have been cohabiting before marriage, and some of our parents and relatives are offended at our decision to have a public wedding celebration.

1. Our families agree completely with the type of wedding ceremony (civil or religious) we want to have.
2. Our families are aware of our difficulties in choosing a type of ceremony, but they support our decision.
3. Our families do not agree with the type of ceremony we'd like to have, but they will live with it.
4. Our families have brought additional pressures and complications to bear on our choice of a wedding ceremony.

1. There is no question about the future religious upbringing of any of our children.
2. We are undecided about the future religious training of our children, but that doesn't present an immediate problem.
3. There is some question about the future religious training of our children, but we have agreed that they will be raised in the faith of the more practicing partner.

4. There is much concern between us and among our families about the future religious training of our children.

Total Religion _____

FAMILY BACKGROUNDS

1. We come from intact families.
2. One of us comes from an intact family, and the other comes from an amicably divorced or single-parent family.
3. One of us comes from a divorced/remarried/stepfamily situation wherein there are serious complications and estrangements.
4. We come from divorced/remarried/stepfamily situations wherein there are serious complications and estrangements.

1. Our families have gotten to know each other, seem to like each other, and have gotten together on several occasions.
2. Our families know each other, have gotten together on occasion because of us, but don't seem to be particularly fond of each other.
3. Our families don't know each other very well, having met only once or twice.
4. Our families hardly know each other at all and will meet for the first time right before the wedding.

1. Each of us has a good relationship with our parents and siblings.
2. One of us has a good relationship with his or her parents and siblings; the other's relationship is strained.
3. Both of us have strained relationships with our parents and siblings.
4. One of us is totally estranged from the family of origin, so that family will probably not attend the wedding.

1. Our families are happy for us and fond of the partner we've chosen.

2. One of our families is happy for us; the other seems to be lukewarm.
3. Neither of our families seems thrilled about our decision to marry, but they have accepted it.
4. For whatever reason, one of our families is openly opposed to our decision to marry and threatens not to attend the wedding.

1. Because our families are so congenial and so much alike, we anticipate few disagreements over matters of taste, style, and tradition in the wedding.
2. Our families are generally congenial and somewhat alike, but individual tastes and traditions will have to be carefully considered.
3. Our families are markedly different in tastes, style, and tradition, so we will have to work very hard to keep everybody happy.
4. Our families are so very different in tastes, style, and tradition that it is impossible to please them all, so we'll simply try to please ourselves.

1. Everyone agrees that we, the couple, are in charge of the wedding regardless of who's paying for it.
2. Everyone says that we, the couple, are in charge of the wedding, but both families expect to play a role in some of the decisions.
3. Everyone says that it's our wedding, but we all know that whoever is paying for it expects to call the shots.
4. At least one of the mothers, or families, is poised and ready to take full control of the wedding if we allow it.

1. We will choose our attendants from among our closest friends.
2. We will choose our attendants from among our siblings and friends.
3. We have more close friends and siblings than we can possibly have in the wedding, so we will have to find other ways to make everyone feel special.

4. We have more attendants than we need or want, and already feel resentful about those we "have to have."

1. The guests at our wedding will be composed of equal numbers of relatives and friends of both sides of the family, and our own friends, as well.
2. The guests at our wedding will be mostly our own friends, with a limited number of relatives and friends from each side of the family.
3. Due to circumstances beyond our control, the guests at our wedding will include some of our friends and a lopsided number of relatives and friends from one side of the family.
4. Whether we like it or not, it looks like the guests at our wedding will be almost entirely the relatives and friends of only one side of the family.

Total Family _____

COMPLICATION FACTOR SCORING:

Few 8–16   Some 17–23   Many 24–32

YOUR WEDDING PROFILE TOTALS:

Personal Background	16
Cultural Background	10
Socioeconomic Background	19
Religious Background	_____
Family Background	_____

Your scores in each of these areas affect the type of wedding you can reasonably plan. Wherever you have high complication factors due to significant differences identified in "Your Wedding Profile," refer to the "Contemporary Solutions" sections in each chapter. There you will find alternatives to solving your particular problems.

In the nineties, complications are more the rule than the exception. Remember, the best defense is a strong offense.

CHAPTER 2
It's Official!
The Engagement

Whether he proposed to you or you proposed to him or there was simply spontaneous agreement, you've made the big decision to marry. And, once you inform the families, your engagement becomes official. You'll probably want to tell other close relatives and friends, too, so they can share the excitement you feel, but you *do not* have to send announcements, have a party, buy a ring, or publish the news in the local paper in order for your engagement to be considered official. Of course, you may want to do any or all of these things, but you are engaged because the two of you say you are, and you're ready to make wedding arrangements. That's all there is to it.

There is no prescribed length for the period of engagement, though most couples who want to have anything more than a very simple wedding will find themselves engaged for at least one year and often longer because it generally takes that long to plan the nuptial. Couples who have known each other for quite a while, or those with pending military or career changes, may have considerably shorter engagements. Those who have educations to complete or other goals to accomplish might be engaged for two or more years.

The length of the engagement doesn't really matter. What does matter is that you use this special period in your lives to strengthen and solidify yourselves as a couple and to establish the quality of your relationship as the number one priority.

Putting Each Other First

You can begin the lifelong labor of love now, during the engagement. If you can establish a pattern of open, honest communication wherein you each learn to listen, really listen, to what the other is saying, then you will be able to handle together what you might not be able to handle alone.

You're entitled to enjoy your engagement, the romantic interludes and sentimental tears, the unexpected congratulations and the spirit of good will, but the time to "savor the moment" will not always readily present itself. You will have to make the time. If you're like most couples, work, school, travel, and personal and professional obligations already keep you going full tilt. The very thought of trying to squeeze in a wedding, much less taking the time to actually enjoy it, strikes you as an impossible dream. "I thought this would be the happiest time of my life and it's one argument after another" is a plaint we hear all too often. It does not have to be that way for you if you establish priorities from the beginning.

Having It Your Way

The first and often greatest obstacle to experiencing the excitement and enjoying this wonderful period in your lives together is a lack of self-confidence. Maybe you haven't ever furnished a home before, or thought about managing career and family, or thrown a party for a couple of hundred people. So what? You can do it. If your complication factors are minimal, it will be easier to accomplish because your families and friends will help pull together your shared vision with maximum support.

"Your Wedding Profile" (page 4) will alert you to any potential problems, permitting you to investigate solutions to the big conflicts now before they arise. Even if you're among the lucky few whose similar backgrounds pose little likelihood of disagreements, you should still decide, together as a couple, approximately when you would like to be married and what kind and size of ceremony and reception you would like to have. Do that before you sit down for serious discussions of wedding plans with any family members. If you have the slightest suspicion that your mother or his, or anybody else, will attempt to take over, then you need to be that much more definitive about what the two of you want from day one.

Planning a wedding is about being in control, and enjoying an engagement is about being in love and feeling good about the arrangements the two of you make for *your* wedding. You're entitled to this, so don't let anyone take it away from you. There are plenty of options in this book to help you achieve just that.

Informing the Families

Mark and Liz chose the auspicious occasion of a Saturday afternoon garage sale at her family's house to inform her parents of their decision to marry.

"I think you know how Liz and I feel about each other," Mark said to Liz's dad as the two of them unpacked a dusty lamp. "So, I guess I should make it official. May I have your daughter's hand in marriage?"

Her dad stopped what he was doing and looked straight at the young man. "Well . . . no," he said.

"No?" Mark was astonished.

"No," her father continued with a spreading smile. "I'd really prefer you take the whole person, not just her hand."

If your families live nearby, it's nice to tell them it's official in person, together. Chances are, unless you've been incommunicado, they won't be all that surprised. Some men still feel, as Mark did, that they should formally ask the father, or mother, for the bride's hand in marriage, and that's a nice touch of tradition if your fiancé is disposed to do it and if it is appropriate to the bride's situation.

If either one of you has children, they should be told first. If your own parents are divorced, then a visit or call is made first to the parent closest to you, then to the other. (Ideally, divorced parents should decide between them how they will handle any wedding obligations.) If one or both of the families live far away, a phone call or note with your news will be fine. In any event, try to arrange for the two of you to visit with families soon, especially if one of you has never met the other's parents before. (Even if the two of you are cohabiting now, don't expect to share sleeping quarters when you visit parents' homes overnight if they indicate discomfort with this.)

Shortly after both sets of parents have been informed, it is customary for the groom's mother, or father, to call the bride's mother, or father, to welcome the new daughter into the family. Don't stand on ceremony, though. If the call hasn't come in a couple of weeks, or if you think his parents might not be aware of the convention, it is perfectly okay for the bride's family to make the overture.

It's also essential to meet with all parents shortly after the engagement is official to discuss your plans and everyone's expectations. Full disclosure of budget parameters and assignment of expenses, as well as the style and size of wedding and the allocation of the guest list, should be clearly stated to avoid erroneous assumptions later on. If distance makes this difficult, use the phone and the mail to clarify these matters up front.

In the meantime, you'll want to do everything you can to help smooth the way so that all immediate family members can share in the excitement and feel a part of the event. This effort is especially necessary for the groom's parents (unless they are hosting the wedding), for your children, or for either family that lives far away from the center of the festivities. Unless they are long-time neighbors or friends, both sets of parents are bound to be a bit apprehensive about gaining a daughter or son and a whole new set of in-laws, or even step-grandchildren. Be sensitive to that, and try to remember that whatever they do or say is prompted only by their concern for the happiness and well-being of their own children, the two of you.

CONTEMPORARY SOLUTIONS

CULTURAL, RELIGIOUS, FAMILY

❦ *If you anticipate that either family will not be happy about your decision to marry or will not approve of the choice of spouse, then it is best that they be informed privately by their own child.* While it's true that you will have to deal with your in-laws for the rest of your lives, even if only in a cursory way, problem parents remain the primary responsibility of their own child.

Before either of you makes the announcement to problem parents, be sure you're prepared to hear the worst: that one or both of them won't attend the wedding or participate in any way. Your stand should be that you want all parents present and that you expect them to reconcile their objections for your sake, but if they can't, so be it. In that case, you will have to plan whatever kind of wedding you can afford without them. Above all else, remember your priorities; commitment to one another is primary. No one should be allowed to ruin the celebration affirming that pledge.

FAMILY

❦ *Parents are divorced and there's animosity between them.* This is particularly difficult if the warring couple is the bride's parents, who generally host the wedding, because they may set either/or conditions on their level of participation. "I'll pay for the wedding, but not if he or she is there," or "I'll host the reception, but I won't pay for his or her family and friends."

Don't get caught in this because, no matter which way you go, you'll be perceived as disloyal to one of them. Try asking a close family friend or relative to deal with the two of them on your behalf. If the groom's parents are willing, or your grandparents or an aunt and uncle, graciously accept their financial assistance and plan to contribute as much as possible yourselves. Your wedding arrangements may have to be scaled back from the fantasy ideal you've had since childhood, but complications like these require realistic compromise.

❧ *Parents are divorced and one of them has a "significant other."* Here the retort is often, "I won't attend the wedding if your father/mother brings _____." Essentially, this is still a problem of feuding parents, but with an additional twist.

Really, unless the "significant other" is close to you, he or she should have the good grace to stay at home on your wedding day, and you are within your rights to say so. A compromise might be to let "the other" attend and to seat him or her in the manner of any other guest. Either way, someone who is not legally a member of the family should remain inconspicuous during the ceremony and reception.

❧ *You have a stepparent who has raised you or to whom you are closer than to your natural father or mother.* The stepparent may assume the official role of host or hostess at the wedding, including walking you down the aisle. The natural parent may attend as a guest, or not at all, as you wish.

❧ *One or both of your parents are remarried, but you're not close to the stepparent(s).* A solution for accommodating everybody is to have your mother, alone or with her spouse, host the wedding, and your father, alone or with his spouse, host the reception. Invitations are worded accordingly. All may stand in the receiving line, or just your mother and the groom's mother, while your father, his wife, stepfather, and groom's father circulate among the guests. Another alternative: only you two receive the guests.

One more possibility is to have your father and mother issue the wedding invitation together; your father *or* mother, with or without spouse, host the reception immediately following the ceremony; and the other parent, with or without spouse, host another type of reception the next day or even after the honeymoon. In this case, separate invitations would be issued to the second reception.

SOCIOECONOMIC, FAMILY

❧ *Your parents are divorced, and one of them "pleads poverty" regarding sharing the costs of the wedding.* Whether it's true or not, you have to accept the fact that his or her priorities lie elsewhere. Budget the wedding with the one who is cooperating, and let that parent issue the invitation alone. Here, too, you both and/or the groom's parents may offer to share costs, a gesture the single parent will undoubtedly appreciate.

Be prepared to deal with the alienation that comes from these unfortunate family difficulties, but don't dwell on it. Go forward with plans for the kind of wedding you can afford with the resources you have.

You will have to be very tough in these hurtful confrontations, but you simply cannot afford to give in to emotional or financial blackmail. You might put off informing problem parents until you're sure you can stand your ground. Sometimes, if you don't waffle, families will eventually resolve their differences and come around. You can hope, but you can't insist. Nor can you placate unreasonable demands now without paying a terrible price later.

Spreading the News

Of course you'll make phone calls or write notes to siblings and other close relatives and friends, and if there's no question about the number of attendants you'll have or who they will be, you can invite those special people to participate in your wedding when you inform them of your engagement. But what about everybody else, everyone you want to know or anyone who may be affected by your news?

If you will need time off from work for wedding planning or an extended honeymoon, you'll have to inform your colleagues and superiors, in a courteous, professional manner, about your decision to marry. If your work is seasonal, or in any way subject to peak periods of activity, you need to consider that in setting a wedding date. Likewise, you might also check with other key people concerning their commitments—graduations, wedding anniversaries, births, etc.—before settling on a date to avoid competing with another special event on your day.

Formal engagement announcements are made by the parents of the bride-to-be at an engagement party (or by the parents of the groom-to-be or any other family member or friend who, for some reason, hosts an engagement party). The parents of the bride, or you yourself, may also submit an announcement for publication in the newspapers of the cities in which you and your families live. Neither engagement parties nor newspaper announcements are absolutely necessary, or even always advisable, and there is no prescribed time when either must be done.

The word on sending out printed or engraved engagement announcements is DON'T. They appear to be nothing more than a request for gifts. Some people, family members and those closest to you, may give you engagement gifts because they love you and are sincerely happy for you, and that's lovely, but "engagement gifts" as such are not to be expected, not even from guests at an engagement party (where, ostensibly, the news of your engagement is only just being announced to those present).

CONTEMPORARY SOLUTIONS

PERSONAL

🐚 *A public announcement of an engagement is never made if the prospective bride or groom is still legally married to someone else.* Having been married and divorced or widowed before, however, in no way affects your right to an engagement party or newspaper announcement.

🐚 *If an engagement is broken, all gifts* **must** *be returned with a note from the bride or groom, depending on who received the gift.* Extensive explanations are not necessary. A simple one will do: "Regretfully, _____ and I have broken our engagement. Therefore, I am returning your gift."

FAMILY

🐚 *If the bride's parents are deceased or in some other way indisposed to announcing the engagement, another close relative or the couple, themselves, may make the announcement.* If the bride is a foreign national in whose country engagement traditions are different, the groom's parents may make an announcement in their own hometown paper and may even host an engagement party.

❧❧ *To Have or Have Not* ❧❧

Newspaper Announcements

If you choose to have a published announcement, it may appear immediately after the engagement, at the same time as an engagement party, or as little as six to eight weeks before the wedding. Announcements may appear in your hometown paper, his hometown paper, and any paper in the location(s) in which the two of you live and work.

Often, newspapers regularly publish instructions for submitting announcements. If not, contact the society editors of each publication for information on fees (some charge), deadlines, and what's to be included (some will send a form to be filled out). Some papers print only the briefest announcements, while others include detailed information on family members, educational backgrounds, and employment. Although some newspapers request the street address of the bride's parents, you may wish to tell them not to include it. You will not only receive junk mail, but it may attract attention to the fact that valuables will soon be pouring into your home.

The usual form:
Mr. and Mrs. John Doe of Atlanta (hometown or street address) announce the engagement of their daughter, Sally Ann, to Mr. Jim Smith, son of Mr. and Mrs. John Smith of Charlotte, North Carolina. A June wedding is planned.

When the bride's parents are divorced:
Mrs. Mary Doe of _____ announces the engagement of her daughter, Sally Ann, to Mr. Jim Smith, son of Mr. and Mrs. John Smith of Charlotte, North Carolina. Miss Doe is also the daughter of Mr. John Doe of Atlanta. A June wedding is planned.

When a parent of the bride is deceased: (Announcement is made by either the mother or the father)
Mrs. John Doe of _____ announces the engagement of her daughter, Sally Ann, to . . . . Miss Doe is also the daughter of the late John Doe. A June wedding is planned.

When the bride has a close stepfather:
Mr. and Mrs. Frank Carter announce the engagement of Mrs. Carter's daughter, Sally Ann Doe, to . . . . Miss Doe is also the daughter of Mr. John Doe of Atlanta, Georgia. A June wedding is planned.

When the bride's parents are divorced and the mother is remarried:
Mr. John Doe of _____ and Mrs. Frank Carter of _____ announce the engagement of their daughter, Sally Ann Doe, to . . . . A June wedding is planned.

When the bride has been raised by a relative:
Mrs. Robert Jones announces the engagement of her niece, Sally Ann Doe, to . . . . Miss Doe is the daughter of _____ (or of the late) _____. A June wedding is planned.

When the bride has been married before:
Mr. and Mrs. John Doe of _____ announce the engagement of their daughter, Sally Doe Robb, to . . . . A June wedding . . . .

When the bride has no living parents or relatives:
Announcement is made of the engagement of Miss Sally Ann Doe, daughter of the late ____, to Mr. Jim Smith, son of Mr. and Mrs. John Smith of ____. A June . . . .

When the bride is estranged from her parents:
Announcement is made of the engagement of Miss Sally Ann Doe of ____ to Mr. Jim Smith of ____. A June . . . .

When the bride is a foreign national and the groom's parents make the announcement:
Announcement is made of the engagement of Miss Sally Doe, daughter of Mr. and Mrs. John Doe of London, England, to Lt. Jim Smith, son of Mr. and Mrs. John Smith of ____. A June . . . .

Remember: *Never* announce an engagement when either partner is still legally married to someone else.

Engagement Parties

Traditionally, the bride's family gives the engagement party to announce to relatives and close family friends (those who will also be invited to the wedding) the good news of their daughter's betrothal. The party can be large or small, formal or informal, at home or out, and at any time of day. Whatever pleases the couple and the family, from a brunch to a barbecue, will be appropriate.

At some point in the festivities, the bride's father (or the mother if the father is absent) will make the "official" announcement in a toast and will welcome the future son-in-law into the family. The groom's parents should be invited and, if they attend, may also be introduced at this time. The "official" toast is just a formality, of course, as guests generally get the message early on from the bride-to-be with a ring on her finger and a man on her arm.

Invitations are not for "an engagement party" per se, but "in honor of." They may be formal or informal, or even issued by phone. Invitations read something like this:

> You are invited for
> _____
> in honor of
> Sally Doe and Jim Smith

It is the prerogative of the bride's family to host the first official engagement party, though subsequent parties (for different sets of guests) may be held by the groom's family, other close friends or relatives, or even the couple themselves. If the bride's family is unable to hold the party for some reason, the groom's family may do so instead.

Those who know about the announcement in advance might bring gifts to the engagement party, but gifts are not to be expected. Whatever is brought should be opened in private, so that guests who did not bring gifts will not be embarrassed, and thank-you notes should be sent promptly. You also should send a thank-you note or small gift of appreciation to the hosts after the party, even if the hosts were your own parents.

The Engagement Ring

Time was when a young man was expected to propose and to slip a ring on his intended's finger all in one dramatic motion, but not anymore. First of all, some women don't even want an engagement ring, and second of all, those who do have pretty fixed ideas about what they want. With the average engagement ring costing $2,200 today, the smart man shops around with his intended before he shows up with a surprise, unless he's absolutely sure he knows what will please her.

"Diamonds are a girl's best friend," and diamond engagement rings, designed to be worn in combination with a matching or complementary wedding band, continue to be the overwhelming choice of most brides-to-be. But they aren't the only choice. Rubies and sapphires are also popular, as are birthstones and even the new colored diamonds (yellow and orange, pink, green, or blue) that are available at jewelry specialists.

The International Gemological Institute recommends that a man spend two to three months' salary on an engagement ring, but your fiancé knows best what he can really afford. The two of you should spend some time casually looking around at rings first, and then your fiancé should make an appointment for the two of you at a reputable jeweler (preferably one that is a member of the American Gem Society), telling him in advance what the budget is. That way, you will be shown only what your fiancé can afford, thus preventing any awkwardness.

You don't have to give your fiancé an engagement ring, though there is a trend toward this today. But you may want to give him some other piece of jewelry for sentimental reasons.

QUESTIONS TO ASK

1. What is the specific weight, quality, shape, and color of the stone?
2. What about the metal content and design specifications of the setting?
3. Will all of this be identified on the sales receipt or on a certificate of authenticity for insurance purposes?
4. What about warranties, guarantees, and repair services?
5. What care will this ring require, and what kind of repairs might I expect to make?
6. May I have the ring's quality and value verified by an independent appraiser before the final sale?

Note: Be cautious about bargain prices that seem too good to be true. The quality of the stone may not be as represented, and you'll have little recourse if you find that out after paying for it. Choose a jeweler who has a reputation you can trust, and check with The Better Business Bureau before you buy if you have any reason to doubt the jeweler's integrity.

CONTEMPORARY SOLUTIONS

SOCIOECONOMIC

❦ *What you really want, he can't afford*. You have three choices: (1) go for a larger stone of a lesser quality; (2) go for the glitz with a fake until you can afford "the real thing"; or (3) don't settle, wait. You can get an engagement ring anytime, even for your tenth anniversary!

PERSONAL, FAMILY

❦ *You don't care for the ring that belonged to his grandmother, which he so lovingly and graciously wants you to wear*. Be honest. Emphasize the sentimental value of the stones, and suggest having them reset into something more flattering to your hand.

PERSONAL

❦ *You don't want an engagement ring, but he absolutely insists that you have one*. Steer him in the direction of a nontraditional style, an unusual design, or a dinner ring that can be worn on the other hand after the wedding.

🌺 TO HAVE OR HAVE NOT 🌺

The Diamond Engagement Ring

The Five Cs

CUT—refers to shape and to the skill and precision with which a rough diamond is transformed into a brilliant, faceted gemstone. The six most popular cuts are:

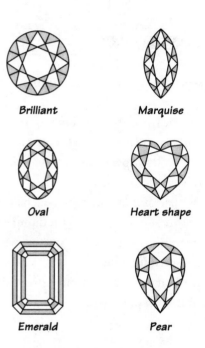

Brilliant   Marquise

Oval   Heart shape

Emerald   Pear

CLARITY—the absence of serious flaws or blemishes. Flawless diamonds are rare and expensive; very slight flaws are acceptable and are not visible to the naked eye. Let your jeweler guide you.

COLOR—body color, not reflected light. Color can vary from clear white to tinges of yellow. Color is graded by letter according to the Gemological Institute of America.

CARAT—the weight of the stone. A carat weighs 100 points, so a 10 pt. stone is 1/10 of a carat. Get the exact weight in points, not in approximations (quarter carat, half, etc.).

CERTIFICATION—provides proof of the diamond's identity and grade. Get it.

Settings should show the stone(s) to advantage and be flattering to the shape and size of your hand. Usual choices include yellow gold, white gold, platinum, and silver. The higher the karat number in gold settings, the higher the proportion of gold in it: 24K (100 percent gold); 18K (18 parts gold to 6 parts other metals); 14K (14 parts gold, 10 parts other); and 10K (10 parts gold, 14 other). For quality and durability, choose 14K or 18K.

Metals may have several finishes: polished—shiny and standard; matte—soft and muted; Florentine—surface texture; or diamond cut—etched with designs for a brighter appearance. Different finishes can be combined in the same setting, or in combination with a wedding band, for a distinctive look.

Wedding Expectations

Large or small, formal or informal, few other events pose the particular challenges, and joys, of planning a wedding: the requisite rituals, the eclectic guest list, the accommodation of a diversity of tastes, and the necessary coordination of all major elements and minor details into a reflection of your own personal style.

Having agreed with your fiancé, at least in principle, on the type, style, and size of wedding you want to have, you both need to put together a plan and develop a realistic outlook before getting your families actively involved. To make the process go as smoothly as possible, acknowledge from the very beginning that some compromises will have to be made as you go along.

During this early stage of engagement, have a casual, preliminary chat with each of your families to see just how close their vision of the wedding comes to yours.

QUESTIONS TO ASK

1. Do your families want the wedding to be a proper, dignified affair, full of ritual and tradition? Do you also want that, or would you prefer a more spontaneous celebration that you know *your* friends would enjoy?
2. What kind of food and fare do your families expect at the reception?
3. Will one family assume most of the cost, with the other making slight, if any, contribution, or will both families share the expenses?
4. Will the two of you make financial contributions as well?
5. How much is everyone prepared to spend, and on what?
6. Roughly how many guests does each family expect to invite?

With some indication of the type and size of wedding agreed upon, you and your fiancé can "let your fingers do the walking" to give you a more realistic picture of what things cost. Consult local advertisers and people you know who have had weddings or parties recently. Call around to inquire about price ranges and packages. Early phone calls will not only indicate what adjustments may have to be made in your expectations, but they also will save you legwork later on by eliminating now places that don't meet your basic needs.

QUESTIONS TO ASK

1. What size party can your establishment accommodate?
2. Will mine be the only wedding in progress?
3. Do you have catering on the premises? Kosher service, or any other special dietary needs?
4. Do you have a liquor license?
5. Are there parking facilities, wheelchair access, or any other guest conveniences I require?
6. What are the "package" or per person price ranges? What does that include?
7. Do prices vary with the time of day, day of the week, or month of the year?

Getting "Real"

With this information in hand, you and your fiancé can "get real" about your wedding vision. The two of you will have facts and figures ready to support the choices you've made when you sit down with your families to develop the actual wedding plan and budget.

This sounds simple, and it can be, if you remain logical and in control as you trade off one choice for another. Everybody falls victim to some emotions and some fantasies when talking about a wedding, but few people actually have the unlimited resources with which to indulge them all. Paradoxically, the more realistic and reasonable you can be about your wedding plans from the very beginning, the more likely you are to have the kind of wedding dreams are made of. When you lose control so that the wedding runs you instead of you running it, when you give in to a vendor's irresistible sales pitch or a pushy relative's "have to have," then you risk feeling overwhelmed and manipulated.

This is your wedding, not a birthday party or a sweet sixteen dance that your mother planned for you as a child or teenager. Families are a part of it all, to be sure, and their wishes, along with the convenience and enjoyment of your guests, merit serious consideration. But when all is said and done, this wedding celebration, like the marriage it proclaims, belongs to the two of you. Keep it that way.

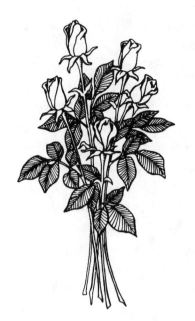

CHAPTER 3

The Wedding Budget

At the height of the "happy days are here again eighties," conspicuous consumption was in, restraint was out. The now famous Tisch-Steinberg wedding reception, held in 1988 at New York's Metropolitan Museum of Art, featured 50,000 French roses and a ten-foot-high wedding cake, among other indulgences, for a reported cost of $3 million. The affair was touted by *New York Magazine* as "one of the most ostentatious parties since the legendary Vanderbilt costume ball of 1883."

Then the decade turned, the recession spread, and America went to war. Suddenly, the nation's mood changed, and people looked again to simple old-fashioned values like family, nature, and patriotism. Everybody lowered their expectations a little; some people lowered them a lot.

So now, in these more moderate days, how much is a wedding done with good sense and good taste supposed to cost? Well, certainly less than $3 million, if that's any consolation. It all depends on where you live, what style of entertaining you, your

family, and friends are accustomed to, and how many of your "nearest and dearest" you expect to entertain. Some define a wedding as a gigantic party, with the amount of food, the liveliness of the music, and the duration of the dancing being all important; others see a wedding as a more dignified occasion, with attention to detail and understated elegance as hallmarks of success. There is simply no one, right way to define a wedding. What's appropriate for you can only be determined by your own style and taste exercised within the context of personal and/or local custom.

Today, the average cost of a wedding for approximately 200 guests is $17,000. In the smaller cities of the South or Southwest, a wedding for 200 could be less than half that; in the major cities of the Northeast, the cost of the same affair could easily double the national average. Wherever you live, a formal wedding with many guests and substantial food is expensive. How do you adjust expectations to fit your economic conditions?

Before you discuss wedding expenses with your families, try to be honest with yourselves about your financial situations. There may be economic realities that will affect everyone's ability to contribute to the cost of the wedding.

1. Is anyone unemployed?
2. Is anyone just recovering from a failed business venture?
3. Is anyone still paying off medical, legal, or educational bills?
4. Has there been recently, or is there about to be, another wedding or big celebration in your immediate families?
5. Do you feel that monies spent on a wedding are well spent, or would you really rather have the funds available to put toward a house or condo? How would your parents feel about that?

Economic pictures do change, of course, and lifestyles adapt accordingly. But even if you plan a long engagement, you still must deal with situations as they are today, not as they might be six months from now. No one should have to go into debt to finance a wedding, and no one should expect the guests to "pay their own way" by giving enough money in wedding gifts to defray the cost. You do not need a major party to have a meaningful ritual, but if you *invite* guests to the celebration, you must be prepared to pay for the whole affair. It's not what you spend, after all, but how you spend it that will distinguish your wedding from all others.

Setting Parameters

To be considerate and set reasonable parameters for everyone's contributions, you must adjust your own expectations to match what you think you and your families can realistically afford. If you've made preliminary inquiries, you now have a better idea of what things in your area cost, at least the food and fare for the reception. Recognizing that the reception constitutes fully 50 percent of the total wedding budget, simple multiplication will give you a quick estimate: per-person price quote × approximate number of guests × 2 = the total approximate cost of your wedding.

How does it look? Did the total knock you off your chair? If it did, you're not alone. Couples throughout the country complain about the high cost of weddings. Most of them are totally unprepared for even the basic expenses, much less for the myriad related costs, so that all too often, as their shopping progresses, their budget balloons—and finally flies away.

We don't want that to happen to you. That's why it's so important to do some preliminary pricing *before* you attempt to set spending guidelines. And that's why it is absolutely essential that everyone involved be honest about what they're prepared to contribute, and what they expect in return for that. If you have any reason to believe that one of your families is being less than candid about its financial situation or expectations of the wedding, or if one of them (particularly the groom's family) is significantly more affluent than the other, but not forthcoming, then perhaps you and/or the groom alone should talk to this family privately before you get everyone together. The one luxury you cannot afford on any budget is a big surprise later on.

You also can't afford clashing opinions or hurt feelings at this early stage of wedding planning. Money is a very sensitive topic for most people, and attitudes about how it should be spent, and on what, can vary greatly even within the same family. So, address the budget battles up front in an effort to cultivate an atmosphere for communication that is reasonable, honest, and considerate.

Apportioning the Cost

The following pie chart indicates a general breakdown of wedding expenses. You may wish to spend more on some areas and less on others. That is why it's important to begin with an average and individualize according to your preferences.

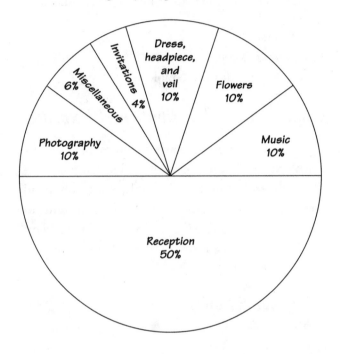

"Miscellaneous" includes optional items such as a video recording, limousines, related wedding parties, printed programs and napkins, guest favors, and other extras. Since the groom generally pays for the rings, his own attire, the fees for the clergy or officiant, and the honeymoon, and since the attendants usually assume the costs of their own attire (dresses and formal wear rentals), those items aren't included in this breakdown.

Obviously, if some expenses can be reduced or eliminated out of hand, such as wearing an heirloom dress, then those percentages can be reapportioned elsewhere. The whole idea of working within a budget, though, is to make sure that you don't spend more in one category than you've managed to save in another. You have to stay flexible without ever losing sight of the bottom line.

Who Pays for What?

Today, assumption of responsibility for wedding costs depends more on who's willing and able than on who's "supposed" to do what. For some families, cultural values and ethnic traditions can be more of a factor than their financial condition in influencing what they are prepared to contribute. In addition, couples marrying today are older, more mature, and better educated than ever before. In most cases, they have their own well-defined values and lifestyles, along with the incomes that enable them to exercise their preferences, so that they will assume a greater share of the wedding costs right along with the decision making.

Basically, there are four ways costs can be handled: the bride's family absorbs the bulk of the expense; the bride's family and the groom's family divide the costs; the couple assumes some of the expenses along with the families; or the couple pays for everything. Incidentally, it is not unheard of, or improper, for the groom's family to assume almost total responsibility. As noted earlier, an aunt, uncle, or grandparent may also offer a specific wedding contribution.

To facilitate your discussion with families, here are both a traditional and a more contemporary breakdown of responsibilities for wedding expenses. Remember, these are only suggested guidelines; whatever distribution is agreeable to all involved is perfectly proper.

Traditional Distribution of Expenses

The Bride
1. Wedding ring for the groom
2. Wedding gift for the groom
3. Personal stationery
4. Accommodations for out-of-town attendants
5. Her physical examination and blood test
6. Gifts for her attendants

The Groom

1. Wedding rings for the bride
2. Wedding gift for the bride
3. The marriage license
4. His wedding attire
5. Gifts for the best man and ushers
6. Flowers: bride's bouquet and going-away corsage; corsages for the mothers; boutonnieres for the men in the wedding party
7. Accommodations for out-of-town ushers and best man
8. Gloves, ties, or ascots for men in the wedding party
9. His blood test and physical examination
10. Fee for the celebrant
11. The honeymoon

The Bride's Family

1. The entire cost of the reception: food, wedding cake, beverages, gratuities for the bartenders and waiters, decorations, music, flowers, parking costs, and coat-check fees
2. A wedding gift for the newlyweds
3. Bride's wedding attire and trousseau
4. The wedding invitations, announcements, and mailing costs
5. The fee for engagement and wedding photographs
6. Ceremony: rental of sanctuary; fees for organist, soloist or choir, and sexton (sometimes included in charge for premises but, if not, these people have set fees); aisle carpets and/or canopy; and any other additional costs for decorations
7. Bridesmaids' bouquets
8. Transportation for bridal party to the wedding ceremony and from ceremony to reception
9. Bridesmaids' luncheon
10. Optional: rehearsal dinner

The Groom's Family

1. Their wedding attire
2. Any traveling expenses and hotel bills they incur
3. Wedding gift for the newlyweds
4. Optional: rehearsal dinner or any other expenses they elect to assume

The Attendants

1. Wedding attire
2. Traveling expenses
3. Wedding gift for the couple
4. The bachelor dinner (best man and/or ushers)

The Guests

1. Traveling expenses
2. Wedding gift for the couple

Contemporary Distribution of Expenses

If you're going to redistribute expenses in a way that will alleviate the lion's share of the burden traditionally assumed by the bride's family, we recommend that you allocate responsibility for certain items to those who have offered to contribute. Those items should then be billed and paid for directly. An example might be:

The Groom's Family

1. All beverages
2. Limousines
3. Music for the reception
4. Photography and/or videography

The Bride and/or Groom

1. Her attire and trousseau
2. Wedding flowers
3. Bridesmaids' get-together
4. Invitations, announcements, and personal stationery
5. Entertainments and courtesies for out-of-town guests

The Bride's Family

1. Ceremony site fee, including fees for any assistants to the officiant
2. Ceremonial music
3. Reception food and any site fees (rental, service gratuities, etc.)
4. The wedding cake

These are rather arbitrary breakdowns, but they give you an idea of how a more equitable division of expenses is possible. Ultimately, the costs should be assigned based on preference and ability to pay.

Another suggestion is to pool the monies from all sources and open a wedding bank account. You and your fiancé can then be in charge of all disbursements.

CONTEMPORARY SOLUTIONS

CULTURAL

❦ *In some cultures, the "traditional" division of expenses between families is entirely different.* The Chinese, for example, consider the groom's family to be the hosts and, therefore, they pay for the wedding; Italian families typically cohost the celebration and split the cost fifty-fifty. Think about how these cultural traditions might affect the willingness of your families to assume certain wedding costs.

❦ *More considerations about budget to bear in mind:* A family from a rural area may be unprepared for the costs, and the customs, in "the big city." It's your job to find out, with as much tact as possible, what kind of expenditure seems reasonable to them and to make sure they understand the likely cost of any budget item they volunteer to assume. You might also have to accept their inability to contribute anything because even traveling to the event is a financial strain.

SOCIOECONOMIC

❦ *Perhaps one family is intimidated by the apparent wealth and social savvy of the other.* If both families are sharing total costs, then each can elect to pay for whatever it (and you) consider essential to the wedding celebration. But, if only one family is shouldering the financial burden, then the other has no right to dictate how the money should be spent.

In all budget decisions, the two of you must arbitrate what you'll have and what you'll spend because the wedding should reflect your combined wishes, not those of any one family. If some choices and selections really don't matter to you, then you can adopt a "you want it, you pay for it" policy where those incidentals are concerned.

Guest Estimates

A simple rule of mathematics is the not-so-simple rule of holding down reception expenses: the cost of whatever you have will increase in direct proportion to the number of people you invite. The more relatives and friends, the more food and beverage, the more tables, chairs, and centerpieces, and the more cars to park. The larger the guest list, the larger the space to accommodate them, the larger the staff to serve them, and the larger the wedding cake. The guest list will be drawn from five sources: the bride's personal and professional friends; the groom's personal and professional friends; the friends and associates the two of you share as a couple; the bride's parents' relatives and friends; and the groom's parents' relatives and friends. You *must* have a preliminary estimate from each of these sources so you can calculate the total before you look for a site for your ceremony and reception.

Years ago, the rule of thumb for dividing the guest list was fifty-fifty between the two families, but that was when brides and grooms were younger with a limited circle of friends of their own. Bearing in mind that a wedding is not an occasion for repaying social obligations or developing business contacts, the majority of the guests should be family and friends who are close to the two of you and with whom you really want to share your special day. The older and more established you two are in your personal and professional lives, the greater the percentage of the guest list that will have to belong to you. Dad will just have to find some other way to entertain his important clients. Neither mom nor dad should expect to invite relatives with whom you've had little or no contact throughout the years.

Most locations are very specific about the minimum and maximum number of people they can accommodate (due to fire laws, building codes, and profitability). The range doesn't usually allow much room for adding or subtracting. A large site may specify 200 standing guests, but only 150 seated, for example; a smaller location will have a much smaller range, perhaps 50 standing, 35 seated. Change your numbers after you've booked, and you may find yourself out of a reception site, as well as a deposit.

When you're hosting the wedding yourselves, the guest list won't be a particular problem or that likely to change, except for the inevitable "If Suzy is invited, then we ought to have Sally, too." But you can deal with that kind of dilemma later when the actual list-making begins. For now, resolve the issue of the overall size of the guest list with your families, and make sure that they know what percentage of the total belongs to them.

CONTEMPORARY SOLUTIONS

CULTURAL

❦ *One family lives far away and will have only immediate family members present at the wedding.* In all fairness, you shouldn't expect that family to contribute significantly to the reception costs of entertaining strangers, especially if they will be hosting a party or reception for you where they live later on. Do send invitations to close relatives and friends, though, even if you know they can't attend. You might also consider sending wedding announcements to more extended family and friends.

FAMILY

❦ *One of the families is extremely large, and the other is extremely small.* The guest estimates from the two are vastly different, and the wedding is going to seem lopsided.

You can apportion the guest list any way you want, provided all the relatives and friends are really close to at least one of you, in which case their names would probably appear on your own list, as well as on your parents'. But if the list goes beyond the number of people who can be accommodated, the family will just have to reevaluate inviting the third cousins four times removed.

It all comes down to how big a wedding the two of you want. Given the answer to that, your choices are either to apportion the guest list, and adjust the financial obligations, on the basis of ability to afford, or to figure out a way to limit the larger list. Some families do this by deciding to eliminate those beyond siblings or first cousins, by not inviting dates of single guests, and by not including children.

PERSONAL, FAMILY

❦ *When the location of the ceremony has limited space, only very close family and friends are invited.* A larger reception held immediately afterwards, or later, may include many more guests. Invitations to the reception are mailed to the entire guest list. An enclosure card indicating the time and place of the nuptial service is inserted into the envelope of those invited to the ceremony. You may always have more people at the reception than at the ceremony, but *it's tacky to do the reverse!*

The Art of Compromise

At this point, the "big picture" should be getting clearer, and while you may not yet like what you see, don't get discouraged. At least now you have a better idea of how close everyone else's vision of your wedding is to your own, and now you can see where the greatest challenges in planning are. You'll have to budget time, as well as money, so the sooner you determine the trade-offs, the more pragmatic you can be about organizing your time and achieving your goals.

The art of effective compromise depends on finding a way to let all the principals know that their feelings are being considered without really sacrificing the substance of what is most important to you both. This can be tricky, but it can be done.

Take a common example: your Italian future in-laws absolutely insist that a Viennese Table (lavish dessert buffet) is a must at a decent wedding. Since you plan to cut and serve the wedding cake for dessert, you can't understand this additional expense at all.

Now stop and think. Maybe what they really want is a touch of their own ethnic traditions in the festivities. Suggest putting a bowl of sugared almonds (an Italian symbol of the bitter and the sweet in marriage) on each table after the meal and passing a platter of traditional Italian pastries when the cake is served. That way, you keep costs under control, and they uphold a custom.

Clashes of opinion during wedding planning are not always about the specific issue that caused the controversy; rather, they may reflect a deeper concern: family, pride, or religious faith. If compromise is genuinely sought, it can almost always be found. Little things do mean a lot. Begin your family merger by working together to find symbols to incorporate in your celebration that will enhance the ritual while also helping your clans come together as one.

With family discussions behind you, and bank overdrafts looming ahead, you're ready to set a budget and to begin the greatest, most exciting, most romantic shopping spree of your life. Never again will you find so many people—friends, relatives, colleagues, vendors, service personnel, or even casual acquaintances—more interested in plans for your happiness, or more willing to tell you how to achieve them.

Use the percentage pie earlier in this chapter to help you fill in the figures on the budget checklist that follows. Then, make a list of local resources to call and/or visit. (You'll find a section devoted to regional resources in every issue of *Modern Bride*.)

QUESTIONS TO ASK

Give yourselves plenty of time to talk about "the vision" of the wedding as you two see it now.

1. Is this wedding going to be large (more than 200 guests)?

2. Is it going to be formal, with a traditional white gown and our attendants in gowns and tuxedos?

3. At what time of day do we picture the wedding taking place, and where?

4. What kind of reception would we really like to have for our guests?

5. Can we all really afford what we're contemplating?

6. Where might some compromises have to be made?

It's important to think about these questions now, before you start to commit yourself to vendors and suppliers, since by making one choice, others are necessarily precluded. Remember, all elements of a wedding must work together for a unified whole. You wouldn't choose an elaborate wedding gown with a train if you expect to be married outdoors and to serve beer and barbecue at the reception.

The time of day, the location of the ceremony and reception, and the attire you choose for yourselves and your attendants must be appropriate and compatible with the degree of formality. Once you make a commitment to any one of these choices, you limit your options with regard to the others.

Think about all of this as you prepare your budget and get to work. Once you begin to obtain estimates from vendors and services, fill them in to determine if it is possible to splurge in one area by cutting back another.

Finalizing Your Budget

Before we leave money matters, and before you fill in every space on the budget checklist with an approximation that exhausts the amount you have to spend, you should know that incidentals and surprises can add up fast. Just so you're prepared, here is a list of unexpected, usually unbudgeted expenses beyond the obvious miscellaneous items—favors, attendants' gifts, postage, etc.—that may very well require reserve funds.

RELATED WEDDING EXPENSES

- Trips home to meet or confer with families (can be big bucks if families live far away).
- Long-distance telephone calls, particularly if you and your fiancé don't live in the same city.
- Additions to your wardrobe for wedding-related parties, luncheons, etc.
- Prenuptial medical, dental, legal, or financial fees.
- Beauty costs for haircuts, manicures, make-overs, diet or exercise programs.
- Entertainments for visiting relatives and friends, both during the engagement and in the time surrounding the wedding.
- Additional gifts as "tokens of appreciation" for those who help you in a special way with the wedding (your parents, favorite relatives, friends who house or entertain out-of-town guests, service people who go above and beyond, etc.).
- Rental cars for you or members of your family, if the wedding is being held away from home.
- Courtesy gifts (baskets of fruit, flowers, candy, etc.) in the hotel rooms or a hospitality suite for out-of-town guests.
- Tickets, tokens, fares, or rentals for special transportation for guests to ceremony and/or reception (train, bus, trolley, boat, ferry, etc.).
- Dinners out because you're too tired to cook.

YOUR BUDGET CHECKLIST

	Budget	Approximate Cost		Budget	Approximate Cost
STATIONERY	$_____		**TRANSPORTATION**	$_____	
Invitations		_____	Limousines		_____
Announcements		_____	Parking		_____
Thank-you Notes		_____	**WEDDING PARTIES**	$_____	
Reply Cards		_____	Bridal Luncheon		_____
At-home, Pew Cards		_____	Rehearsal Dinner		_____
PHOTOGRAPHY	$_____		Out-of-town Guests		_____
Formal Portraits		_____	**FEES**	$_____	
Engagement		_____	Church/Synagogue		_____
Wedding		_____	Officiant		_____
Wedding Album		_____	Assistants		_____
Parents' Albums		_____	(cantors, altar boys)		_____
Extra Prints		_____	**GIFTS**	$_____	
Videography		_____	Maid of Honor		_____
RECEPTION	$_____		Best Man		_____
Food		_____	Bridesmaids		_____
Beverages		_____	Groomsmen		_____
Wedding Cake		_____	Other		_____
Gratuities and Taxes		_____	**FLOWERS**	$_____	
Escalation Clause		_____	At Ceremony		_____
Valet Parking		_____	Bridal Bouquet		_____
Coat Check		_____	Attendants' (male, female)		_____
Ladies' Room		_____	Mothers' Corsages		_____
Police Officer		_____	Reception		_____
MUSIC	$_____		**EXTRAS**	$_____	
Wedding		_____	Monogrammed Napkins		_____
Reception		_____	Matches		_____
BRIDAL ATTIRE	$_____		Guest Towels		_____
Dress		_____	Favors, Groom's Cake		_____
Headpiece and Veil		_____	Rice Bags, Garter		_____
Undergarments		_____	Hotel Accommodations		_____
Jewelry		_____	**HONEYMOON**	$_____	
Shoes		_____	Transportation		_____
Trousseau		_____	Accommodations		_____
WEDDING			Daily Allowance		_____
CONSULTANT	$_____				
			Total Budget	$_____	
			Total Estimated Cost		$_____

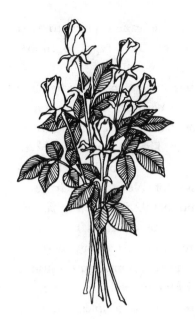

CHAPTER 4
Developing a Wedding Plan

It took Anne Sagnelli and her fiancé, Keith, 18 months, from start to finish, to plan their wedding in a university chapel followed by a formal, buffet dinner in a private club for 135 guests. "I shudder to use the word," she laughs, "but it was perfect. The whole thing went without a hitch. I'm still getting calls and notes from people telling me that ours was the most beautiful wedding they had ever attended."

No ordinary feat for a couple mixing Lithuanian/Italian/Irish families and orchestrating a wedding at the height of the season in June. But then Sagnelli is no ordinary woman: She's been a corporate special events manager for seven years. "No question about it. That experience helped," she admits.

Unlike Sagnelli, most brides-to-be are novices at planning an affair of the size, and the importance, of a wedding. Even a woman with considerable experience in entertaining will find her leadership ability tested, her sense of taste and style challenged, and her mind totally preoccupied with wedding details during the engagement period.

In focus groups conducted for *Modern Bride*, newlywed women aged 18 to 30 complained of having found the process of planning and preparing for a wedding to be more stressful, tedious, and fraught with conflict than they ever had anticipated. They also admitted to battles with parents, in-laws, shopkeepers, vendors, and sometimes their own fiancés, over choices related to the kind of wedding they wanted and over trying to maintain control.

Those who work regularly with bridal customers often comment that people shopping for weddings are not merely trying to secure the items and services they need, but are really trying to buy a dream. That's what makes the entire process of planning so complicated, but also so much fun. The whole must be greater than the sum of its parts, greater than the dress or the food or the flowers or the music alone. And the whole exists, at least in the planning stages, only in the imagination of the creator.

"It's a bride's and groom's sense of themselves, of who they are and what they want to project to their families and friends," says Marcy L. Blum, noted New York City wedding consultant. "A wedding is taking the ephemeral and making it real."

33

Living Your Fantasy

Let's talk a minute about fantasy and reality, because weddings are a bit of both and, inevitably, something happens to a woman when she starts to plan her own. As she translates her private joy into a public proclamation of love and commitment, the girlish notions of romance and make-believe reassert themselves. Sometimes, relatives and friends help that happen: the mother who wants her daughter to have the wedding she never had, or the former roommate whose recent nuptials rivaled Princess Di's. Sometimes, fantasies are awakened by the possibilities a bride-to-be never knew existed, possibilities pictured in magazines or touted on television. No matter how or when they occur, sentimental longings can prompt even the most no-nonsense, no-frills woman to make totally uncharacteristic choices and decisions.

Even couples who initially agree that they want a simple affair soon discover that, when it comes to weddings, there are many different definitions, and price ranges, of simplicity. A "simple" choice like the color or fabric content of tablecloths suddenly takes on epic proportions. Everything matters, because everything is a "once in a lifetime" decision, a personal reflection, a statement of your couplehood.

The tug of war between fantasy and reality, reason and emotion is normal, and it will probably happen to you. That's okay. The trick is to know it, to be prepared for it as a consumer and, through developing a plan and knowing what to expect, to prevent one whimsical moment from creating a chain reaction that overextends your resources.

Nobody said this was going to be easy, but then few worthwhile things ever are. If you can keep your wits and your sense of humor about you, though, planning a wedding can not only be managed, it can be enjoyed.

The Religious Ceremony

The centerpiece of the wedding celebration is, of course, the marriage ceremony, so that's the logical place to start. It's also the easiest place to start because you only have two basic types to choose from: civil or religious.

Among *Modern Bride* readers, the overwhelming majority, 87 percent of first-time brides, have a religious ceremony. Maybe that's because Americans are so pervasively religious: The National Study of Religious Identifications (directed by Barry Kosmin of the City University of New York Graduate School, 1989-90) found that 92.5 percent of Americans claim some religious identification. Or, maybe it's because only a religious ceremony, with its accompanying rituals and traditions, can do justice to the spiritual nature of the marital commitment.

Whatever the reason, most couples and their families, even those who may not practice their faiths regularly, find that they want to "sanctify" their union with the blessing of their clergy in the tradition of their faith. And indeed, for many denominations, anything less than a religious service constitutes no marriage at all.

If you envision a religious wedding ceremony, you'd not only better "get to the church on time," but you'd better get there ahead of time. Places of worship, like other popular wedding sites, are booked well in advance, plus they have the added demands of regular services, liturgical seasons, holy day observances, and other restrictions on their availability. If the two of you are of the same faith and have no impediments to marriage in that faith, then your initial visit with the clergy will be a routine matter of checking schedules and setting a date. And you must have a wedding date before you can set anything else!

QUESTIONS TO ASK

1. When is the earliest we could be married? (Some clergy/congregations/dioceses have minimum engagement periods.) What dates are open for the month/year we're considering?
2. Are there any papers to be filed, banns to be posted, or premarital preparation programs to be completed before the wedding?

3. Can you perform the ceremony for us in a location other than this house of worship? (This could also be a legal issue if you want an officiant from out of town.)
4. Are there liturgical restrictions? Will we be able to personalize our ceremony if we wish? In what ways?
5. When should we meet with you again regarding specific ceremonial arrangements?

If you both are Christian, as 86.5 percent of Americans claim to be, remember that there can still be differences in requirements among the different denominations. Some will not marry any Christian who does not uphold the sacramental nature of marriage; some insist that you believe in the Trinity; some consider divorce an impediment to remarriage. The point is, you never know until you ask, and you need to ask right away.

Be sure to integrate whatever guidelines and requirements the clergy gives you into your overall wedding preparations. Once you've set the date, you're on your way. Just don't forget to consider the tone and degree of formality the ceremony will establish when making subsequent wedding choices.

CONTEMPORARY SOLUTIONS

RELIGIOUS

❦ *If you are of markedly different faiths and hope to mitigate that difficulty between your families with a concelebrated wedding ceremony with clergy from both, then it is imperative that you contact them both immediately.*

Don't automatically assume that your differences can't be reconciled. You'll find most clerics eager, and maybe more able than you think, to help you work things out provided you've allowed them enough time to do so.

❦ *If neither of you identify with any one faith, or if you as a couple can't meet the specific requirements of a particular faith, but would still prefer a religious ceremony, then one of the nondenominational churches or nonsectarian chapels may be your answer.*

A ceremony there will bring a spiritual dimension to your ceremony without the religious requirements.

❦ *You've found a priest and a rabbi who are willing to co-officiate, but your Jewish family won't be comfortable sitting in a church and your Christian relatives won't be at ease in a synagogue.*

Choose a neutral location, such as a nonsectarian chapel on a university campus, or pick a reception site at which you can also hold the wedding ceremony. Some Catholic dioceses do not allow ceremonies to be performed outside of a church, but the priest may assist at a ceremony anywhere. Rabbis willing to co-officiate the marriage rarely have the same restrictions so, in this case, the rabbi becomes the main officiant.

You should know that in any co-officiated ceremony, only one of the clergy is, in fact, the official, legal celebrant. The other is, in essence, offering a blessing.

The Civil Ceremony

If you are not particularly religious, or if you have problems resolving Christian/non-Christian backgrounds, you should consider a civil ceremony. Marriage is one of the more enjoyable duties of most civil officials, and you don't have to settle for the 60-second special at City Hall.

Several officials are empowered to perform a marriage: judges, justices of the peace, mayors, county clerks, and superior court clerks. They usually hold the ceremony in their own offices or chambers but, if contacted in advance, most will be happy to officiate in any location you choose.

Some officials are quite eloquent and try to embellish the simple civil ceremony with their own wisdom and humor. If one of them is a personal or family friend, so much the better; you can work together to create the kind of individualized ceremony you want. You might also consider simply being married downtown with just immediate family and witnesses present, and then having a larger reception later in the day.

Contact the office that issues marriage licenses in your city to find out who is qualified and how to get in touch with them.

CONTEMPORARY SOLUTIONS

CULTURAL

❦ *Sometimes, a couple will have both a civil and a religious ceremony*.

This is a common practice in states that border Mexico, for instance, since Mexican law separates church and state and does not empower the clergy to perform a "legal" marriage. If one of you is a Mexican citizen, or a citizen of any other nation with similar legal/religious separations, you must have two ceremonies for the marriage to be recognized in the other country. (Contact the appropriate foreign consulate for specific information.)

In this situation, some couples choose to have the civil ceremony first, with just immediate family and friends, and then the religious ceremony and a large reception later, perhaps the next day. They may have two celebrations on two consecutive days, and the bride may wear two different, white wedding outfits. However, traditionally religious couples will not consider themselves married until the nuptial has been sanctioned by the church.

Still another alternative is to have the church wedding first, and then to have a civil official perform the legal ceremony and sign the pertinent documents at the reception immediately following the church service. Arrange your dual ceremonies in whatever way is most convenient and pleasing to you and to your family and friends. Issue separate invitations if you're having two separate celebrations.

WHO CAN OFFICIATE?

States differ in whom they will authorize to perform marriages and how "official status" is defined. A sampling of authorized officiants from the various states includes:

- Justices of the peace (sometimes called magistrates)
- State and national Supreme Court Justices
- Mayors
- County clerks/notaries
- Tribal chieftans
- Clergy "in good standing"

Call the county clerk's or registrar's office *in the location in which you plan to be married* to find out who is authorized there. In some states, authorization does not extend beyond a specific municipal or county line.

Being an Informed Consumer

The bridal market fuels $32 billion annually in retail sales. That's right—$32 billion, and growing. What that means for you is a tremendous array of goods and services available, probably more than you ever imagined, and a fierce competition for your business, which give you considerable leverage as a shopper.

Americans are the best-educated consumers in the world. Even as a novice in wedding planning, you can navigate this industry and make the range of choice and level of competition work for you, provided you bring the same consumer awareness to shopping for your wedding as you ordinarily bring to shopping for everyday goods and services.

Reputable suppliers have a vested interest in your satisfaction because your wedding will become, in effect, a word-of-mouth advertising campaign for whatever they're providing. When you and your guests are impressed with the food, service, or ambiance, word gets out. (You may, in fact, be making some of your own wedding selections on that basis now.) Customer satisfaction means more than momentary success; in the bridal industry, it means longevity, and that's what you want to look for.

Fair Lane, the Henry Ford Estate in Dearborn, Michigan, is a baronial mansion built in 1915, now a National Historic landmark. It is also typical of an enterprise that doesn't need to advertise a great deal. "Our clients are mostly automotive executive families and we do lots of repeat, word-of-mouth business," says Alice Cerniglia, public relations coordinator. "Between our historic location and our reputation for excellence in food and service, we are booked up to two years in advance."

Cerniglia's comments bring up another key factor that affects your position as a consumer: time. It can work for or against you, depending on how much of it you have. Popular services and prime locations in preferred seasons can be booked well in advance, so it pays to start shopping as early as you can, particularly for your reception needs. It is possible, of course, to plan a lovely wedding in under six months, but you may find some resources entirely unavailable, and you may have to pay a premium price for others. A tight planning schedule almost always precludes the wider range of choices and alternatives open to the couple with ten months to two years ahead of them.

To be a savvy consumer, you also need to understand the difference between economy and value. Economy is achieved when you have the time to shop around, to compare costs for a specific product or service from one source to the next. That kind of comparison shopping, of course, depends on knowing *exactly* what you want so you don't get less quality or service than you deserve.

That's where value comes in: getting what you want and wanting what you pay for. For instance, a super reception package may seem like a good buy until you realize that you don't care about the personalized napkins, matchbooks, cake boxes, and guest favors that are part of it. In that case, there's no value in the deal for you because you are being charged for something you really don't want.

A combination of comparison shopping and recognition of value will ensure that you get the most for your money. And you can do this without necessarily sacrificing style, because there are many ways to "cut back" without "cutting out." You just have to allow yourself enough time to consider the available choices and alternatives without feeling unduly pressured to "sign on the dotted line."

One final tip: Educate yourselves in this particular market. Attend bridal store shows sponsored by retailers in your area, as well as bridal expositions that travel throughout the country. You can also write for the numerous booklets and brochures offered in *Modern Bride*, many of them free. The more you learn about the quality and price of competing products and services, the better your choices will be, and the happier you will be with the choices you make. Gathering information costs you little, but it can save you a lot.

❧ TO HAVE OR HAVE NOT ❧
"On Line" Assistance

If you're already plugged into the computer for most of your business affairs, why not let your PC help with wedding tasks? Software packages are available specifically for that purpose (see magazine ads or visit your local software dealer), or you can adapt programs you may already own:

desktop calendar
planning & organizing, deadlines & social events

spread sheet
budgeting & comparing costs

data file
directory of resources, guest list, gift records

word processing
correspondence with vendors & suppliers

desktop publishing
designing maps, directions, schedules, program for ceremony, or even a bridal newsletter to keep attendants and out-of-towners informed

laser printer/fancy fonts
calligraphy for invitations and addressing envelopes

Considering a Wedding Consultant

There's no question about it: Wedding planning is time consuming. Good organization and a range of reliable resources are essential to pulling it all together. If your time is at a premium or if distance is a problem, a professional wedding planner is well worth the fee. With so many details to look after, a planner's experience can take the worry out of coordinating everything, save you costly oversights and

mistakes—and even provide hand-holding and mediation with obstinate relatives and friends.

Most wedding planners and consultants charge on either a flat fee or a percentage basis. Some may get discounts from vendors which, in turn, are passed along to you. Flat fees can range from several hundred to several thousand dollars, depending on the size of the wedding and the complexity of the tasks to be performed; percentage fees are based on the total wedding and reception cost and can range from 10 to 20 percent.

A successful wedding planner should be able to pass along enough savings to you to at least defray his or her own fee. Some can save you a great deal more than that because they know where to look for solid services at competitive prices, and because they have the added leverage of being a regular, repeat customer for those services. The bigger and more elaborate your wedding, the more savings you should realize overall. Most important, a good planner will work within the budget you've already set and ensure that you get the most in goods and services for the money you have to spend.

In addition to purchasing power and a knowledge of the marketplace, a truly creative consultant offers you the advantage of professional advice in matters of taste and style. He or she can help you add elements to personalize the more traditional ceremony and reception, or help you bring flair and ingenuity to a theme wedding. A consultant can suggest ideas you never thought about, find resources you never knew existed, and orchestrate a cast of thousands into a cohesive whole for weekend parties and related wedding events.

"What the couple is contracting is practical knowledge and design expertise," says Robbi Ernst III, president of June Wedding, Inc., in San Francisco. "Hanging out a shingle because you've been through one wedding is not enough." He cautions couples to interview wedding planners just as thoroughly as they would any other professional adviser to determine if they feel comfortable about the kind of care and experience the consultant can provide. "A wedding is too important, and too personal, to turn over to someone you're not completely sure you can trust," says Ernst.

Reputable consultants will always tell you up front whether or not it's worth your while to employ them for the size and type of party you're planning, and most will also agree to give you a one-time consultation, for a one-time fee, to help you get organized if you want to do the wedding yourselves. Expect to sign a contract for more extensive services, and before you do, make sure the contract stipulates exactly what the responsibilities and liabilities of the consultant are.

QUESTIONS TO ASK

1. Is the consultant a member of a professional party planning association or local business organizations?
2. What is the planner's background and experience?
3. Is there a list of client references you can contact?
4. Has the consultant been written about, at least in the local press?
5. Just how much, or how little, of the wedding is the consultant able to supervise?

Note: Check the consultant's reputation with area vendors and service personnel, and call the Better Business Bureau to see if any complaints have been lodged.

Setting the Date

While it's seldom possible to please everybody, you do want to think carefully about how your choice of wedding date will affect your family, friends, and attendants. Holiday weekends, for example, can be a blessing for some people—those who have to travel and won't have to take an extra day off from work—but a curse for others—those who might find babysitters hard to find or those who would have preferred to get away for a few days.

Generally speaking, the so-called "family holidays," Thanksgiving, Christmas, Easter/Passover, or the 4th of July, are not recommended times for weddings. Secondary holiday weekends, Memorial Day, Labor Day, or Columbus Day, are more acceptable, though you should expect that guests who only learn of your wedding when the invitation arrives may well have other plans. Likewise, choosing semester breaks or weekends from mid-May to mid-

June presents problems for those on different school-year schedules.

The greater the distance people have to travel, and the greater the diversity of age and obligation among them, the harder it's going to be to find a convenient wedding date. That's even true at more ordinary times of the year and when most of your guests reside in your area. Sunday night means some have to work the next day; Friday night means some will have to leave work early; mid-week means both.

These are the realities of the way we live today. About all you can do is take the lifestyles of your friends and families into consideration, and check the date in advance with those you care about the most.

Wedding Transportation

From a horse-drawn carriage to a London taxi, from a standard stretch limo to a classic Rolls-Royce, today's livery services can "get you to the church on time" in whatever style suits you. Over 72 percent of all couples employ hired transportation for their weddings, and the elegant white limousine is the conveyance of choice 85 percent of the time.

Wayne J. Smith, president of the National Limousine Association, the professional organization representing 900 member companies across the country, attributes the rise in hired livery service for weddings to both romance and reality. "For one thing, couples are sophisticated," says Smith. "They know that their choice of transportation can enhance their overall wedding style. But, more than that, they are also concerned about safety for themselves and those they love. They want everyone to feel free to celebrate, but they also want a safe wedding."

Besides being safe and comfortable, a special wedding-day conveyance is, to most couples, the ultimate luxury. Those with formality and elegance in mind will choose the traditional white, silver, or black limousines; those with a sense of romance might choose a nostalgic "replicar." (See more under "Theme Weddings" in Chapter 16.) Often, couples will even hire one or two additional vehicles for their bridal parties and their parents, so that all VIPs will arrive and depart in style and safety.

Wedding transportation is not a necessity, but it is an affordable luxury that alleviates some of the worry over getting everyone everywhere on schedule, especially with the wedding-day jitters. To that end, though, you'll want to be sure that you deal with an established, reputable company, and that you inquire about more than price when comparing various services.

Mr. Smith offers the following guidelines:
• Get word-of-mouth recommendations from people/businesses you know who have used a service before (or call the National Limousine Association for referrals; see Appendix).
• Set up a face-to-face meeting with the owner/manager of the company.
• Verify the insurance protection and the qualifications of drivers.
• Be sure that the company is licensed by the appropriate licensing authorities (state and municipal); this is especially important if the vehicles will be crossing state or county lines during your wedding service.
• Check to see if the company is a member of the National Limousine Association; this is some indication of reliability and service standards.
• Know what the liquor laws are in your area and *don't* expect any exceptions for your wedding. (In many areas, the use of alcoholic beverages is prohibited in vehicles, and that includes champagne!)

During peak wedding/prom/party seasons, the demand for transportation, especially for exotic vehicles, can easily surpass the supply, so you will want to start interviewing companies far enough in advance to allow for adequate choice and comparisons (three to four months should suffice). Be wary of companies who rely solely on phone answering machines, or who don't respond promptly to your initial inquiry. This could indicate poor reliability. Discuss your plans in general terms over the phone, and then make an appointment for a personal visit with those companies who seem able to meet your needs.

Finally, in the interest of romance, don't share your limousine ride from the ceremony to the reception with anyone else. These few minutes together are likely to be the only ones the two of you will have alone all day, and they are the first few minutes of your married life. Savor them, and keep them private.

QUESTIONS TO ASK

1. Are you fully licensed and insured?
2. How many and what type and size of car(s) will be necessary to appropriately transport us and our party?
3. May I select the exact vehicles to be used?
4. How are your rates structured? Is there a minimum number of hours that must be committed?
5. What services/amenities are included in these rates?
6. What are your policies on tipping?
7. How will the drivers be attired?
8. What deposit is required, and when is the balance due?
9. Do you take credit cards? (Most do.)

What Will It Cost?

Livery fees are structured on an hourly basis and will, of course, vary with availability and demand. In general, prices for luxury sedans to accommodate the couple alone start at around $40 per hour. Larger, more opulent vehicles are more expensive, so that a super stretch limousine accommodating six or eight people might run $85 to $90 an hour. Exotic, rare, or one-of-a-kind models often rent for considerably more.

In return for these rates, you have a right to expect that the car and driver will appear on time

at the designated locations; that the driver will be mannerly, knowledgeable, and appropriately dressed; and that the vehicle will be in pristine condition. The car should have been freshly cleaned and waxed, all appliances (television, stereo, etc.) should be in working order, and the bar (ice, soft drinks, champagne, whatever you've agreed upon) should be fully stocked.

KNOW YOUR CONTRACT

Expect to sign a written contract for limousine services that specifies the following:

- The date, time, and place(s) of service
- The number of people to be transported
- The number and types of vehicles to be used, including the vehicle identification number of the one(s) you've selected
- The liability, for both you and the company, for accidents and damages
- The hourly rates for each vehicle, and the total number of hours contracted
- Any additional fees (taxes, tips, etc.)
- The amount of deposit paid, the cancellation policy, and the date when the balance is due

---

About Valet Parking

While you're thinking about wedding transportation, it's also a good idea to think about valet parking for your guests. If your reception location can provide it, then all you need do is secure those arrangements through it. But if yours is to be a large affair at an off-site location, a private club, or home where no services are available, you may want to consider contracting a valet parking service for the convenience and security of your guests.

Such services do exist in most urban areas, and you'll find them advertised in the bridal supplements of your local paper. A representative of the service will visit your reception site, determine the best parking plan, and advise you on the number of attendants you'll need. Most services can also provide security and lighting, if needed.

Parking attendants should be appropriately dressed on the day of your wedding and provide courteous, efficient service. The company should be fully insured and licensed to do business, and all arrangements, including hourly fees and specific services, need to be contained in a contract.

If you're having a large wedding at a private residence, call the police department to check local ordinances and get their advice on parking and security on city streets. In some areas, where traffic congestion could be an issue, you will need a flagman (usually an off-duty police officer), a valet service, or some other certified person directing traffic and parking. Find out so your guests don't get ticketed, or worse.

Your Wedding Planning Checklist

12 to 24 Months Before the Wedding

☐ Together, visit the clergy. Set the date for the ceremony.

☐ Discuss expenses with all concerned and establish a firm budget.

☐ Decide on the size and the degree of formality for your wedding.

☐ Interview party planners/wedding consultants, if you plan to use one.

☐ Look for unusual locations in which to hold the celebration, if that's one of your preferences. Contact your local parks department or historical society. You can find listings in the nationwide directory *Places*, available at some libraries or directly from the publisher (see Appendix).

☐ Select the place you'd like to hold the reception. Make reservations if it is in a club, hotel, catering hall, or restaurant. If it is to be at home or at a place that does not provide food, check into

catering services and book them. Ask to see a variety of possible menus; inquire if a cake is included or if it must be arranged for separately.

☐ For an outdoor wedding, make alternate plans in the event of inclement weather. Options include a very sturdy tent and a platform that withstand rain, or an indoor alternative location indicated on the reception invitation.

☐ Shop for your wedding dress, complementary headpiece, and veil.

☐ Invite relatives and/or friends to be in your wedding party. Discuss finances with them and be considerate of their financial limitations.

☐ Select two or three possibilities for your attendants' gowns and arrange an appointment with the shop to bring your attendants in to see the choices. Because they pay for their own dresses, it's thoughtful to do this, if possible, but the final decision is definitely yours.

☐ Buy calendars for attendants and immediate families and mark important wedding-related dates for them in red. As other dates are made during the planning, they can plug them into the calendars.

☐ Draw up the guest list. Notify your families to do the same.

☐ Interview photographers, videographers, musicians, and florists. Make a separate folder for *each* service you select. Keep contracts, notes, questions, and all pertinent data in them for quick reference.

6 to 12 Months Before the Wedding

☐ Have your fiancé ask his attendants to be in the wedding.

☐ Select and order your invitations. Include extra envelopes in case of mistakes and a few extra invitations to have as mementoes for you and your family. If you want calligraphy and find handwork too expensive, look into computer resources. Ask for envelopes to be delivered early so you can address them leisurely. At the same time, order personal stationery (an ample supply of both letter and note paper) for writing thank-you notes.

☐ Have mothers select their dresses. Your mother has the privilege of first choice of the color and style she prefers. The groom's mother chooses a dress similar in formality and in a complementary color. Both should blend with your bridal party color scheme.

☐ Decide on the men's attire. Accompany your fiancé to a formal wear specialty shop in your locale to get expert advice on what the groom, best man, ushers, and fathers should wear.

☐ Register with the bridal gift registry in your favorite store. Meet with the director of the registry and the trained staff for help in choosing china, silver, crystal, linens, and other household preferences. Indicate engagement and shower gifts, as well as wedding presents.

☐ Discuss honeymoon destination possibilities. Send for brochures.

☐ Reserve the rehearsal dinner location.

4 Months Before the Wedding

☐ Address invitations and announcements. All addressing, stuffing, and stamping should be completed in time to mail the invitations four to six weeks before the wedding. If you have an "A" and a "B" list, you may mail "A" eight weeks in advance. When you receive regrets, you may invite people on "B" four weeks (and no less than three weeks) before the wedding.

☐ Prepare maps and directions to include with your invitations.

☐ Check with the post office for the postage needed to mail the invitations when all the pieces are enclosed in the envelope. Buy pretty "Love" stamps.

☐ Meet with the caterer to firm up the menu and all the details. If any guests require special food, arrange that now. Be sure all your expectations are clearly defined in a written contract, which should include taxes, service charges, and additional fees to bartenders and waiters, if not included in the package. Also, be certain that the location carries basic liability insurance protection.

☐ Engage a baker to create a special wedding cake if you want something more elaborate than what your caterer offers. Inquire about a cake-cutting charge if you bring the cake in from elsewhere.

☐ Investigate having air-conditioning in a tent when the wedding is to be held in warm-weather months.

☐ Plan a rehearsal dinner. Members of the wedding party, their spouses, fiancés, or significant others should be invited along with both of your immediate families. If possible, invite out-of-town guests, too.

☐ Arrange accommodations for attendants who do not live in town. If neither you, nor family, friends, or neighbors, can house them, make hotel reservations. Your fiancé should do the same for his attendants.

☐ Reserve a block of rooms at a hotel for out-of-town guests. Most hotels offer discounts for guests for a wedding weekend. Before mailing invitations, write to your guests and enclose the hotel information so they can make their reservations directly. Also provide them with a complete information package, including city maps, transportation schedules and prices, sights to see, and suggested restaurants.

☐ Ask a friend or relative to check on your out-of-town guests to be sure they are comfortable and to answer any of their questions. Provide that person's name and phone number in your letter because you will be busy those last few days.

☐ Visit your florist with dress-color swatches to help with the selection of flowers for your wedding and reception. Ask about providing the aisle runner. Again, be sure everything is clearly itemized in a contractual agreement.

☐ Decide on your honeymoon destination. Consult a travel agent. Traditionally, the groom makes these arrangements, but if you're better at that, don't hesitate to offer.

☐ Hire limousines.

☐ Investigate resources for designing and printing a program to distribute at the ceremony. Desktop publishing should make that possible at reasonable cost.

☐ Consult with your officiant about any restrictions on photography and videography during the ceremony.

☐ Discuss with helpful family or friends the possibility of their inviting out-of-town guests to dinner the night before the wedding, if you can't include them at your rehearsal dinner. Also, they might host a breakfast or lunch for travelers, if the wedding takes place late in the day.

2 Months Before the Wedding

☐ Compile a list of people you would like invited to showers.

☐ Tell the hostess for parties in your honor where you are registered. That store may be indicated on any invitation *except* the wedding invitation.

☐ Mail your wedding invitations.

☐ Record gifts. Note the giver's name, address, type of gift, date received, and date acknowledged.

☐ Write thank-you notes promptly. Within two months of return from your honeymoon, all gifts should be acknowledged.

☐ Confirm the date and time of rehearsals with your officiant.

☐ Notify attendants and family of the time and place.

☐ Send invitations to the rehearsal dinner.

☐ Plan a get-together in honor of your attendants.

☐ Select gifts for attendants. Your fiancé does the same for his.

☐ Choose your going-away outfit and honeymoon clothes.

☐ Begin trousseau shopping for lingerie and clothes you'll need wherever you plan to live afterward.

☐ Purchase a wedding guest book for friends and family to sign.

☐ Check with local authorities if a blood test is needed for a license.

☐ Make an appointment with your doctor for a complete physical. Be sure to see your dentist as well.

☐ Meet with the organist and anyone else who will play or sing at the service to determine the music.

☐ Meet with the musicians or DJ engaged to play at the reception to plan the selections you and your fiancé want, from "your song" to the dance tempo you expect them to maintain. Plan a variety so there's something older guests will enjoy, as well as what's hot among your peers. Caution them about excessive volume—it can ruin a reception. Tell them about any ethnic favorites you may want so they'll be familiar with the music. Inquire about breaks, continuous music, and overtime. Get it all in writing.

☐ Speak with the caterer about the food you want to serve to your photographer and musicians. Something simple to eat, a beverage, and a place to sit that's away from your guests are sufficient.

☐ Meet with the person handling your reception and firm up every detail. If rental equipment is required, make those arrangements now.

☐ Select the wedding ring(s). Arrange for engraving.

☐ Set a date with your photographer for a formal bridal portrait four weeks before the wedding.

☐ Discuss having a portrait of both of you done for the newspaper announcement. This is a contemporary alternative to the traditional photo. Or, you may submit a wedding photo of the two of you taken on your wedding day.

☐ Check with your local newspaper for the form and timing of your wedding announcement submission.

☐ Select party favors to present to your guests to thank them for sharing your happiness. For this purpose, a groom's cake, in traditional fruitcake or deep chocolate, may be ordered from your baker. Guests take a piece home in little boxes.

☐ Give thought to your cake top. Porcelain figurines are beautiful and will be a lasting memento. A creative baker will have other ideas to present.

☐ Talk about personalizing your ceremony and discuss your ideas with your officiant.

☐ Check with the church sexton and manager of the reception location for accessibility to accommodate handicapped or elderly guests. Inform ushers of this.

☐ Buy fake rings to sew on your ring bearer's pillow if you're having one. (The best man carries the real rings in his pocket.)

1 Month Before the Wedding

☐ Finalize plans with your photographer and make a list of pictures you want taken during the ceremony and reception.

☐ Ask a relative or friend who knows the family well to help the photographer identify the people to be included in your photos, especially if there is a divorce and remarriage or any type of sticky situation among parents of the couple.

☐ Develop an orderly system of tracking guests' responses and any special information you need to remember about them.

☐ Discuss the bachelor party with your fiancé. Suggest that the event be scheduled at least a week before the wedding day so there's plenty of time for your groom to recover from the revelry.

☐ Have final fitting of your gown and make certain it will be ready for your bridal portrait sitting.

☐ Make an appointment to have your hair styled just before your formal portrait is taken and again the day before or day of your wedding.

☐ Check apparel for the wedding party. Have bridesmaids' gowns fitted. Get swatches of material and have shoes dyed to match. If any attendants live out of town, send their dresses to them to be fitted. Check on the mothers' dresses and accessories.

☐ Call the caterer and make a final decision on the reception menu. Be sure that the cake has been ordered. Give a reliable estimate of the number of guests expected, so they can give you a written confirmation of cost per person with an itemized accounting—to the smallest detail—of what they promise to do.

☐ Confer with the florist to be sure everything is ordered. Confirm the time flowers will be delivered and decorations will be completed.

☐ Arrange transportation.

☐ Select groom's wedding gift. He does the same for you.

☐ Go over all procedures of the ceremony and receiving line. Make seating plans for the rehearsal dinner (if it is large), for the ceremony, and for the reception. Write out place cards, if you plan to have a bride's table and a parents' table. Decide who will be in the receiving line and plan positions.

☐ Keep gift checklist up to date and *write thank-you notes daily.*

☐ Consult movers for estimates on moving your gifts and personal belongings to another town if you're relocating. Be sure you are insured against any damage or loss while in transit.

2 Weeks Before the Wedding

☐ Make a date with your fiancé to get your marriage license.

☐ Be sure clothing and accessories for all members of the bridal party are in order.

☐ Complete the wedding announcement forms for your newspaper and your groom's hometown paper to submit with your photograph. Mail it soon.

☐ Take care of name changes on your bank account, Social Security card, license, insurance, etc.

1 Week Before the Wedding

☐ Finalize your rehearsal dinner arrangements or other plans.

☐ Wrap gifts for your attendants and groom. Present them at the festivities following the rehearsal.

☐ Make plans to transport gifts brought to the reception, to parents' home, or other designated place.

☐ Call guests who have not responded to the invitation to ask if they'll be attending the reception. Add last minute acceptances and phone caterer with final count.

☐ Confirm vocalists and musicians, and recheck your selections.

☐ Arrange your gift display. All cards should be removed. Checks are not displayed, but a card stating "Check from Aunt Louise" may be substituted. Insure gifts against loss or theft.

☐ Invite friends and relatives to drop by to see your gifts.

☐ Give a small gift or write a note of appreciation to friends and relatives who did special favors to make your planning run smoothly.

☐ Make a final check with florist, caterer, sexton, clergy, musicians, photographer, and videographer.

☐ Begin honeymoon packing.

1 Day Before the Wedding

☐ Have a manicure, pedicure, and even a massage to pamper yourself and help you relax.

☐ Attend the rehearsal. Review all duties with the principals in the wedding party.

☐ Give ushers the list of guests to be seated in the reserved section.

The Wedding Day

☐ Rest and thoroughly relax in a nice warm bath.

☐ Allow plenty of time to dress—about two hours before you have to be at the ceremony or ready for photographs.

☐ Have a wonderful day and enjoy every beautiful moment!

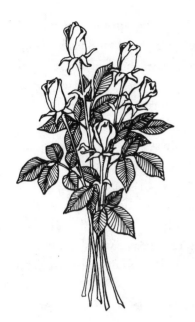

CHAPTER 5

Reception Options

With a wedding size, budget, and date determined, and with a vision of the type of wedding ceremony and reception pretty much formulated in your mind, you're ready to begin shopping for all the related goods and services. We recommend tackling the reception next, because securing the site for the date you want is so important, especially if your ceremony is to be performed there.

Depending on what's available in your area, your reception possibilities are: a hotel or catering establishment, a club or restaurant, a community center or meeting hall attached to a church or synagogue, a private home, or an unusual setting, such as a park, boat, historic site, etc. Each type of location offers a particular ambiance and distinct advantages and disadvantages, as you will discover when you visit them.

Most couples find shopping for their reception fun because they often are treated to dinner, or at least invited to sample the menu items. They can also arrange to visit clubs to hear musicians play or receive videotapes of reception locations and parties that were held there. Along the way, you're sure to learn a lot about the hospitality industry, and to refine your tastes and define your style. Maybe, with a bit of luck, you'll even meet a banquet manager with whom you have an instant rapport and in whom you can place your total confidence.

On-Site Locations

Reception sites fall into two basic categories: on-site and off-site. On-site means that the place can provide most, or all, of the reception services you'll need: food, beverage, staff, tables, linens, china, maybe even the flowers, the music, and the cake. On-site locations include hotels, restaurants, clubs, and catering halls; some church and community centers, historic settings, and more unusual places may have on-site capabilities as well, or will at least have caterers and suppliers to recommend based on a history of successful performance.

Obviously, the convenience of one-stop shopping is what makes on-site locations so popular with wedding couples, particularly those planning very large affairs. Catering directors or program coordinators at these places are experienced party professionals. They will not only work with you to coordinate all the major elements of your reception, many will even coordinate related details with all other outside suppliers, like musicians, florists, photographers, and limousine drivers. Because they orchestrate special events all the time, they know how to keep things running smoothly and efficiently, and how to remember everything you might be likely to forget, especially on your wedding day.

The flip side to the convenience of one-stop shopping is that, by booking an on-site location, you are also booking the services offered there. You may not be allowed to bring in your own wedding cake or florist. You may be forced to choose from among several, preset "wedding packages," and your wedding might not be the only affair in progress at the time. In the end, only you can decide whether the services and conveniences offered meet your needs.

Off-Site Locations

Off-site locations are those that offer no services on the premises. You have the space (a private home) or you pay a rental fee for it (a loft, historic site, etc.), and you have to bring in everything yourself. While an independent caterer may be able to provide much of what you need in addition to the food and beverage, some cannot. You'll find that the term "caterer" can mean anything from someone who prepares only specialty food items to a full-service company that comes complete with tents and air conditioners.

The good news about an off-site location is that you can have it all your way. You will choose and coordinate all the details, and you will be virtually guaranteed of a wedding that is quite unlike anyone else's. If that distinction is worth the extra cost in time, and often money, to you, then it is the way to go.

Tented Affairs

The use of party tents for weddings is becoming increasingly popular, particularly for "at home" cel-

ebrations or those held on the grounds of historic mansions and parks. With big weddings back in style and spaces to accommodate them at a premium, people have looked to see what's new in tent technology, and they've been surprised, and delighted, at what they've found.

Want archways, pathways, or bridges? Chandeliers, parquet floors, or stained-glass panels? Ladies' rooms, men's rooms, or air-conditioning? How about two or three or more tents, all connected by covered marquees and color-coordinated, perhaps to match your wedding? These days, you don't have to settle just for a tent; you can build your own community!

"Couples don't realize the possibilities tenting offers to create a truly individualized ambiance and atmosphere," says Jacquelynne O'Rourke of Edelweiss Caterers, Inc., in Danbury, Connecticut. She and her husband, James, began strictly as caterers, but soon found themselves coordinating more and more tented affairs. Now, 10 years later, their expertise in both food and facilities has been put to the test at weddings as large as 500 in New York, New Jersey, and upper New England, as well as all over Connecticut.

"We have so many beautiful natural sites in this part of the country, including the lawns and gardens of private homes," she points out. "People want to take advantage of them."

And they do—in every season. Today's tent specialists come with their own generators for heating, cooling, cooking, and dancing to DJs or live music. The O'Rourkes work with several companies, each with different capabilities and in various price ranges. They also supervise the construction and coordinate all the fittings and furnishings.

"Creating your own site can get very involved," O'Rourke admits. "*Everything* has to be obtained from a supplier, and somebody needs to be in charge of putting it all together."

The cost of a tented affair will run about the same, or maybe a little more, as a similar function in an established location because all necessary items are rented, and priced, separately. If you're considering a tent wedding, here's what you'll need:

- At least one tent, 40' × 100' or 60' × 60' for 200 people
- Any additional tents for the ceremony, cocktails, cooking, or restrooms
- Covered walkways or connecting marquees
- Generators for heating, cooling, lighting, cooking, or musical equipment
- Additional equipment for cooking or sound hookups, also back-up generators and porta-johns
- A dance floor, hardwood flooring, or ground cover
- Chairs and tables
- Table linens and chair covers
- China, flatware, and glassware
- A complete staff, including any supervisory personnel required by safety codes
- Any permits required by local ordinance

Fantasy Locations

Successful weddings of all sizes have been orchestrated in so many unusual locations that it is virtually impossible to discuss them all. Consider:

- Yachts, paddlewheelers, and cruise ships
- Lofts, galleries, and museums
- Wineries, ranches, and racetracks
- Theaters and studios, movie sets, and amusement parks
- Zoos, wildlife preserves, and botanical gardens
- Corporate centers, historic sites, and college campuses

An extraordinary location will offer extraordinary charm, but it may mean an extraordinary planning effort, as well. You'll have to deal with the logistics of transportation, parking, and guest accessibility. You'll have to consider what is and is not available on the premises; most have adequate facilities for caterers, but some might require setting up your own kitchen. Then there's the interior. What

---

RECEPTION TRENDS

Party planners and catering directors around the country report these trends. Some seem destined to last.

Food and drink—a preference for poultry and seafood, wine and champagne, because of health awareness and a distaste for "conspicuous consumption"; the return of basic "meat and potato" dishes for economic reasons

Resurgence of the cocktail party—especially in large cities where time, space, and money are key factors

Renewed formality—whether it's a garden wedding during the day or a black-tie affair in the evening, a mood of elegance prevails

Theme weddings—everything, down to the last decorative detail, is orchestrated with a period, ethnic, or design motif (see Chapter 16)

Nontraditional wedding cakes—in a variety of shapes, flavors, and colors; also serving groom's cake in chocolate, German chocolate, or carrot

Wedding weekends/multiple receptions—a series of coordinated parties and events for wedding guests; usually done because the majority of family members and friends are from out-of-town, and therefore must go "on location" to share the couple's special day

---

will you need to do to customize the decor and provide for guest convenience?

Fantasy locations are especially suitable for "theme weddings," and that's often why such sites are chosen. Experienced party planners are accustomed to dealing with the problems inherent in

CONTEMPORARY SOLUTIONS

PERSONAL, FAMILY

❦ *Your guest list includes enough men, women, and children to populate a small city, but the two of you still don't want an elaborate, formal wedding.*

No problem. The size of the wedding doesn't automatically make it formal or informal; the setting has a significant influence, as well. Strive for warmth and originality over pomp and circumstance in your ceremony, perhaps by personalizing your vows, using contemporary musical selections, and choosing an informal reception site that will be conducive to fun and gaiety. Reinforce a casual tone with appropriate selections of attire, food, music, and decorations.

PERSONAL, CULTURAL, RELIGIOUS

❦ *One family objects to serving alcohol at the reception, and the other can't imagine its relatives and friends celebrating without it.* The real question is: How do the two of you feel about it?

Here are some possible solutions: (a) serve nonalcoholic beverages (sparkling grape juice and cider or nonalcohol-based punch); (b) pour glasses of champagne only for the bridal toast; (c) have an open bar in a separate area and let the family who wants liquor available for its family and friends foot the bill. Toast with sparkling grape juice.

The bar bill can be a significant reception expense, but under *no* circumstances should any of your guests be subjected to a cash bar to reduce reception costs. They should not be expected to tip bartenders either; that should be included in the gratuities in your contract. (Appoint someone to remove any tip receptacles that appear on the bar at the last minute.)

Of course, a family's objections might not be on monetary grounds at all, but for religious or personal reasons. If you two are nondrinkers and do not plan to serve alcohol in your home, then you are not obligated to have it at your wedding.

PERSONAL

❦ *The chapel for your ceremony and the private club for your reception are both available on the same day, but with a significant lapse of time between the two events. What can you do with your guests for the hours that intervene?*

With the overwhelming popularity of certain choice locations, this is an increasingly common problem. There are several answers. Guests who live locally can probably amuse themselves for a few hours, or they might be invited, along with out-of-town guests, to your parents' home or that of another relative or friend. A hospitality suite at the hotel comes in handy in this situation, too. If many guests are visitors to your city, you could even rent a bus or van and arrange a sight-seeing tour.

unusual locations, of course, but are you? When you start bringing in outside contractors, costs can quickly get out of hand, and important details can get overlooked.

If you've always dreamed of a truly unique setting for your wedding celebration, then by all means investigate whatever is available in your area. Contact the local parks and recreation department, historical societies, or the Chamber of Commerce, or talk to a professional party planner who is known for "the theatrical." Just be sure you know what's involved before you commit.

QUESTIONS TO ASK

These are general queries to make on your initial visit to a site. You can get more specific about menu items, service, taxes and gratuities, and other details later on before you finalize the contract.

1. Is this site appropriate to the style and tone we visualize for our wedding, and is it conveniently located to the site of the ceremony?
2. Is there a rental fee and, if so, what exactly does it include?
3. Are we getting the most for our money in terms of the time of day, day of week, and month of the year?
4. What is the maximum number of guests the site can accommodate, seated and unseated? Is there a minimum number that must be guaranteed?
5. If my wedding will not be the only affair in progress, how will privacy be ensured and for how many hours will I have the space?
6. Are there facilities for music and dancing (piano, dance floor, microphones, etc.)?
7. Are there regulations or restrictions regarding music, photography, decorations, etc.?
8. If this is an off-site location, are there adequate facilities for food preparation and service? Are there charges for those facilities? May I choose whatever independent caterer and service personnel I wish?

9. If on-site, what is the approximate price per person for the kind of food and beverage service I want? What else does that price include?
10. What is the standard service staff-to-guest ratio?
11. Are there adequate parking and guest facilities, including wheelchair access and convenience for elderly guests?
12. Is there an area for the ceremony, special changing rooms, or any other separate spaces I'll need?
13. If an outdoor site, what will we do in case of inclement weather?
14. Does this location carry liability insurance in case a guest is injured during my affair or in an accident resulting from DWI after leaving the reception?
15. What kind of a reservation deposit is required? What are the payment terms and the refund/cancellation policy if my plans should change?

Ways to Save on Your Reception

1. Investigate your "dream" location. It may be more reasonable than you think, and it doesn't cost anything to inquire.
2. The same reception (fare) at a different time of day can be less expensive. This is definitely true on weekdays and during less popular months. Explore alternatives.
3. Take advantage of coordination services offered by catering managers at your reception site. They have a vested interest in the success of your affair, and will often work with, and recommend, outside suppliers.
4. Buffet service can be more expensive than passed or plated service because of the additional amount of food required for a fresh-looking display. Check.
5. Buy hors d'oeuvres by the piece, not by the platter. Who knows what size tray will be used?

❧❧ TO HAVE OR HAVE NOT ❧❧
Reception Fare

Today, individuality and flexibility are in, rigidity is out. You need not have a particular type of reception just because others are having it, although some types of receptions are more typical in one region than in another. Adapt your own plans to your style and budget, but here are general guidelines for receptions of any size. Of course, wedding cake is served regardless of how little or how much other food you provide.

Time of Day	Type of Reception	Reception Fare
Morning 10 A.M.–1 P.M	Champagne breakfast Buffet brunch	Simple, but varied: coffees & teas, sweet rolls, muffins & buns, croissants & crepes, quiche, berries with custard or fresh cream
Midday noon	Brunch or lunch Sit-down or buffet	Same as above, plus salads, pastas, cold poached salmon or chicken, light sorbet, sparkling wines
Mid-afternoon 2 P.M.–5 P.M.	Tea or open-house style	Light buffet with champagne punch, teas & coffees, miniature sandwiches, assorted cheeses and fruits, sweets & tarts, nuts & mints
Early Evening 4 P.M.–7 P.M.	Cocktail or food station buffet	Eclectic: seafood & pasta, brochettes, carving stations, cheese & fruit, wine & champagne
Evening 6 P.M.–on	Traditional sit-down dinner	Cocktails & hors d'oeuvres, three or four course dinner including appetizer, soup/salad, meat, poultry, or fish entrée with mélange of vegetables & a light dessert
Late Evening 8 P.M.–on	Sit-down or station buffet	Hearty hors d'oeuvres or light supper: fish or chicken stir-fry, vegetable pastas

6. To save on liquor, limit open bar service to one hour of cocktails and serve wine/champagne with dinner.

7. If your wedding is during a holiday season, check to see what decorations might be in place at the site. You may not need more.

8. Ask hotels about complimentary bridal suites, discounted room rates for guests, and special honeymoon packages at related properties.

9. *Always* note the "escalation clause" when booking far in advance. Most places will reserve the right to raise quoted prices in accordance with the latest Consumer Price Index at the time of final payment. Try to negotiate a ceiling. (See sample contract, p. 55.)

About Contracts

When you've made all the decisions on what, when, and where, you're ready to make a commitment. That means a contract or a sales agreement. Expect to sign one with every single supplier with whom you deal: stationer, reception site, caterer, bakery, bridal salon, musicians, florist, photographer/videographer, decorator/designer, limousine service, and wedding consultant (if you have one).

Everything should be covered in the contracts, from types, sizes, and numbers; to dates, times, and delivery schedules; to taxes, gratuities, and other "extras"; to payment plans, cancellation fees, and refund policies. (See specific concerns under discussions of individual wedding services.) Read all contracts carefully, and be sure you understand exactly what is being promised and how, and when, the bill is to be paid. If you have any qualms about the suppliers with whom you're dealing, call the Better Business Bureau to see if any complaints have been registered against them.

With a clear contract in hand, you have something to rely on when lines of communication get crossed. Of course, there's no retake on a wedding, and going to court later can't help you recapture those lost moments when things go wrong. That's why it is so necessary that you deal with reputable business people. Phone or visit your vendors at agreed upon intervals, and use your contracts as you go along to verify that products and services are being prepared as you've agreed.

Catering Contracts

Careful consideration of the contract is especially important for the reception services because charges for food, beverages, waiters, and waitresses are not the only ones you're likely to incur. There may also be space rental, fees for linens and china, costs for staff to set up and take down, or even surcharges for heat and air-conditioning! Everything, down to the last canape, must be specified.

You'll probably be asked for a deposit of 10 to 25 percent at the time you reserve the site or service. This percentage is figured on the initial estimated cost (base price per person or minimum package) for your size party. As a rule, there is a three payment schedule: the next installment is due a few months later, and the final payment is made anywhere from 8 weeks to 10 days before the wedding, after specific menu selections have been made. Often, that final payment (the last 50 percent) is required in cash or certified check. As much as we would like to advise you to use a major credit card as a recourse to withholding final payment if your agreement is not fully satisfied, the fact is that few establishments permit this.

With full payment made in advance, the obvious question is, "What if . . . ?" What if the food, service, or delivery is not as promised? Unfortunately, there's not a great deal you can do after the fact except to make mental notes of what went wrong and hassle with them about it later, perhaps through an attorney. Your position will be much stronger if you have *everything* in writing, including the final menu selections. If it isn't written down somewhere, don't expect it; if it is, do everything possible in advance to make sure you get what you are paying for.

The terms of payment now standard in the industry for many wedding services also make a case for the advantages of hiring your own bridal consultant (see next section). Not only can the independent consultant provide invaluable guidance in your selection of vendors and suppliers, but his or her "repeat buying power" can protect your financial investment. "A good reputation is still the best insurance," says Gayle Labenow of You Are Cordially Invited on Long Island, New York.

Reputation and good faith work both ways, of course, and many fees and payment policies, which may seem unfair, have resulted from honest business people too often being stuck with bad checks, changed minds, and unreasonable expectations. The bridal industry is a service-oriented industry, and that makes everyone vulnerable. But brides, or mothers, or anyone who's planning an affair like a wedding within a limited time frame and with little or no experience, are the most vulnerable of all. They are likely to make commitments in haste, or out of desperation, and live to regret it.

Labenow advises couples to thoroughly investigate their resources, to speak up, and to learn to negotiate contract terms. "If you can't do that," she says, "then get someone to do it for you, *before* you make any commitments. Once people have already signed contracts with sites, caterers, musicians, etc., even the best, most influential consultant can't be hired later to change the terms or redress the grievances."

Guidelines for Standard Contract Terms and Conditions

Forms may vary from one establishment to another, but *all* catering or reception contracts will include the following sections. Look for them.

AGREEMENT AND DEPOSIT: A deposit (usually 25 percent) of the anticipated total bill, based on an estimated number of guests, is made at the time the agreement is signed. The contract is made for a certain space or location to accommodate a minimum number of guests at an average per-person cost.

COSTS: Total cost is based on an average per-person charge within certain menu selections. To this will be added applicable state and local sales taxes, and gratuities (usually 15 to 20 percent). Contracts also generally contain an "escalation clause"; that is, the caterer reserves the right to pass along any increase in costs to him that may occur between the time the contract is signed and the day the event takes place. Often the increase is tied to the Consumer Price Index; regardless, a ceiling (usually 3 to 5 percent) should be stipulated.

GUARANTEES: A minimum number of guests are guaranteed, not to exceed a maximum number based on the space. Final guest count must be given three to five days before the event.

PAYMENT AND REFUND POLICIES: Balance due on the remaining contract is expected before the event takes place, anywhere from two weeks to a few days before, often when the final guest count is given. Any additional expense incurred at the affair itself (overtime, additional food or beverage, etc.) will be payable upon completion of the function.

XYZ PRIVATE FUNCTIONS AGREEMENT TERMS AND CONDITIONS

1. Patron hires Caterer to provide the services as described in this agreement and Patron agrees to pay therefore as herein provided. The Patron guarantees payment for the minimum attendance and agrees to notify the Caterer at least 3 business days prior to the event of any increase in such minimum. Parties are booked in locations with limited capacity, and therefore, increases of over 3% may only be accepted with consent of the Caterer.

2. If Patron cancels the function or this agreement, or if Caterer cancels the function because Patron has violated this agreement and if Caterer has been unable to rebook the space, Caterer shall charge as a cancellation fee the difference between the total contract price hereunder and the cost of performance of this agreement, plus actual expenses reasonably incurred. The remainder of the deposit will be returned to Patron; without interest. If Caterer can rebook the space, the cancellation fee shall equal 5% of the contract price (but not more than $100) plus actual expenses incurred. The foregoing cancellation fee shall be consistent with the requirements of the NYC Department of Consumer Affairs—Reg. No. 518.

3. Patron agrees that it will not permit the consumption of alcoholic beverages at the function by any person under 21 years of age, and further agrees to cooperate fully with the Caterer in seeing to it that no person under 21 years of age is permitted to drink alcoholic beverages on the premises.

4. The gratuities set forth in paragraph 11 of this agreement and applicable State sales taxes are in addition to the prices herein agreed upon, except as specifically stated otherwise.

5. Patron will pay a deposit on signing of the contract and other deposits as requested by Caterer. The balance due on the full contract price will be payable two weeks before the date of the function unless other arrangements for payment have been made in writing. Any amounts due in excess of the contract price will be payable upon completion of the function.

6. Performance of this agreement is contingent upon the Caterer's ability to perform, and the management shall not be responsible for failure to perform due to labor troubles, government acts and regulations, fires, acts of God, and other causes, whether or not similar to the foregoing, beyond the Caterer's control. Caterer reserves the right to change the room location of the function.

7. The Patron agrees that the Caterer's rules for functions, as set forth below, will be strictly complied with by the Patron and his employees, agents and guests.:
   a) No beverage, food, floral decorations or entertainment of any kind will be permitted on the premises without permission of the XYZ Catering Department. The Caterer's regular charges for the handling of any such arrangements will be paid by the Patron on demand.
   b) The function shall begin promptly at the scheduled time and the function room shall be vacated promptly at the indicated closing time. Should the time be extended, the Patron will bear the additional costs resulting therefrom.
   c) The Patron shall be responsible for any damages and losses to the Premises of XYZ or others, caused by the Patron or any of the Patron's employees, agents, guests or other persons attending the function.
   d) The Patron shall not put up any display on the premises or entrances without the written consent of the Caterer.
   e) The function shall be conducted by the Patron in an orderly manner in full compliance with all the rules of the Caterer and with all applicable laws, ordinances and regulations.
   f) Games of chance will not be permitted unless proper legal permission has been requested and obtained from local authorities by the Patron.

8. The Caterer shall not be liable for damages to, or loss of, any merchandise, samples, equipment or any goods or personal property exhibited, displayed or left in any room, or other areas of the Caterer.

9. Due to increases in costs of goods, labor, taxes or foreign currencies at the time of the function, the prices quoted may be increased, or reasonable substitutions of menu items may be made.

10. In the event this agreement is signed in the name of a corporation, partnership, association, club or society, the individual signing same represents to the Caterer that he or she has full authority to sign and deliver this agreement.

11. A gratuity of twenty percent (20%) of the total food and beverage charges will be added to the Patron's bill, of which 13.5% is to go to the captains, waiters, waitresses, and where applicable, bus-boys and/or bartenders engaged in the function, and 6.5% for supervisory, sales and other banquet personnel.

12. Patron agrees to protect, indemnify, defend and hold harmless Caterer and his agents and employees, against all claims, losses or damages to persons or property, government charges or fines, and cost (including reasonable attorneys' fees) arising or connected with the function, including, but not limited to, the installation, removal, maintenance, occupancy, or use of the premises, or part thereof, by Patron or any guest, invitee or agent of Patron, or any independent contractor hired by Patron, except those claims arising out of the sole negligence or willful misconduct of Caterer.

_____
(Caterer)

AGREED AND ACCEPTED BY PATRON:

NAME _____

TITLE _____

If the patron cancels the affair after the contract has been signed, the return of the deposit and any other prepayment is contingent upon the caterer being able to rebook the space for that date and time. Even then, some will retain part of the deposit as a "cancellation fee." Make sure any fees or percentages are specified.

ALCOHOLIC BEVERAGES: No alcoholic beverages may be brought onto or removed from the premises without the consent of the caterer or establishment. As an alcoholic beverage licensee, the caterer is subject to the rules and regulations of the State Liquor Authority; therefore, the patron must agree that no guest under legal age will consume alcoholic beverages on the premises.

DISPLAY AND DECORATIONS: All decorations and entertainment are subject to the approval of the caterer. Displays, floral arrangements, decorations, musical equipment, etc., must be of a type that will not damage the premises, and all must be set up and removed as required by the caterer.

SECURITY AND LIABILITY: The patron agrees to be liable for any damage or breakage caused by the guests. The caterer, in turn, is not responsible for any loss of or damage to property any guest brings onto the premises.

INDEMNIFICATION: The patron agrees to "hold harmless" the caterer or establishment and their employees against all claims, losses, or damages to persons or property, fines or fees (including attorneys' fees) arising out of or connected to the event, except those arising out of sole negligence or willful misconduct on the part of the caterer. (This means any claim brought by you or your families, individual guests, or independent contractors: musicians, photographers, etc.)

Rethinking the Reception

As you visit sites and make final decisions, take note of architectural details, color schemes, and menu

---

SERVICE TERMS YOU NEED TO KNOW

FOR FOOD:

buffet—guests serve themselves from one central food display

butlered (passed) service—hors d'oeuvres passed among guests on waitered trays

food stations—guests serve themselves from various locations, each devoted to a specialty (seafood, pasta, carved meats, etc.)

French service—seated diners are served individually from a tray of food, held by one waiter, served by another

gratuities—a fee for tips for all service personnel (usually 15 to 20 percent)

maitre d'—terminology differs according to place; may mean head waiter, captain, or person in charge of all food and beverage service staff

plated service—prearranged plates of food are set in front of seated diners

Russian service—seated diners are served individually by one waiter alone, who both holds and serves the food from a tray or tureen

staff ratio—the ratio of waitstaff to guests; 1 to 10 or 12 guests is considered good for seated affairs; 1 to 15 or 18 for buffet service

FOR DRINK:

consumption bar—same as open bar, except the host is charged per drink based on a running bar tab. This is practical only when the majority of your guests are not drinkers.

corkage fee—fee per bottle charged to open and serve liquor you bring in

mixed drinks—drinks that take exotic mixes or fancy equipment to make; may be more expensive than simple drinks

open bar—wine, beer, or spirits available by request for a prescribed length of time (during the cocktail hour) or for the entire evening. Host pays a flat rate based on the average per-guest consumption calculated in advance.

> **poured drinks**—simple drinks that do not require mixing, stirring, or shaking
>
> **premium** or **"name" brands**—well-known or quality brands of liquors, imported or vintage label beers and wines
>
> **tableside** or **barside service**—beverage service provided at the table by a waiter or by a "rolling" bar, as opposed to the guest having to get up and go to the bar

possibilities at the places you've chosen. Is there a decidedly French, Italian, or other influence? Does the setting evoke another historical period or imply a certain degree of formality? Brides often select their gowns, pick their colors, or decide to incorporate a theme into their wedding because of the style and tone evoked by the ceremony and reception sites.

This is a good time, then, after you've made these preliminary selections, for you and your fiancé to recall the "wedding vision" you discussed earlier. How well are the choices you've made so far fitting that vision?

Certainly, you won't want to make any subsequent choices (in menu, music, flowers, invitations, etc.) that will clash with the dominant character of a particular site. For example, an ornate ballroom with marble columns and moldings in gold relief might be best left unadorned so as not to overwhelm; whatever appointments or decorations you choose must reflect the elegance of the room. By the same token, a Spanish mission or a country farm might cry out for the casual, for wildflowers in wicker baskets and table appointments in bright colors with accents in pottery and straw.

Or perhaps you have the opposite concern: a barren space that will take considerable embellishment. In this case, you'll enjoy more freedom to cre-

ate the ambiance you want, but you'll have to start thinking now about what will be needed to bring some style and character to a nondescript place. Again, you'll want to choose your own attire and your wedding colors with that challenge in mind. Remember, throughout your decision making, every choice has to work together to create a pleasing whole.

Here are some aesthetic touches you might want to consider:

- Drape fabric or rent artwork to cover wall flaws or add character.
- Use topiary trees, cascades of ribbon, or floral garlands to accentuate arches and pathways.
- Rent columns, screens, or pedestals to lend architectural interest.
- Use votive candles, rented lamps, or tiny white lights to create mood and atmosphere.
- Consider professional lighting effects and sound systems.
- Print menus or frame artistic table-assignment cards that guests can take home as mementoes.
- Have cocktail napkins, matchbook covers, even soap in the restrooms monogrammed with your initials or names and wedding date.
- Use multi-layered table linens, pinned or draped with bows, in your wedding colors.
- Coordinate menu selections with an eye toward color appeal, degree of formality, and an ethnic or design motif.

You can get some other ideas from the chapters on theme weddings and ethnic celebrations, but these suggestions should make you aware of the kinds of things you can do. Creative visualization and attention to detail are the hallmarks of successful party planners everywhere. With some time, some imagination, and yes, some money, you can bring that touch to your celebration yourself.

CONTEMPORARY SOLUTIONS

PERSONAL, FAMILY

❦ *You've narrowed your choices for a reception to either an elegant club with mediocre food and service, or a restaurant with great food and service in a less-than-desirable atmosphere. The cost of both are about the same. Which should you choose?*

The choice between food or atmosphere is a familiar dilemma for all of us who dine out. It really depends on what you value the most and on what other commitments, in terms of style and budget, you may have made already.

If the elegant club is more appropriate to your wedding style, then keep menu selections there simple and service requirements uncomplicated. A buffet or "house specialties" might be the best bets. But, if food and service matter most, then call in a floral designer or professional party planner to see what can be done to enhance the surroundings at the restaurant. You may have to cut your budget somewhere else in order to afford this assistance, but you can probably hope to do more to improve the atmosphere at a site than you can to improve food and service.

PERSONAL, SOCIOECONOMIC

❦ *Reception costs are exorbitant at the only place available for your date and your size wedding. The expense promises to throw the whole budget out of whack. What can you do?*

First, be sure you've compared costs at this location for different times of day and different menus, and that you have thoroughly investigated other alternatives in your area, including tents and private caterers. If none of these suits you, there are three choices: (1) change the wedding date so that more options will be open to you; (2) reduce the size of your guest list so you can go somewhere else; or (3) absorb the unexpected reception expense by revising your budget downward for all other wedding costs: gown, flowers, music, etc. We caution, however, that the panic of having to book a place because there seems to be nothing else is a dangerous situation to let yourself be drawn into.

FAMILY, CULTURAL

❦ *Your ethnic family expects the food and fare they're used to from "the old country," but your own tastes are considerably more sophisticated. How can you have the "classy" wedding and reception you want without disappointing many of your relatives and family friends?*

No one culture has inherently "more class" than another. It all depends on how you translate the traditions into a modern social setting. You can have a "classy," even a very formal, wedding while still allowing your guests to enjoy *gnocchi* or dance the *hora*. Perhaps you can use symbolic colors or flowers in your decorations, or integrate an ancient ritual into a personalized marriage ceremony. Such signs of respect for your family heritage can enhance the true meaning of your celebration by emphasizing the value of preserving tradition as each new family is formed. (See "Ethnic Customs," in Chapter 16, for more ideas.)

Reception Protocol

Each family has its own style, and each celebrates in its own way. Some are reserved and dignified; others are fun-loving and festive. You'll have to consider the combined character of your collected relatives and friends when determining not only what you will have at the reception, but how you will have it.

We realize, of course, that some situations are difficult: estranged parents, feuding relatives, etc. But you can't force people to be other than who they are, so there's no point in trying. What you can do, though, is to plan for the comfort, convenience, and conviviality of the majority of your guests at the reception and try to head off any altercations with some sensible precautionary measures.

Think about the following:

- Will the time of day and location you've chosen present a problem for elderly relatives? One bride we know hired a van to transport her aunts and grandparents who lived two hours away.
- Will your guests have to wait outside during the picture taking? More and more couples are taking pictures earlier, *before* the ceremony, to avoid this.
- Will a receiving line at the reception cause a bottleneck? Some couples receive their guests right after the ceremony (in the back of the church, temple, or synagogue); others limit the participation to the mother of the bride, the mother of the groom, the couple and the female attendants. Fathers mingle. In some circumstances, the couple alone greet their guests.
- Will you want everyone to sign a guest book? If so, let them do that as they enter.
- Are some of your guests elderly or handicapped in a way that makes it difficult for them to walk or stand? Assign an usher or a friend to give them special assistance, and bring them into the reception site first.
- Will there be many small children at your reception? A separate sideroom with toys and games for them, supervised by teenage sitters, could be a godsend—for everybody.

- Do some guests have special dietary needs (vegetarian, kosher, diabetic, etc.)? If yours is a seated reception, give the caterer a list of those people, and arrange for their meals in advance.
- Do your families and friends have gourmet palates or more pedestrian tastes? Make menu selection so that all will be sure to find something they enjoy.
- Will there be dancing? Make sure there is music for all ages, including any ethnic numbers your guests will expect.

Wedding Cakes: Having Yours (and Eating It, Too)

The one thing that's universally served at every wedding everywhere is wedding cake, and you'll be happy to know that the traditional, sometimes dry, white wedding cake is no longer expected. The creative confections provided by bakers and caterers today are a feast for both the eyes and the palate.

Most couples still choose a traditional-looking wedding cake, although what it tastes like may come as a surprise: carrot cake with cream cheese, pound cake with lemon filling, chocolate cake with mocha mousse, classic genoise with white chocolate icing, even cheesecake or ice cream! And, while most wedding confections are still predominantly white, fanciful designs and colorful accents can turn them into visual and edible masterpieces.

A wedding cake large enough to serve 200 guests could cost anywhere from two hundred to several thousand dollars, depending on who designs it, who bakes it, and how elaborate it all becomes. You can have whatever kind of cake you want, as long as you can find someone to create it and as long as you're willing to pay for it.

Go to the baker prepared with specifics about the size and type of wedding you're having, as well as particulars about the reception location. Room decor, ceiling height, temperature, lighting, linens, and wedding colors all will influence your choice of cake. You should also bring the names and numbers

⚜ *TO HAVE OR HAVE NOT* ⚜

Reception Traditions

You may have any, all, or none of these, as you wish.

- A photo display of events in the couple's childhood and courtship on a bulletin board at the entrance to the reception.
- A bridal portrait display, usually on an easel or framed and sitting on the table with the guest book.
- A receiving line: mother of the bride first, then mother of the groom, then father of the groom, then father of the bride (if he doesn't choose to circulate as host), then the bride, then groom, then maid/matron of honor, then bridesmaids, if you wish. (Note that the best man and ushers do not stand in the receiving line, but circulate among the guests.)
- Toasting: done first by the best man for the couple, then by the groom for his bride, then by anyone else.
- The first dance: reserved for the newlyweds alone.
- The second dance: the bride with her father; then, the groom with his mother-in-law, the bride with her father-in-law, and the bride's father with the groom's mother. Then guests join in.
- Cutting the cake: the bride and groom, his hand over hers, cut the first slice of wedding cake. She

takes the first bite, then feeds him the second. The caterer cuts the balance to be served to guests. (If a buffet reception, this is usually done right after the toasting; if a sit-down, it is done after the meal.)

- Tossing the bouquet: all unmarried women assemble behind the bride as she tosses her bouquet over her shoulder. (This may be done right after the cake has been cut or toward the end of the reception before the couple leaves.)
- Tossing the garter: the groom removes the garter from the bride's leg and tosses it over his shoulder to all unmarried men. (The bachelor who catches it may then put it on the leg of the woman who caught the bride's bouquet.)
- Taking leave: if you're merely going upstairs to a hotel suite, your leaving signals the end of the reception; if you are going away, then the two of you will sneak off to change clothes, and reappear to bid a final good-bye in a shower of good wishes often accompanied by rice or bird seed or rose petals or perhaps balloons.
- Reception favors: mementoes for guests to take home may include special candy or groom's cake, inscribed glasses, plants, menus, framed photographs, etc.

Receiving line

Mother   Mother   Bride   Groom   Bridesmaids
of bride   of groom

CONTEMPORARY SOLUTIONS

FAMILY

❦ *Your father and his new wife are hosting the reception, and arrangements among all concerned have been very difficult. Yet, the wedding is formal and you want a receiving line. How can you arrange it so relationships don't get even more strained than they already are?*

As the celebrated couple, you two are "the stars of the show," and you two alone, or with your maid/matron of honor and/or attendants can form the sum total of the receiving line. If your father is the host, he could be circulating among the guests anyway, and his new wife will be with him.

❦ *You have adoptive parents or step-parents who have raised you and whom you love, but a natural parent has come back into your life and you are now close with him or her. Should all these people stand in the receiving line?*

Probably not, unless the relationships among them all are exceptionally forgiving and accepting. The parent(s) who raised you and who have contributed the emotional (and maybe the financial) support that makes your wedding possible deserve to have the place of honor.

of your caterer, florist, wedding planner, and anyone else the baker may wish to consult to coordinate details and delivery.

Start shopping for the wedding cake three to four months before the date, even earlier if your requests are highly unusual, if the bakery you've chosen is very popular, or if you're being married in a peak season. Make sure that you're familiar with the style and quality of the chef's work before you buy.

QUESTIONS TO ASK

1. Approximately what size cake will be needed for my number of guests? (Don't forget to consider the overall menu and the amount of food being offered, what time of day or evening the cake will be served, and whether or not it will be your only dessert.)
2. Will the kind of cake we love (chocolate, carrot, fruitcake, etc.) be equally appreciated by our guests, or should we consider a more universal flavor? (You can have different layers made in different flavors, all frosted alike.)
3. Do you have actual photographs of some of your creations so we can make our choice? May we have a "taste test"?
4. What are the cost estimates for the designs and types of cakes we like?
5. Will there be additional charges for delivery and/ or set up, or rental fees for stands, columns, or supports? (If your caterer or reception site usually provides the wedding cake, then don't forget to ask about the "cake-cutting" charges they may impose if you bring your cake in from elsewhere.)
6. What deposit is required, is it refundable should our plans change, and when is final payment due?

When you place your order and make your deposit (usually 50 percent), get a written agreement or contract that specifies the kind of cake, filling, and frosting, the number of people it will serve, the design details you've agreed upon, and the delivery date, time, and procedure. Also put in writing any additional fees or rental charges, and ask how the final payment is to be made (check, cash, credit card, etc.).

Finally, if your cake promises to be the eighth architectural wonder of the world, be sure you establish in advance the manner in which it will be cut and served. Special creations require special assurance that they will be expertly handled. You also will want to inform the caterer if any part of your wedding cake, usually the top 6" layer, is to be set aside and frozen for you to enjoy on your first anniversary. (Some couples prefer to have their baker recreate a fresh, miniature version of their wedding cake for that first-year celebration.)

Reception Seating

Once your responses are in, you'll have to plan the guest seating for your reception. If yours is a stand-up affair, then you need only a few tables and chairs around the room; but if it is a seated reception, even a small one, you'll have to provide place cards or numbered table assignments so your guests will know where to sit. At a very large affair, you may even need a host or hostess to help people find their places.

Even in uncomplicated situations, planning guest seating takes some social savvy. You'll want to be sure people are placed conveniently and seated with others whom they know or whose company they will enjoy for several hours. It's also nice to consider things like age, marital status, and proximity to the dance floor, buffet tables, restrooms, and exits when assigning specific friends and relatives.

Make (or obtain from the reception site) a sketch of the overall floor plan, determine the number of tables you'll need, number them, and arrange them on the plan. With a visual aid in front of you, it will be much easier to make a list of appropriate seating assignments, especially for very large affairs. Ask your mother or future mother-in-law to help you with any guests you don't personally know.

Usually, there is a main table or bride's table, sometimes situated on a dais, at which you and the groom are in full view. The bride sits to the groom's right, with the best man next to her and the maid or matron of honor next to the groom. Other attendants fan out in man/woman fashion around the rest of the table. The parents and the clergy may also be at the main table, although at large receptions, parents generally have tables of their own nearby with the clergy and other close relatives.

It doesn't have to be this way, of course. We know of receptions where the bride and groom sat alone at a romantic table for two, or where they sat with their parents while the attendants and their partners who were not in the wedding had their own table. If you have divorced or separated parents, you might be well advised to seat them separately with their own friends and family members. There are simply no rigid rules about reception seating. When traditional guidelines don't work for you, use common sense.

❧ TO HAVE OR HAVE NOT ❧

A Groom's Cake

An old Southern tradition, the groom's cake is gaining popularity throughout the country. Early wives' tales had it that a single woman guest could place a slice under her pillow and conjure dreams of her future husband; later, in pioneer days, cakes were baked by the groom's parents for weary traveling guests to enjoy on their trip back home.

Today, a groom's cake might be served at the rehearsal dinner, or at the wedding reception, or boxed as guest favors. It can be in any flavor, color, or shape (chocolate or fruitcake is traditional); often, the cake is designed to reflect the groom's particular interest, occupation, or background (a football, a book, a cowboy boot, etc.).

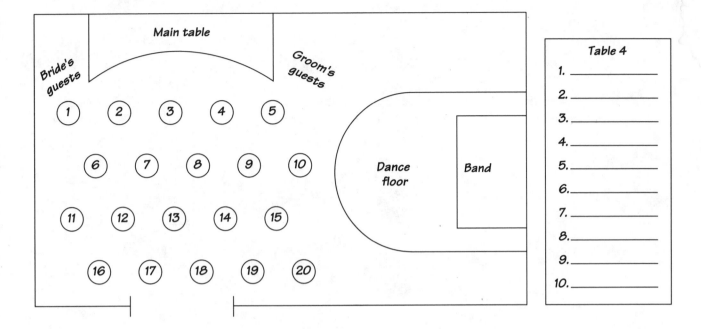

The Schedule of Events

In order to avoid costly overtime charges and to keep things running smoothly, you'll have to set a time schedule for food service, music, and reception traditions. If you don't have a wedding consultant, work this out with your catering manager and with the master of ceremonies (usually the director of the band), if you have one. A DJ can do this, as well.

A timetable for a typical, 5-hour sit-down dinner reception might look something like this:

7 P.M.	Everyone arrives, guests go through the receiving line, candid photos are taken.
7–8:30 P.M.	Cocktails and hors d'oeuvres are being served, soft music plays.
8:30–9 P.M.	Guests find their seats, the bride and groom enter, toasts are made, the first courses are served, dancing begins.
9:30 P.M.	The entree is served.
10:30 P.M.	The cake is cut, the bouquet/garter are thrown, coffee and dessert are served, dancing continues.
11:45 P.M.	The bride and groom take their leave.
midnight	The last dance is played, parents bid farewell to guests, the reception ends.

Adjust your schedule to fit your own time frame, but make sure that someone, if not an MC, is in charge of signaling the progression of events and making announcements to the guests.

CHAPTER 6
Wedding Dressing

We all have one. You know, the one favorite outfit that you pull out of your closet every time you want to look and feel your best, when you think eyes that matter will be on you, when you really want to wow them. Maybe it's a flattering business suit or a sexy cocktail dress; maybe it's one of those "investment" pieces that you agonized over buying, but have worn for years. Whatever it is, you know that special feeling when you put it on: it's right, it's you, this is as gorgeous as you're gonna get.

At no time is that feeling more important than on your wedding day. The dress has to be right, it has to be you, it has to be "as gorgeous as you're gonna get." True, you will probably wear it only that one day, but what a day! It may, in fact, be the only time when all eyes are absolutely guaranteed to be on you and when you do, in fact, really want to wow them, even if you're basically shy.

On your wedding day, you deserve to look like a million. You can be original, you can be fantastic, you can be whimsical, you can be romantic. And you may wear white, regardless of your age, size, or marital history.

For many, a wedding dress will be the single most expensive garment ever purchased. However, a great look doesn't always depend on a great price. Notwithstanding the four-digit extravaganzas created for soap opera stars and mega celebrities, even the best-known bridal designers have styles in popular price ranges. And, despite all the bad press bridal retailers and manufacturers have suffered in recent years, it is still possible to buy a quality gown, custom-fitted to you, without breaking the bank or getting ripped off.

The Inside Story

There are over 200 bridal manufacturers in the United States, not including European importers or ready-to-wear companies that make formal wear suitable for a bride. As with every other aspect of the fashion industry, quality, style, and price points vary, and new designs and designers come and go. There's a lot to be said for staying power in this business, and those who endure generally do so because they consistently deliver high quality and trusted service for the price.

The average wedding dress costs $780. Add a veil or headpiece, at an average of $150, plus the shoes, undergarments, and other accessories, and you're pushing $1,000 no matter where you live. There are ways to buy it all for less, of course, but not without some trade-offs and not always without some risk.

How to Shop

Before you go anywhere, first peruse the pages of bridal magazines. These publications are virtual catalogues of wedding attire available in the marketplace today. Manufacturers' ads will give you an idea of "the look" each house is known for and will almost always identify the retail stores in your area that carry their lines. (If they don't, call the manufacturer directly and ask for the names of stores nearby.) Fashion editorial pages will focus on design details and quote prices, as well as identify the designers and manufacturers.

Studying magazines is the best way to familiarize yourself with what's being shown, and to develop a sense for coordinating accessories, attendants' attire, and the style of the wedding. You should also take the time to attend bridal fashion shows held by retailers in your area, usually in the spring and fall when the new lines have been introduced. While refining your tastes and developing an image of "the look" you'd like to achieve, you'll also gain a realistic perspective on what you're likely to have to spend.

Even if you don't find *the* one gown you love, take notes and set aside pictures of those with features that appeal to you, whether it's a neckline, waistline, sleeve, or a fabric. As you begin to compare the notes and pictures in your collection, a pattern of preferences will emerge. This pattern will give direction to an experienced salesperson, so be sure to take them with you when you shop.

You should know that good bridal stores put their staff through rigorous training programs. A sales consultant in a reputable salon will know her lines, know what can be done to customize a particular gown, and understand the psychology and emotion involved in this all-important purchase. Her knowledge and experience should enable her to be both sensitive to your needs and objective in her advice. If you don't find that, go somewhere else.

Besides the quality and workmanship of the gown, much of what you're paying for in a full retail establishment is service. Bridal attire is about the last apparel industry left in which customized, made-to-order garments are still routine, and the profit margin on such individualized service is a lot slimmer than you might think given the cost of the gowns. Proper measurements must be taken, expert alterations made, and a perfect fit achieved. If anything goes wrong in quality, workmanship, fitting, or delivery, a reputable retailer will stand by the customer and make it right. We've seen some go to Herculean efforts for a bride, even when the snafu wasn't the store's fault.

And so it is in any marketplace: when you deal with people of integrity who value their own reputations, you *do* get what you pay for. When you don't, you shop at your own risk. In a free-market economy, the choice is always up to you.

A Dozen Dos for Dress Shopping

1. Take only one person with you when you shop. That person may be your mother, a friend, or your fiancé, but whoever it is, be sure she or he can be objective.
2. Label magazine pictures with page number, name of magazine, and date of issue. Bring along the pictures of gowns you like, as well as any special accessories (heirloom veil or headpiece, jewelry, etc.) that you plan to wear with your gown.
3. Be ready to explain the style and type of wedding you're having to the sales consultant: size, theme, time of day, location of ceremony and reception.

4. Wear suitable undergarments, hose, and heels of the approximate height you're likely to choose for the wedding. Also, do your hair and makeup so that you look like your "better" self. All of this will add to your total impression of the gowns.

5. Be honest about your price range. Tell the salesperson what you'd ideally like to spend, and what your outside limits are. Be firm, and bear in mind that the gown itself is not the only expense for your total wedding attire.

6. Make an appointment, give yourself plenty of time, and expect to try on at least six to eight different gowns in each salon you visit. Brides in larger cities with many retail establishments to choose from often shop around for three weeks or so before making their final selection.

7. If you're not comfortable in the shop, or don't feel a certain confidence in the consultant there, go elsewhere.

8. Do not get sidetracked by accessories and attendants' attire. You can shop for those things later, after you've chosen your own gown.

9. Inquire about alterations and fitting fees. Every dress will have some. Make sure seamstresses are experienced with the intricacy of bridal work.

10. Tell the salon when you'll need the dress (for coordination of other elements, for the bridal portrait, etc.) and ask about delivery and fitting schedules.

11. Be sure you understand all terms, guarantees, and refund policies *before* you put down a deposit on a gown. (Usually, the deposit is a nonrefundable 50 percent when you order, and the balance is payable when the dress comes in before it is fitted. Alterations, even minor ones, are almost always extra.)

12. Start shopping early; six to eight months is recommended, much earlier if you have special fitting needs or an unusually large bridal party to plan for. And *never* put down a deposit on a dress that you haven't tried on, no matter what your size or fitting needs.

Where to Shop

Shopping for a wedding dress is a unique experience, and most women find it extremely enjoyable, as it should be. After all, how many other times in your life are you likely to spend as much money for one ensemble, or to receive such special, undivided attention while doing it?

There are many ways to find the dress of your dreams, and we suggest you think about these various avenues carefully before you start to shop so you know what to expect from each source. The horror stories everybody hears are born out of consumer ignorance; they don't have to happen to you.

• **The full-service bridal retailer.** If you want quality, attention, and expertise, this is the way to go. Indeed, many leading manufacturers are very choosy about the stores they will allow to carry their lines, so that the appearance of a retailer's name in a manufacturer's ad is generally an indication of some reputation and reliability.

A full-service retailer handles everything: consultation and advice, customizing and modification of design, fittings and alterations, accessories and coordination, and the ordering and fitting of attendants' attire. Those that have been around awhile and have a reputation to protect will do whatever they can to ensure a happy bride. In fact, sometimes a consultant in one of these salons will voluntarily oversee floral bouquets or male attire, or even show up before the ceremony to be sure every last detail is in place!

Full service, of course, means full price, unless you're lucky enough to be a sample size (typically 8-10-12) and manage to find the gown you love at one of the sample sales retailers hold once or twice a year. (Large retailers who stock gowns in broader size ranges for immediate purchase also put their in-house stock on sale periodically.) Sales at reputable salons can save you 40 to 50 percent of the full retail price, yet the store will still provide all its usual services because you've purchased the gown from them. If you can afford to wait for a sale, it's worth considering.

• **Very large retail establishments.** These stores can sometimes show you the same gown you've seen elsewhere for as much as 10 percent less. This is not discounting; rather, it is realistic pricing given the enormous sales volume of the store or chain. They can simply afford to sell for a little less. The trade-off for a price break in a large store is perhaps a less personalized, less intimate atmosphere, although a full range of services will still be available.

• **Department stores**. Major department stores, such as Saks Fifth Avenue, Marshall Field's, Woodward & Lothrop, etc., have bridal salons in their larger stores. The quality, prices, and services available will reflect the quality, prices, and services in their overall merchandising niche.

Department stores that don't have bridal salons will almost certainly have evening wear departments. Some brides, particularly those who are planning less formal weddings, will find the dress of their dreams in that department, charge it to their store credit card, and live happily ever after.

• **Discounters.** This group includes stores that advertise as discounters, so-called "bridal closeout sales" at hotels, sales out of the homes of discount representatives, and telephone orders placed to central buying offices that claim to buy directly from manufacturers (a claim most manufacturers staunchly deny). Can you save 20 to 40 percent by going this route? It's possible. Are you sure to save by going this route? Not necessarily. Here's the deal on discounters.

Closeout sales are exactly that, closeouts. Gowns sold this way have probably been languishing in storerooms or tried on as samples a hundred times before they ever show up on racks in front of you. So, these sales are a strictly cash-and-carry

operation. There are usually no identifying labels or tags, no way (unless you've become a bridal gown expert) to be absolutely sure of what you're buying and what the true retail value ever was, and no recourse whatsoever should you get the gown home and find that it is damaged, imperfect, or a knockoff of what you thought was "the real thing." Finding someone to do alterations and fittings is *your* problem, and the Better Business Bureau and consumer protection laws can't redress grievances, since these dealers don't take credit cards or even have permanent addresses.

Mail-order discounters or those with home representatives may be a little less risky, provided you know exactly what you want down to the last digit of the style number. Of course, the only way to know that, and to know how sizes run and whether or not a style will flatter you, is by first taking advantage of the good faith of your local full-service retailer. To take the time of staff the retailer trains and pays, and to try on merchandise they stock, then to purchase the dress from someone else who made no investment whatsoever undermines the whole concept of retail service.

So, in order to buy successfully this way, you'll either have to be dishonest about your intentions in a bridal salon, or you'll need the luck of the Irish to buy a gown sight unseen, which is probably not the way you usually shop. And there's no recourse after the fact. You'll pay in full up front, plus shipping and handling, and the gown will be sent directly to your home. Alterations are your problem and, if the dress is delayed, damaged, incorrect, or otherwise below your expectations, you'll have a hassle on your hands.

• **Vintage clothing stores and consignment shops**. For a distinctive look from a bygone era or a fabulous designer gown at a frankly affordable price, you can check antique clothing shops and secondhand apparel stores. Such places are not always easy to find, but some women swear by them. You will probably be able to use credit cards, though you may not be able to return the dress once it's purchased. Refurbishing and alterations can be expensive, and clothes should be in good condition to begin with. Check with an accomplished seamstress or with a dry cleaner that specializes in refurbishing and preserving wedding gowns before you buy so you'll know what you're getting into, what's possible, and what isn't.

• **Wearing someone else's dress.** Whether it's a family heirloom or a dress that belongs to a friend, you'll have to take it to a seamstress or a good dry cleaner to see what has to be done to make it suitable for you, and how much time and money will be involved in doing it. If the gown belongs to a friend and she wants it back, there may be a limit to the alterations that you can reasonably expect to make. Also, how will you feel about not owning your wedding gown?

• **Rentals.** If not owning doesn't bother you, then you might consider renting a gown from one of the women's formal wear rental shops that have begun to spring up in major cities. Those with bridal gowns typically rent even the most lavish creations for between $200 and $400. Like men's rentals, minor alterations and cleaning are included in the charge.

• **Custom-made.** Consider having the gown made or making it yourself. Major pattern companies and better fabric stores sell everything you need to create a complete bridal outfit. The only thing you have to supply is the expertise, and that is considerably more sewing ability than is required to make a simple skirt or sundress. If you or someone you know is an expert seamstress, and if your sense of style is so unerring as to make you completely confident about the end result, then you can probably have the dress of your dreams for less than half the cost of buying it retail.

Those are your choices. Whatever way you go, remember that price doesn't always mean value, and that mistakes and mishaps can be twice as costly in the long run.

QUESTIONS TO ASK

1. May I see this particular gown I'm interested in, or if not this style, other samples from this manufacturer? (If they don't carry the line you want, don't shop there. When a store tells you they can get a dress from a manufacturer they don't ordinarily carry, beware. They may be involved in a practice known as "transshipping," which means they'll obtain the gown through a third party. This is illegal.)

2. How long will it take to get the dress I want, and what kind of modifications and alterations will be necessary? How long will those take, and what will they cost?

3. Who is the manufacturer of the gown I like, and what can you tell me about its reputation and reliability?

4. How long have you been in business, and have you serviced other brides I may know? (Bridal salons do go out of business. If yours does after you've put down the deposit, you can lose your money and be without a dress.)

5. What, if anything, is included in the price of the gown?

6. What kind of a deposit do you require, is it refundable, and can I put it on a credit card? (Federal consumer protection laws ensure that goods and services purchased by credit cards will live up to their promise. When they don't, you may not have to pay the bill, provided you have honestly tried to correct any dispute with the merchant, and provided the purchase was made within 100 miles of your home. Use credit cards whenever possible.)

7. Can you guarantee that the gown will be here and ready by the time I need it? What if something goes wrong?

CONTEMPORARY SOLUTIONS

PERSONAL, FAMILY

❧ *You or someone in your wedding party is either a large woman (size 18 or over) or extremely small.*

Call around before you shop to find out how much of a selection you'll have, and start shopping that much earlier to allow for the extra fitting time. The bigger, full-service retailers usually have stock from petites up to size 20, and some major manufacturers cut their gowns up to size 44. Most are attuned to the needs of the larger woman and have many designs that can be custom fitted just for her.

In general, American women are getting larger and bustier, and bridal houses are well aware of that. Look for special bridal fashion shows for the full-figured woman, and rest assured that an experienced staff in a reputable salon will know how to help every bride look truly beautiful on her wedding day.

❧ *You've always dreamed of wearing your mother's dress, but it's too small or not exactly your style, even discolored or deteriorating. What can you do?*

Take the gown to a good dressmaker and ask for recommendations. A simple gown can be given some opulent additions, like beadwork, an elaborate veil, or a long train, and turned into a gown befitting the most formal setting. The converse is also true: a shortened sleeve, an altered hemline, or a streamlined bodice can simplify an extravagant gown. Provided it's in good condition, an heirloom dress can almost always be refashioned and updated, and today, there are miraculous processes for restoring natural fabrics to their original state (see Appendix).

PERSONAL

❧ *You were having your gown made, but that's turned into a disaster (fabric didn't come in, seamstress got sick, dress didn't look like you thought it would, etc.). How fast can you purchase the kind of dress you really want?*

Go to the biggest and best full-service retailer in your area and explain your predicament. Maybe they'll have something you love in stock; if not, the retailer probably has a special relationship with at least one manufacturer who can be called on for a favor in an emergency. We've known brides to find, fit, and wear a dress, all in the space of 72 hours, though that's hardly a stress-free way to make it down the aisle.

What to Wear

The size of the wedding, the time of day, the location, and the formality of the bride's dress are what determine the style of the wedding. This chart is a guide to assist you with everyone's attire, but it is always subject to changes in fashion. For example, styles in menswear have become more versatile. Local formal wear specialists throughout the country can advise you on the newest choices for rental or purchase. Your preferences, guided by your bridal consultant's advice, will help you plan a beautiful wedding. In a second marriage, the bride should feel free to follow her wishes, and white is a valid choice.

TYPE OF WEDDING	BRIDE	MEN	BRIDESMAIDS	MOTHERS
FORMAL DAYTIME	White, ivory, or delicate pastel-tinted, floor-length wedding dress with a cathedral or a chapel (sweep) train. Long veil covering the train or extending to train length. Or ballroom dress with full skirt and optional sweep train. Bouquet or prayer book; shoes to match gown; long gloves with short sleeves, otherwise gloves are optional.	**Traditional:** cutaway coat (either oxford gray or black) with striped trousers, gray waistcoat, wing-collared white shirt, and a striped ascot. **Contemporary:** black or gray contoured long or short jacket, striped trousers, wing-collared white shirt; gray vest (optional). Jacket in selection of colors, matching pants and coordinated shirt.	Floor-length, ballerina, tea-length, or short dresses; hat, wreath, or decorative hair comb, gloves to complement length of sleeves; shoes to match or blend with dresses; honor attendant's dress may match or contrast with other attendants' dresses.	Street-length dresses, small hats (optional), shoes, gloves, and corsage to harmonize. The mothers' ensembles should complement each other in regard to style, color, and length.
FORMAL EVENING	Six o'clock is the hour that separates the formal evening wedding from the formal day wedding. Wedding dress is the same as for the daytime; fabrics and trimmings may be more elaborate.	**Traditional:** black tuxedo or a dinner jacket, black striped trousers, coordinated vest or cummerbund, and bow tie. Ultraformal: black tails, white tie, and accessories. **Contemporary:** contoured long or short jacket, matching trousers, wing-collared shirt, vest or cummerbund, bow tie.	Long or ballerina-length evening dresses; accessories same as daytime. Fabrics can be more elaborate.	Floor-length or ankle-length dresses, small head covering; dressy accessories—furs, jewelry.
SEMI-FORMAL DAYTIME	White or pastel floor-length or ballerina dress. Veil: elbow length or shorter. Same accessories as formal wedding.	**Traditional:** gray or black stroller, striped trousers, gray vest, white shirt, gray-and-white striped tie. **Contemporary:** formal suit in a choice of colors and styles, matching or contrasting trousers, white or colored shirt. Bow tie, vest, or cummerbund.	Same as for formal wedding, although style and fabric should be simplified.	Same as for formal wedding.
SEMI-FORMAL EVENING	Same as daytime. Fabrics or trim may be more elaborate.	**Traditional:** dinner jacket, black trousers, vest or cummerbund, white dress shirt, bow tie. In warm weather: white or ivory jacket. **Contemporary:** formal suit (darker shades for fall and winter, lighter shades for spring and summer); matching or contrasting trousers. Bow tie to match vest or cummerbund.	Long, ballerina, tea-length, or short evening dresses; accessories same as daytime. Fabrics may be more elaborate.	Same as for formal wedding.
INFORMAL DAYTIME AND EVENING	White or pastel floor-length, ballerina, or tea-length dress or suit. Short veil or bridal-type hat. Small bouquet, corsage, or prayer book. Gloves and complementary shoes.	Black, dark gray, or navy business suit. In summer, white or natural jacket, dark tropical worsted trousers; navy blazer, white flannel trousers; or white suit.	Same length dress as bride wears; however, if bride wears floor-length style, it is permissible for attendants to wear a short dress. Accessories should be simple and suitable to the ensemble.	Street-length dress or suit ensemble.

Choosing Your Style

Let's face it: not everything looks good on everybody. Just because an outfit is spectacular on a size 8, 5'7" fashion model doesn't mean it will do a thing for you. To capture your own best look, you'll need to work with the consultant, keep an open mind, and be objective about your physical features.

The saleswoman will begin by asking questions about your wedding: date, time, location, type of ceremony and reception. She may then talk to you about the appropriateness of the style of gown you seem to want for the kind of wedding you have described. If you're concerned about what the rules of etiquette dictate regarding bridal attire, the traditional guidelines are shown on page 71.

Traditional guidelines are fine, but our own experience and our conversations with retailers around the country indicate that when a woman finds the dress she loves, that's the end of it. She will wear that dress regardless of the time of the day, the season of the year, or the size of the guest list.

"All the old taboos—about train lengths, suitability of fabric, beaded dresses during the daytime, and the like—have really gone out the window, and I think it's just as well that they have," says Michele Piccione, leading designer for Alfred Angelo. "Today's bride is better educated, more confident, and more discriminating about quality and workmanship. And, she's making memories, so why shouldn't she have what she wants?"

Piccione cautions a woman not to follow trends when selecting her gown, but to choose a dress that's comfortable, classic, and truly most flattering for her.

"The biggest mistake a woman makes is to select a gown with design features—an elaborate sleeve or an unusual neckline—that completely overwhelm. The dress wears her instead of the other way around," she says. "And then, sometimes the dress is fine, but the headpiece becomes too much. It overpowers both the woman and the gown and throws the whole image out of proportion."

You'll have to think about all of this, and more, when choosing your own wedding attire.

The Feel and the Fit

Unless she's a seamstress herself or accustomed to having her clothes made by one, the average woman has never experienced having a garment custom ordered and tailored just for her. It takes considerable skill, and sometimes considerable patience on the customer's part, to achieve that all-important look and fit.

The bridal consultant will bring you sample gowns in your nearest size to try on, clipping, pinning, or holding them in place so you can get an idea of how the properly fitted dress would look. You'll notice as you try them on that wedding gowns have a different "feel" from ready-to-wear clothes. They may employ stays, boning, wires, crinolines, and linings for shape and contour. Depending on the fabrics and the decorative applications, they can be heavy and constricting. Sleeves and bodices can have complicated closures, and you may need help getting into the dress. You may even have to practice a bit before you feel graceful moving in billowing skirts with weighty trains.

People in the industry refer to constructing a wedding gown as "building a costume," and once you become familiar with wedding apparel you'll understand why. Your bridal consultant may counsel you to put this sleeve on that bodice, or drop this waist or raise that hem. She may show you the same gown available in different shades and fabrications, or the same basic design with more, or less, ornamentation. Such options are what customization is all about.

Your wedding dress will probably be quite unlike anything else you've ever worn before and, since you'll be wearing it for many hours, it is important to consider comfort and convenience, as well as style, when choosing it.

Think about:
- Getting into and out of limousines
- Kneeling, bending, or climbing stairs at your ceremony
- Dining and dancing at your reception
- The weather, and how warm or cold it might be
- The properties of individual fabrics and how easily they might wrinkle, snag, or tear

And, if you intend to preserve your gown as an heirloom for your own daughter one day, then make classic design and quality construction top priorities.

Good fit and construction are absolutely essential. A poorly made garment, or even a well-made one inexpertly altered, can be a problem, or even a disaster, on your wedding day. Besides the hundreds of dollars you're spending, that's one more reason to purchase your gown from experienced bridal retailers and manufacturers who have earned a reputation for quality and service.

The Facts About Custom Fitting and Alterations

Unless you are an absolutely perfect dress size and want no modifications whatsoever on the gown you've selected, you will need some alterations to ensure a proper fit. In spite of reports to the contrary, trust us when we tell you that alterations constitute a salon service, not a profit center. Here are the facts:

- Even the most minor alterations and modifications are time consuming and require sewing expertise: to take in a bodice, waist, or sleeve, for instance, means taking apart all the seams and adjusting them proportionately; to shorten a sleeve, adjust a neckline, or hem a skirt may mean detaching them from major bodice or waistline seams.
- Most dresses are lined, underlined, and/or interfaced; that means alterations must be made on several layers of fabric.
- Style modifications not possible by the manufacturer must be done by the salon; this may involve extensive reworking, rebeading, or refashioning to match the design details of the dress.
- Dresses are always ordered from manufacturers in your next nearest size, not so the salon can make "big bucks" on alterations, but so the seamstress has fabric to work with. It is easier to take in and cut off the excess than it is to let out, especially when standard seam allowances (5/8 inch) aren't sufficient for the expansion.

In short, what may seem like a simple change to you is not always as easy as it looks. A good salon must employ both experienced seamstresses and expert beaders/hand-workers, as well as cleaners and pressers, who can all ensure that the gowns are delivered to the bride ready to wear. Stores also have to provide the trims, fabrics, materials, and equipment necessary for the support personnel to do their jobs.

Thus, a bridal shop may charge a flat fee for routine alterations or structure their fees according to each task to be performed. Either way, charges barely cover their costs in wages, time, and materials.

Figure Flattery

When you've got it, flaunt it, especially on your wedding day. Choose a gown to accent your best features and that automatically will draw attention away from the less-than-perfect ones.

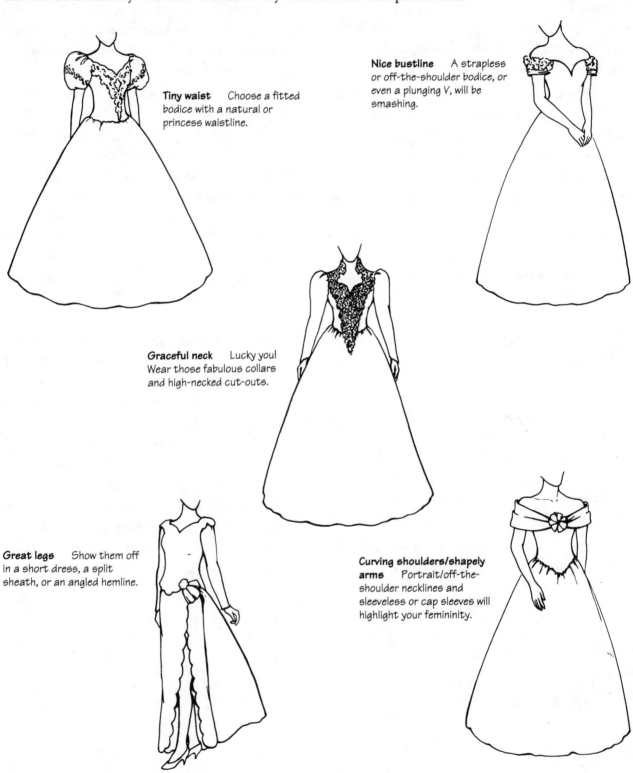

Tiny waist   Choose a fitted bodice with a natural or princess waistline.

Nice bustline   A strapless or off-the-shoulder bodice, or even a plunging V, will be smashing.

Graceful neck   Lucky you! Wear those fabulous collars and high-necked cut-outs.

Great legs   Show them off in a short dress, a split sheath, or an angled hemline.

Curving shoulders/shapely arms   Portrait/off-the-shoulder necklines and sleeveless or cap sleeves will highlight your femininity.

Small hips   Go for the peplums, aprons, bustles, and other hipline interest.

Flawless back   Choose a low or backless dress; accent with strands of pearls or crystals.

Tall and slim   Envy you! A classic sheath will be a showstopper; a full-skirted ballgown, royal and rich.

Small shoulders and arms   Go for the big sleeves; you can get away with it!

Beautiful hands   Wear long sleeves tapered to a point.

CONTEMPORARY SOLUTIONS

RELIGIOUS

❦ *You're not a child or a fairy princess. You'd like to wear a very sexy, very sophisticated wedding dress, perhaps something strapless or slit up the side, but you think the officiant might object. Will you have to change the ceremony or change your vision of the dress?*

Neither one. Ask the officiant up front if there are any rules regarding bridal attire. If there are, and many churches and synagogues do have them, then look for one of the versatile creations being designed expressly to combat this problem. You can find strapless gowns with jackets, coats, boleros, or detachable shawls and sleeves. You'll also find dresses with full or layered overskirts that, when taken off, reveal sheaths or even short miniskirts underneath.

These designs are not only fun, they're practical, and they provide the perfect solution for the woman who wants different looks for her ceremony and reception. Such a choice is also ideal if she is having more than one ceremony or reception, or if she wants a simple, basic dress that can be worn again. (Note: Versatile designs like these are available for bridesmaids, too.)

PERSONAL

❦ *You're having a "theme" wedding, and you'd like to go all out with an outfit that's in keeping with the occasion, yet something that is elegant and still looks bridal. You don't really want to rummage through someone's attic for a dress.*

You don't have to comb antique dress shops to achieve either a "retro" or period look. Bridal creators, like other fashion designers, are influenced by films, art exhibits, historical costumes, whatever catches the public fancy. Many of today's most popular gowns revive a twenties, thirties, or forties look in the most modern, most luxurious fabrics. Tell your bridal retailer about your theme wedding and the look you'd like to achieve. Whether it's Southern belle or Victorian, she's sure to have something along those lines.

Fashion Focus

The most characteristic features of a gown are the neckline, the bodice, and the sleeves. You'll want to give these features extra consideration in selecting what flatters you most. Following are the most popular choices:

Necklines

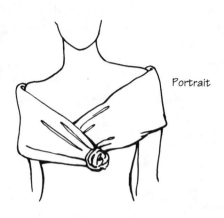

Portrait

Portrait   so called because it frames the shoulders and face and accentuates the bustline; includes off-the-shoulder styles

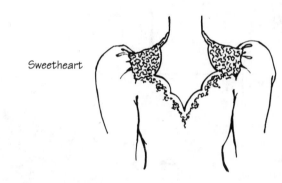

Sweetheart

Sweetheart   an open neckline that begins inside the shoulder line and is shaped like a heart

Queen Anne   a sculptured neckline high on the sides and the back of the neck, then opened into a semi-sweetheart shape

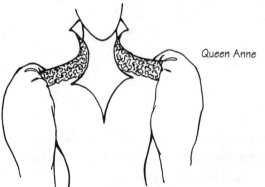

Queen Anne

Sabrina   a neckline that crosses the collarbone

V-neck and scooped neck   as their names describe

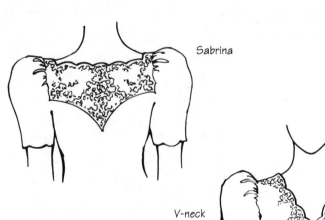

Sabrina

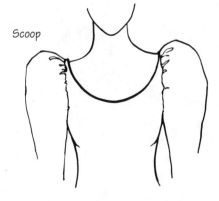

Scoop

V-neck

Almost every woman can wear one of those classic necklines. Others are not so universally flattering.

Jewel   high and round, circling the natural neckline

Band collar   upright collar circling the base of the neck

Decolletage   a plunging V that reveals cleavage

Strapless   reveals the neck and shoulders; usually worn with a shawl, jacket, or cover-up

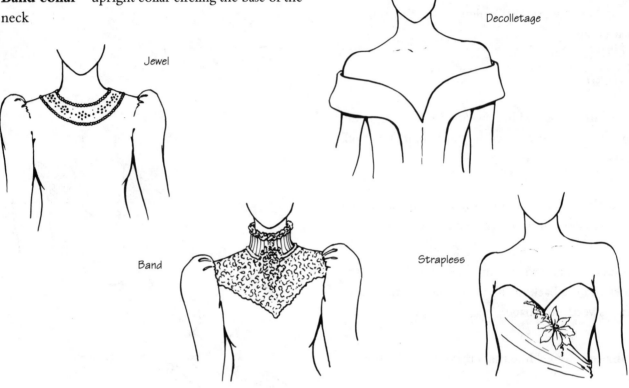

Jewel

Decolletage

Band

Strapless

Bodices

Fitted or ballgown bodice   hugging the upper body, ending in a dropped or natural waist; a classic design that most women can wear

Fitted or ballgown

Princess   a clean design that hugs the upper body, accents the waist without a seamed waistline, then flares into the skirt; also a look becoming to most women

Princess

The basic bodice design can be accentuated with ruffles, pleats, cut-outs, and other details flowing into the waistline:

Natural waistline   bodice and skirt joined and fitted at the natural waist

Basque waistline   elongated bodice, fitted through the waist and dropping to a pointed V in front; most popular of all

Dropped waist   bodice dropped to several inches below the natural waistline; may be fitted or not; perfect for short-waisted brides

Empire waist   shortened bodice with skirt attached just below the bustline

Natural waistline

Dropped waist

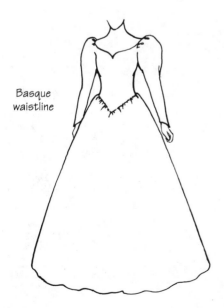

Basque waistline

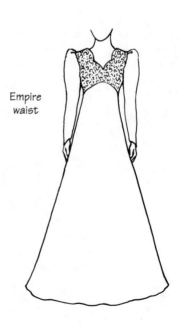

Empire waist

The bodice culminates in a skirt, which can be long or short, full or fitted, or anything in between: straight (sheath, slit, trumpet, or bottom flounced); flared (circle, A-line, bubbled, or full ballgown); or graduated in tiers, drapes, or asymmetrical hems. The total effect, from neck to hem, forms what is known as the line of the dress. The simpler, more classic the line, the more flattering it's likely to be to most figure types. That's why the classic gown with a portrait neckline, a fitted bodice, and a ballgown skirt has become so traditional and so timeless.

Sleeves

Sleeves can range from none (sleeveless) to simple (unadorned cap, fitted short, three-quarters, or long) to elaborate (puffed, winged, or bowed). Often, you'll find the most opulent detailing on the sleeves (beads, lace, sequins, ribbons, bows, etc.), so you'll need to be especially conscious of the size and shape of the sleeve as it affects your overall silhouette, given your particular height and figure type. The most common types are:

Fitted   a natural set-in sleeve, either long or short, without fullness

Long pointed   fitted sleeve ending in a point of lace or fabric on the hand

Full Juliette   gathered into the armline, puffed slightly, then tapered downward; long sleeves may end in cuffs

Leg-of-mutton   full puff at the shoulder, fitted at the forearm; **Gibson** is a softer version of the same design

Gauntlet   detachable wrist and arm cover; worn instead of gloves

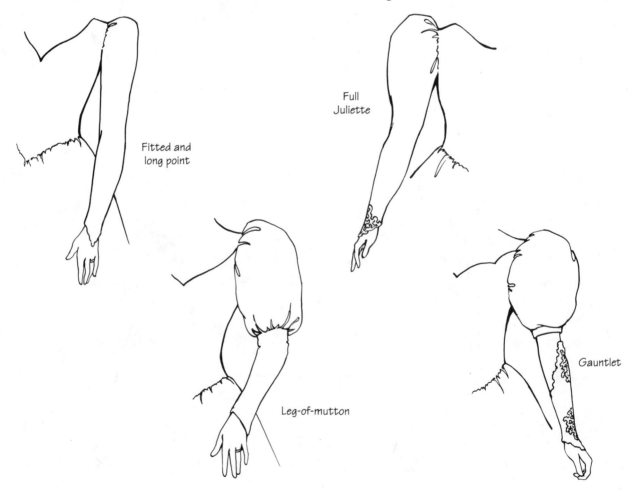

Fitted and long point

Full Juliette

Leg-of-mutton

Gauntlet

TRAIN TERMS YOU NEED TO KNOW

You may choose a dress with or without a train. Most brides want a train because it is regal and it makes the ultimate bridal statement. Be sure the bridal consultant shows you, your mother, or your maid or matron of honor how to bustle your train for unencumbered dancing at the reception. If you prefer, some dresses have detachable trains.

brush—barely brushes the floor

sweep—falls about 6 inches onto the floor

chapel—falls 1 and 1/3 yards from the waist, rests 12 to 18 inches on the floor

cathedral—falls 3 yards from the waist, rests 22 inches or more on the floor

royal—very long, you'll need pages to carry it

watteau—train is attached at the shoulders instead of at the waist

Note: Some brides choose to have their train come from the veil. Lengths of veiling can be layered with Velcro tape and detached for the reception.

Fashion Fabrics and Trims

Modern technology has brought a fabric explosion to the fashion industry and to bridal fashions, as well. The variety of weights, blends, finishes, and fiber contents today means that almost everything except the heaviest velvets or the lightest handkerchief linens can be worn year round.

Satin and silk are, by far, the most popular wedding choices around the country, in every climate, every season, and every time of day. **Satin**, the most traditional bridal fabric, can be in silk-face (expensive) or in blends (less costly), with a high gleam or delustered. **Silk** can be pure (most expensive) or blended (less costly) into chiffon, charmeuse, faille, organza, taffeta, crepe de chine, broadcloth, brocade, or peau de soie, all of which have a lustrous finish and a rich feel.

Natural **cotton** and **linen**, and man-made **polyester** and **rayon** also get their share of the limelight from designers, and you'll be amazed at the patterns and finishes these fabrics can achieve. Fiber content obviously affects the price of your gown, as well as the drape, styling, and durability.

The mind-boggling selection in fabrication is matched only by the endless array of decorative trims: **lace** (imported or domestic, hand finished or machine made); **beadwork** (hand-sewn or glued pearls, crystals, bugle beads, or sequins); **appliques** (attached fabric patterns or lace); **ribbon, cording, braiding, embroidery**, and **covered buttons**. Again, the amount and type of decorative detail, and the manner in which the ornamentation is applied, will affect the overall cost of the gown.

Veils and Headpieces

Though some women choose to wear very little on their heads or in their hair on the wedding day, nothing signifies a bride more than the traditional veil. It can be fashioned simply and attached to a band, comb, cap, hat, or tiara, or it can be constructed elaborately in multiple layers or cascading folds running in length from the tip of the nose to the tip of the train.

The creative flair and incredible diversity of veil and headpiece styling today make it almost impossible to discuss them all. You'll just have to see for yourself. You'll want the headpiece you choose to highlight your features and complement your face shape and hairstyle. You should also make this selection while you are actually trying on your gown to be sure that its size, design, and character achieve a "crowning effect" for your entire bridal outfit.

Here are some hints when shopping for your veil and headpiece:

- A simpler selection looks best with a spectacular gown, a more detailed one with a classic dress.
- Some religious ceremonies will require a face (blusher) veil, and some brides prefer this even when not required to wear it.
- Ready-made headpieces can be changed; custom ones can be fashioned just for you.

- Try to wear your hair the way you will be wearing it on your wedding day.
- Keep in mind that most headpieces are made to sit on the crown of your head.
- Have elaborate veiling made detachable for your reception festivities.

🍒 *TO HAVE OR HAVE NOT* 🍒

"Something old, something new, something borrowed, something blue, and a sixpence in your shoe."

This good-luck bridal tradition dates back to Elizabethan England. To honor it:

something old—an heirloom gown or piece of jewelry

something new—your gown, shoes, undergarments, etc.

something borrowed—a handbag, handkerchief, or jewelry

something blue—a garter, or blue detailing on your undergarments

a sixpence—believe it or not, you can buy a sixpence, but wearing it in your shoe could be a tad uncomfortable

---

CONTEMPORARY SOLUTIONS

CULTURAL

🍒 *You may want to honor ethnic traditions with special bridal accessories: a* **mantilla, lasso,** *or kneeling pillow for the Spanish ceremonies; wedding crowns tied with ribbon for the Greek nuptial; a satin purse for the "money dance," a common reception custom in Filipino, Italian, and other Mediterranean and Eastern European cultures.*

You often find such items in large bridal shops, especially those located in culturally diverse cities or ethnic neighborhoods. Card and party supply stores stock some of these items, too. The Beverly Clark Collection and numerous other mail-order resources (advertised in *Modern Bride*) have catalogues full of these accessories.

Bridal Accessories

As with any fashion ensemble, important details, sometimes unseen, can make a big difference. You'll want to choose the accessories for your wedding attire with extra care.

Shoes

Start shopping for shoes as soon as you've selected your dress, so you'll be sure to have them for fittings, especially when determining hem length. If you haven't looked at evening footwear lately, you're in for quite a surprise. You'll find beautiful fabrics

Your Wedding Attire Checklist

Since you'll be putting together your wedding ensemble over time, you'll need to keep a folder just for that. It should contain all records, receipts, sales agreements, canceled checks, and charge slips, and fabric swatches, color cards, and any pictures of the items you've purchased.

The Gown

Designer _____ Style # _____ Size _____

Description _____

_____

_____

Date Ordered _____ Est. Cost _____

Retailer _____ Phone _____

Salesperson _____

Deposit _____ Balance Due _____

Delivery Date _____

Fitting Date(s) _____

Alteration/Extra Charges _____

Headpiece/Veil

Designer _____ Style # _____

Description _____

Date Ordered _____ Est. Cost _____

Retailer _____ Phone _____

Salesperson _____

Deposit _____ Balance Due _____

Delivery Date _____

Shoes

Description _____

Date Ordered/Purchased _____ Cost _____

Retailer _____ Phone _____

Salesperson _____

Costs for Dyeing/Detailing _____

Date Ready _____

Other Accessories

	Date Purchased	Where	Cost
bra			
slip/petticoat			
panties			
hosiery			
garter			
gloves			
handbag			
jewelry			
earrings			
necklace			
bracelet			
other			

(satin, silk, moire, faille, brocade) in a variety of styles and heel heights (flats, pumps, slingbacks, and sandals) adorned in myriad ways (lace, beads, sequins, pearls, ruffles, ribbon, or rosettes). You might even decide to have your wedding shoes custom designed with bits of lace or trim to match your gown. It's all up to you.

Keep these points in mind when shopping for shoes:
- Choose a style that flatters your leg and complements your gown; high heels or slingbacks for a short dress or sophisticated sheath, mid-heel pumps or flats for a floor-length ballgown.
- Select a heel height you're accustomed to wearing, and *make sure the shoes are comfortable.*
- Consider the location of your ceremony and the activities you plan at your reception (you don't want to sink a spike heel into the lawn or break one while dancing).
- Order shoes in plenty of time to have them available for dress fittings.
- Wear your shoes around the house to break them in.

Undergarments

Beautiful bras, slips, and petticoats do more than make you feel elegant; if chosen wisely, they can also improve your comfort and movement and enhance the line and appearance of the gown. Try on everything with your dress to assure fit and comfort. This is especially important for bras, since backless, strapless, sheer, or cut-out dress bodices may require an unusual type of undergarment that you're not accustomed to wearing. (In some cases, the bra may have to be built into the dress.) Appropriate underpinnings are often available from the bridal retailer where you purchase your dress. If not, the consultant there can tell you what you need.

Hosiery will be one of your last purchases, so try to take a swatch of your dress with you to match the hue. An off-white (ivory or candlelight) dress may need hose with a beige or grayish tinge; a pink or peach cast might look best with very light pastels. Not even all pure whites are alike!

You'll find stockings, thigh-highs, and pantyhose in an array of textures and patterns, including some with rosettes, rhinestones, or even wedding-bell trim! Again, whatever you choose, be sure they're comfortable, and purchase two pair, just in case. . . .

Other Accessories

Gloves are available in varying lengths and fabrications, including kidskin, and may have tiny covered buttons or other design details. Gloves are definitely back in style; wear short ones with long sleeves, longer ones with short, sleeveless, or strapless gowns, and take care to match the color.

Handbags should be small for necessities only; look for interesting shapes and decorative details that coordinate with your gown and shoes.

Jewelry should be chosen carefully to complete the ensemble; pearls are traditional, of course, as are lockets, diamond stud earrings, heirloom bracelets, or that special wedding-day gift from the groom. In general, conservative jewelry complements a classic bridal look, eye-catching pieces accent a more sophisticated or theatrical style. Be sure to try on earrings with your headpiece, and remember, you'll be wearing your engagement ring on your right hand during the ceremony.

A **bridal garter** is worn if you plan to honor the tossing of the garter tradition; it is often blue and is always decorated with ribbon, rosettes, lace, even tiny seed pearls.

Pleasing the Maids

If you've ever been in someone else's wedding, you've probably said it yourself: "I hope she picks something I can wear again!" Since bridesmaids usually pay for their own attire, pleasing the maids is of paramount importance to the considerate bride; it can also be a real challenge when there are many attendants, each of whom has her own particular style, size, taste, and budget.

Fortunately, many of today's designers of bridesmaids' attire are as fashion conscious, and as cost conscious, as the women who wear their creations. Everything we said earlier about the tremendous variety of fabrication, styling, detailing, and sizing available in bridal design is equally true for attendants' attire. Add to that a virtually unlimited range of colors, prints, and patterns, and a real concern for wearability and adaptability, all at affordable prices, and you'll see why choosing the dresses for your bridesmaids is such dizzying fun.

"The special friend or relative who's a bridesmaid deserves to be more than just a block of color in a photograph," says Donna May Cammarotta, a bridesmaid designer at The House of Bianchi. "A woman appearing in another's wedding wants to be stylish, good looking, maybe even a little sexy. She wants to have fun and feel comfortable and, yes, she really does want to be able to wear that dress again."

Bridesmaids' dresses are not just dresses anymore. There are sheaths, suits, and separates, as well as the more traditional formal designs, and the same style may be available in many colors, prints, or fabrications besides the sample you see. Be sure to ask your bridal retailer about all the possibilities for any particular style you're considering.

Selecting Wedding Colors

Most brides think color first when considering maids' attire, as well they should. The color of the attendants' dresses will constitute the single greatest color statement of your wedding. Whether the dresses are solids, prints, or combinations, the dominant color scheme will have to be reflected and repeated everywhere else: in flowers, trims, table linens, china, centerpieces, and cake decorations, even in mothers' attire and the accessories of male attendants. Once you've chosen the bridesmaids' gowns, ask the salesperson to give you color swatch-es you can take with you to coordinate everything else.

QUESTIONS TO ASK

1. What are my favorite colors; which are most flattering to me?
2. Which colors, or shades of color, will most flatter the complexions and hair colors of my bridesmaids?
3. Are the colors I'm considering appropriate to the time of day and degree of formality of the wedding? (Lighter colors or pastel prints are more appropriate for daytime; vivid jewel tones, stark contrasts, or combinations with black are better in, but not limited to, the evening as they tend to be more formal.)
4. Will the color(s) lend themselves to appropriate seasonal flowers and decorations (or ethnic traditions or theme weddings)?
5. Which color(s) will be pulled out of a print as dominant?
6. Will the color, print, or combination of the dresses present a problem in matching shoes, headpieces, or other accessories?

How to Choose Bridesmaids' Attire

It is your prerogative as the bride to choose your wedding colors and, subsequently, what your attendants will wear. It is thoughtful, of course, to also consider those involved. Generally, you will choose their gowns at the same bridal store where you bought your own. (In fact, some retailers will not coordinate bridesmaids' dresses unless you purchased your wedding gown there.)

You might take your maid or matron of honor with you when you shop, but we wouldn't recommend taking the entire bridal party. That gets too confusing. If you want everyone's opinion, pick out several styles you like from magazines, gather your bridesmaids together, and let them discuss which style they like best. Obviously, the more attendants you have, the more difficult a consensus might be to reach.

If your attendants live far away, you also will have to consider the extra time, and expense, required to ship the dresses, to allow for fittings and alterations, and to obtain matching accessories. Your sales consultant can provide measurement forms so each woman can take her own proper measurements for the orders. Or, if you've chosen a style that's readily available from a national manufacturer, your attendants might be able to order their dresses at a salon near them. (Again, stores might not be willing

CONTEMPORARY SOLUTIONS

PERSONAL, SOCIOECONOMIC

🐚 *You really want a dear childhood friend in your wedding, but she's been a bridesmaid twice recently and just doesn't know if she can afford to do it again. Can you offer to pay for her dress without offering to pay for everyone else's?*

This is a common problem among women friends "of the marrying age," and it would be most considerate and generous of you to offer to pay for her attire. Your other bridesmaids do not have to know about any private financial arrangements you make. However, if your friend declines the offer and maintains that she simply cannot participate, you'll have to respect her decision.

PERSONAL, FAMILY

🐚 *Your sister or dear friend is pregnant. You want her to be in your wedding, but there's no telling what she will look like by the date. How can you select a style now that will be suitable for her, as well as for your other attendants?*

Granted, it isn't easy, but there are ways around this situation. She might be your maid or matron of honor (and you may have two maids or two matrons or one of each), in which case she can dress entirely differently from the others. Or, she might wear the same color and fabric as you've chosen for the other attendants, but have the line of the dress modified for her condition.

One joyous occasion should not preclude participation in another, and everyone at the wedding will understand any variation in the pregnant attendant's attire. Get the professional advice of your sales consultant to see exactly what can be done.

PERSONAL

🐚 *One of your closest friends is very heavy and extremely self-conscious about her weight. You want her in your wedding, but you're also afraid that she won't look right in any bridesmaid's dress you choose. What can you do?*

Take your friend to your bridal retailer, and show her the attractive selections available in her size. (Most manufacturers of bridesmaids' dresses can "slope" their designs to fit every figure type from petites to size 44. Call ahead to be sure the dress you're considering is one of those.) Point out to her that certain design features, such as the portrait or off-the-shoulder neckline and the Basque waist, are very feminine and flattering to most women, and are particularly so for the fuller figure. Then entice her to try on a sample, and watch her self-confidence rise as your concern for her "fit" in your wedding party disappears.

to place an order for just one dress. Attendants should inquire about this by phone. If that is impractical, use their measurements to order all the dresses to their nearest size through the salon where you purchase your dress, then mail the dresses to each out-of-towner for alterations. There is always a charge for alterations anyway, so it doesn't matter where it's done. However, if you have only one or two attendants from out of town, you might be able to arrange with the bridal shop to do their last-minute alterations when they arrive the day before the wedding.)

Here's what you'll want to keep in mind when choosing attendants' attire:

- The maid or matron of honor may wear a different color or style.
- Dresses should be similar in line and degree of formality to your own; they may be the same length or shorter than yours, but all their hems should fall at the same place on each woman.
- To flatter various figure types, consider different styles in the same fabric or color.
- To flatter various complexions, consider different colors in the same style, or a "monochromatic" scheme of the same style and color in graduated shades and hues.
- Varying heights can be evened out by allowing each woman to wear a different heel height.
- Headpieces and accessories, earrings, necklaces, gloves, hose, etc., should be the same for everyone; make sure the attendants know what those are and that you consider both the individuals and the dress design when choosing them. Perhaps you could provide one or more of the accessories as your gift to your attendants.
- Let your attendants know in advance if any special undergarments will be required by the dress design.
- It is perfectly proper to have an all-white wedding, or a black-and-white wedding, if you choose.
- Junior bridesmaids (aged 9 to 14) may wear outfits identical to those of the other bridesmaids, or something more youthful.

- Flower girls (aged 4 to 8) may wear long or short dresses appropriate to the style of the wedding; often they are in white with sashes or ribbons in wedding colors.

Outfitting the Men

In the fall of 1886, Mr. Griswold Lorillard, a tobacco heir, shocked his contemporaries by wearing a tailless black dinner coat to the annual autumn ball at the Tuxedo Park Country Club in Tuxedo Park, New York. (He had fashioned this coat after the description a friend had given him of a cut-off coat the Prince of Wales wore in the English countryside.) As appalled as the guests were at this dramatic departure from social convention on such a formal occasion, other gentlemen soon saw the sense of the design and began to copy Lorillard's tailless dinner coat. Thus the tuxedo was born.

Lorillard might himself be shocked at the many colorful, creative interpretations popularly referred to as "a tux" today, but no doubt he would be pleased to see that men continue to dare to assert their own style and to insist on comfort and convenience, even on formal occasions.

The International Formalwear Association does still make a distinction between the "traditional" black tuxedo and its proper variations for the different times of day (the cutaway, the stroller, and the black tails), and their more contemporary versions (colors, patterns, and prints, all of which are accurately called "formal wear suits"). We make that distinction, too, and so will you when you visit your nearest formal wear shop with your fiancé.

The groom should select his own wedding attire, and that of the male attendants, based on the time of day of the wedding and the degree of formality, or propriety, you two are hoping to achieve. He should have your help to do this, and you should both have the guidance of a men's formal wear specialist. Together, you will decide, given your own

FORMAL WEAR TERMS YOU NEED TO KNOW

ascot—a scarf-like tie looped under the chin; worn with a cutaway coat

braces—you know them as suspenders; used to hold up trousers when a cummerbund is worn

cummerbund—a pleated waistcover (worn instead of a vest, with the pleats facing up); usually matched to a bow tie

cutaway—the daytime formal tailcoat (also called a morning coat) in black or gray, worn with striped trousers

opera pumps—patent leather slip-on shoes with grosgrain bows on the toes

pocket square—a small, dressy handkerchief worn in the upper jacket pocket; not worn when men are wearing boutonnieres

slip-ons—plain dress shoes in black patent or smooth leather

stroller—a slightly longer black or gray jacket (also called a walking coat) worn with striped trousers for formal daytime or afternoon weddings

studs—formal shirt fasteners; look like buttons, but are considered jewelry

white tie—the most formal evening attire of the sort that made Fred Astaire famous; a white tie and white piqué vest over a winged-collar shirt, with a black tailcoat and matching trousers

winged collar—the formal dress shirt that sports a stand-up collar with folded-down tips

attire and that of your bridesmaids, whether the men in the wedding party would be more appropriately dressed in a traditional or a contemporary style.

If you choose the traditional look, your choice will be relatively simple: only certain outfits are proper at certain times of the day (see our What To Wear guide on page 71). But, if you choose the contemporary approach, then almost anything goes. You might match ties, cummerbunds, shirts, or even jackets and suits to your wedding colors. You might select interesting fabrics—tapestries, brocades, iridescents, or other textures. You might even go for creative styling, such as double-breasted jackets, shawl collars, capes, etc.

Visit your formal wear shop soon after all the women's attire has been decided so you can appreciate the range of choice and determine what will work best for your celebration. While most stores can arrange rentals with only a few weeks notice, it's not advisable to wait that late should unique fitting problems, special orders, or unusually large wedding parties demand more time and attention. Three to four months in advance is recommended.

Bring along magazine pictures of men's formal wear you both like, also swatches of your colors and your attendants' gowns, and anything else regarding your ceremony and reception that might prove helpful (brochures of the reception site, pictures of the church, etc.). The sooner you and your fiancé finalize this important wedding decision, the sooner you can get on with coordinating everyone and everything else.

QUESTIONS TO ASK

1. Are the style(s) and appropriate accessories we like in stock, or will they have to be ordered?
2. What will be the total cost of this outfit for each man? What amount of deposit is required?
3. By what date will all deposits and measurements have to be in?

4. How do we handle out-of-town ushers? (Most men's formal wear stores have some sort of travel package that contains instructions and a self-addressed measurement form to be returned to them with the deposit. It is an accepted industry courtesy for a man to take this form, sent to him by the groom, to any formal wear store in his area and be properly measured free of charge.)

5. How many days does the rental fee cover? (Typically, for a weekend wedding, tuxedos are picked up Thursday night or Friday, returned on Monday.)

6. When do the final fittings for the wedding party take place? Do you have the capability to make any last-minute alterations or corrections?

7. What are our liabilities for damaged apparel or lost accessories?

8. Do you have a brochure or picture of our selection that we can take with us?

Boys aged 9 to 14 may serve as "junior ushers." They wear what the other ushers wear, but you need to ask your formal wear specialist about sizing for them. Small boys (aged 4 to 8) may be ring bearers. They may wear outfits to match the men's attire, also sized down by the formal wear specialist. Other choices are Eaton suits with short pants and knee socks or fancy breeches for very formal weddings. Resources that design flower girl dresses sometimes have ring bearer outfits, as well. Otherwise, you and the children's parents will have to see what's available for them at a children's shop.

Fashion Focus for Him

Establish the look your groom prefers: very stylish and fashion conscious, more conservative, or somewhere in between. (In summer, the latter is often satisfied by choosing a white dinner jacket with black trousers for a tropical, yet still formal look.)

Determine which style and cut flatters the groom most: single- or double-breasted jacket, European or regular fit.

Agree on whether the groom wants to be distinguished from his male attendants, or prefers to have them in the same combination.

Inquire about the cost of the rentals for his attendants. (Ushers usually pay for their own rentals, which can range from $50 for a basic tuxedo to over $100 for designer styles with all accessories.) The groom might present some accessories (special cuff links, shirts, or studs) to his attendants as gifts.

Does the groom own a tuxedo? If not, will future use make it practical for him to purchase one now?

For an informal wedding, the groom may wear a dark business suit or a blazer and slacks. The other men in the wedding party should dress similarly.

For Moms and Dads

Because they have places of honor on your wedding day, your parents, and grandparents, will want to look their very best. They'll do that within the guidelines you've set for the tone and formality of the wedding.

Fathers generally wear the same attire as the ushers, though if the wedding is formal and either gentleman owns his own tuxedo, it is perfectly proper for him to wear it, matching or not. If your fiancé's father will be serving as the best man, which is an increasingly popular practice these days, then his outfit really should be the same as those of the other men in the wedding party.

Traditionally, the mother of the bride gets to choose her attire first. You may suggest a style or color in keeping with your degree of formality and overall color scheme, but you should allow your mother to select whatever she feels is most flattering to her. She may wear a short dress or suit in the day or in the evening, or a long gown for a formal evening wedding. (A floor-length gown during the day is appropriate when the bridesmaids' gowns are also floor length.)

Once the mother of the bride decides what she is wearing, the mother of the groom may select her attire. Her dress or suit should be of the same degree of formality as your mother's in a shade that becomes her and blends with the wedding colors. Once again, with mothers' attire as with your own, all the rigid rules, such as not wearing beaded dresses before 6 P.M. and so forth, are no longer relevant. Mothers, and grandmothers too, are a lot younger and more stylish these days than they used to be, so they can be trusted to be elegant and appropriate at the same time.

Your mother, and his, may shop for their dresses at your bridal retailer, or anywhere else that carries special-occasion attire. You might offer to accompany each woman if she'd like that. If either one already owns something she feels would be perfect, she should be allowed to wear it.

Elegant Guests

Of course, you have no direct control over what your guests wear to the wedding, but you can send strong signals. The wording and the design of your invitations, for instance, will indicate the style and tone of your ceremony and reception and, by extension, guests will infer appropriate guidelines for their own attire. (See more in Chapter 11, "The Honour of Your Presence.") By the way, these days, it is considered acceptable for female guests to wear black or white to a wedding; it is the style, not the color of the outfit, that is deemed appropriate or inappropriate.

If you're having a very formal evening wedding and you wish your guests to be part of the glamour and high style, you may stipulate "Black Tie" on your invitations. That means all male guests are required to wear tuxedos and all female guests are expected to "dress to the nines."

The only problem with being so explicit, however, is that men who don't own tuxedos, and may not be able to afford to rent them, will feel unwelcome to attend. A more practical solution is to use the words "Black Tie Invited." That way, guests get the message that yours will be a very elegant affair; the women will still go all out, but the men will have the option of wearing either a tuxedo or a dark business suit.

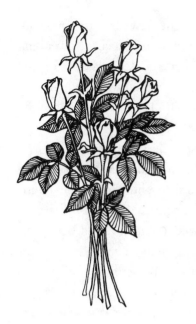

CHAPTER 7
Special Situations

While it is true that only two people wed, it is also true that those who are close to the couple have a vested interest in their well-being. Parents want their children to be happy, to have an easier life, to have wonderful kids and a loving home of their own. Families want to continue traditions, form alliances, and look with pride on the new generations. Friends want to remain friends, to stay close, to gain rather than lose in the marital bargain.

With all this vested interest and emotional involvement, it's not hard to understand why people get crazy when planning a wedding. In wanting the best for the couple, they can't help but define "the best" in their own terms.

Usually, their definition is challenged in small ways, in matters of taste or protocol, wherein everyone will admit to differences of opinion and compromise will ultimately effect a solution. But sometimes, the definition of best is challenged in a fundamental way, in matters of faith, philosophy, or values that cannot be easily compromised. These are the issues that no one wants to discuss because they come to the very center of who we are and what we

stand for. They represent special complications for the couples who face such challenges.

Interracial Marriages

In the 1990 census, 9.8 million people checked "other" in the race category boxes, a significantly higher number than had ever done so before. Just as the waves of immigrants at the turn of this century produced a new generation of Americans of mixed ethnic ancestry, so too have more recent immigration patterns and integration laws begun to produce a new generation of racially, and culturally, blended Americans. As birth records and census data show, more and more people, of bi- and triracial backgrounds, find it difficult, if not impossible, to identify with any one group. And that is part of the fear that surrounds the issue of interracial marriages.

According to the National Center for Health Statistics, 2 percent of all marriages in the United States are interracial; more than half of all American-born Asians marry non-Asians. Yet, in spite of the fact that interracial marriages are increasingly common in the United States, and regardless of the fact that state laws prohibiting it were struck down by the Supreme Court in 1967 (Loving v. Virginia), acceptance by families and communities continues to lag. People are afraid of losing their cultures, their traditions, their distinctions.

"The couple entering an interracial marriage has to be *very* secure in their own relationship," says Yvette Walker Hollis, editor and publisher with her husband, Daniel, of *New People: The Journal for the Human Race*, a bimonthly publication for interracial and intercultural families. "They have to be prepared for unexpected reactions, even from friends and family members who are basically supportive, and they cannot allow themselves to be overly sensitive to the reactions of strangers."

The Hollises themselves are an interracial couple, and they were fortunate to have the acceptance of their families and friends when they married. Ironically, though, it was the small problems in wedding planning that led them to a greater awareness of the bigger issues involved: "There were simply no interracial couples pictured in the magazines," she recalls, "and very few interracial wedding parties. I had trouble picking my wedding colors—we finally decided on black and white to make a statement—and I found myself on a personal quest for an interracial couple cake topper, which didn't exist, but which I was able to have made." (See Appendix.)

The Hollises admit they were lucky; most couples face problems far greater than just wedding details. Another bride, whom we'll call Maggie, has a more typical story.

Maggie is biracial, the product of a Haitian father and a Latin American mother; now she has a white stepfather. She met Keith, an Irish Caucasian, at a sports center where they both were avid runners. Romance ensued. All during their courtship, the couple's visits to her home were warm and friendly, to his home, cool and distant. When they finally got engaged, they kept it a secret from Keith's family.

Eventually, though, the news had to come out because Maggie and Keith wanted a church wedding with approximately 100 guests. When they informed Keith's family, his mother refused to attend, and his sister quit speaking to them. Keith was caught in the middle.

"His mother thought he had some sort of psychological problem because he wanted to marry me," Maggie says, "and she wanted him to get counseling. And because he actually listened to her and considered what she said, I felt hurt and betrayed." Maggie returned the engagement ring.

Time passed. Ultimately, with the help of a priest—"At least we were both Catholic and had that in common," Maggie says—the couple got back together and had the wedding they planned. Keith's mother attended, and so did his sister.

Maggie summarizes the ordeal: "It all worked out in the end, but not without some hurt and sadness along the way. Now that we're married, things are getting better; it's workable, at least on the surface, and I don't feel like I have to bend over backwards to please everyone anymore. The real acceptance will come over time, or it won't. In any event, Keith and I have come to accept the curiosity of others about our relationship, and the complications that might result for us and our children, as part of the society in which we live."

Family bonding, social acceptance, children, housing—all remain personal challenges and political issues for couples of mixed white, black, Asian, or native American unions. Each group has its fears and prejudices, and each group is concerned about its loss of identity. And when the interracial couple also has marked cultural and religious differences between them, the situation is likely to be even more difficult.

These are realities. But we know many couples who are making their interracial marriages work, and they have this advice for others entering such unions:

- Concentrate on your own relationship first and always; the two of you must stay strong and unified.
- Look for what you have in common and build on it: religion, culture, values, professions, etc.
- Don't keep your courtship and engagement a secret; give people time to grow in acceptance.
- Don't automatically assume that any objections or lack of enthusiasm about your marriage are racially motivated.
- Don't project problems before they develop out of your own stereotypical thinking.
- Be up front about the fact that yours is an interracial wedding when dealing with caterers, ceremony and reception sites, honeymoon travel, etc.; you don't want any negative reactions marring your happiness.
- If you know that serious prejudice exists among any friends or family members that might result in hurt or ugliness during your wedding celebration, then exclude them from participation; you deserve a wonderful, problem-free wedding day.
- Look for racially and culturally diverse communities in which to build your future lives together.

Interfaith Couples

Of the many possible differences a couple can face, perhaps none is more sensitive, or more difficult to compromise, than religious differences. The identification with a religion extends beyond mere preference or convenience into the very core of one's existence, into a view of life, a family identity, and sometimes an ethnic heritage. Thus, religion is not an issue that can be discussed easily or in an objective way. Two people don't just give up their ingrained beliefs and settle readily on a third choice.

Furthermore, the dilemmas of an interfaith marriage are rarely limited to just the two partners. Even couples who are not particularly religious themselves soon realize, once their engagement is announced, that the prospect of an interfaith union raises significant issues for their families: the celebration of holidays, the raising of children, the transmission of values and traditions. For the interfaith couple, then, getting engaged can demand more than just finding workable solutions for themselves; it can mean finding acceptable solutions for their families, as well.

Studies since 1985 have found that 52 percent of all Jewish men and women take gentile spouses (from the Council of Jewish Federations), and that a third of all Catholics are involved in what are called "mixed" marriages (from the National Opinion Research Center at the University of Chicago). Rates of intermarriage among various Protestant denominations, Orthodox sects, and non-Christian faiths are not recorded, but the clergy of all faiths share a concern about religious intermarriage.

To them, and often to the families involved in such unions, marrying outside of the faith represents a repudiation of religious values and principles. Ultimately, the question comes down to the children of the union: how can the faith be preserved and the values be transmitted to a new generation raised in interfaith homes? The fear is that they won't be.

Religious leaders are of two minds: (1) that the dilution of religious observance and identification through intermarriage is already a fact of American life and, therefore, that the clergy ought to minimize alienation by helping couples and families integrate their values and blend their traditions; or (2) that religious rules and regulations regarding interfaith marriage need to be strengthened and emphasized, even made more rigid. If you are an interfaith couple, you might find your clergy, and your families, divided along the same lines.

Unfortunately, there is no easy answer to these issues. You may have a difficult time finding a religious officiant for your wedding. You may need to participate in one of the many premarital counseling programs now offered for interfaith couples (see more in "Preparing for Marriage," Chapter 8). One of you may decide to convert to the other's faith, or you may both adopt another religion. In severe cases of disagreement, you may even have to reconsider your decision to marry. "If you really believe that *your* faith, *your* religious tradition is the only true one," cautions a Protestant minister, "then you have to have serious reservations about the viability of an interfaith marriage."

In a world where cultural values are so often confused with spiritual values, the interfaith couples face a special challenge. They must remain true to their individual convictions while serving as an example of tolerance and understanding to their families, their children, and their communities. It is not an easy challenge, but those who undertake it seem to be blessed with a special vision: the ability to recognize the Lord by whatever name you use, be it God, Yahweh, Allah, Buddha, or Jesus Christ.

QUESTIONS TO ASK

1. How much do you know about each other's religious backgrounds? With knowledge comes understanding. Talk about your religious experiences, visit each other's clergy, and consider premarital instruction programs as ways to learn more about the other's faith.

2. What are your faith's laws regarding marriage? Visit the clergy as soon as you decide to marry, and find out what accommodations can be made in the wedding ceremony for interfaith couples. If both faiths will sanction the marriage, and if the ceremony can reflect elements of both traditions, your families and friends will feel more comfortable.

3. What values and beliefs do the two of you share? No matter how disparate your religious backgrounds, it is absolutely essential that an interfaith couple find their common ground.

4. What holidays and religious occasions are important to you and your families? Alienation of their children is what families fear most. You can minimize these fears by planning in advance how you

will celebrate Hanukkah, Christmas, Easter, Passover, and other holidays in your home with your families.

5. How will you raise your children? Most couples agree that children need to be raised with some religious beliefs; how they are implemented may be the single greatest issue that interfaith couples face. Be honest with each other regarding your children's religious future.

6. Are you willing to shoulder your religious responsibilities in the home? When one partner is essentially nonpracticing, the other may not only have to continue practicing his or her faith alone, but may also have to take primary responsibility for the religious training of children. It can be a heavy burden.

The Long-Distance Wedding

In a nation where 18 percent of the population changes residence each year, planning the long-distance wedding is a fact of life for hundreds of couples. Job relocations, educational goals, and changing family circumstances keep everyone on the move. The problem, of course, is that on the move or not, everyone also wants to be part of the wedding, and that usually means physical proximity.

"The more distance you have to cover, the more attention you have to give to staying in touch and the more time you need to do it," says Cheryl, a newlywed, who finally had to settle on "a central location" for her wedding.

She had met her husband, who was from Chicago, while in school in Colorado. At the time they got engaged, Cheryl's father lived in Missouri, her mother and stepfather had just been transferred to South Carolina, and the rest of her family was in Arkansas. Her closest friends, whom she invited to be attendants, were in Illinois, Missouri, Colorado, and Canada.

"Our biggest concern was to plan the wedding so that the most people could participate, and the fewest number would be inconvenienced," she says. "We also knew we had to plan far enough in advance so that everyone who had to travel could budget for the expense."

After much traveling and talking themselves, the couple decided to be married in Missouri because it was "centrally located" and because her father and friends there were more likely than anyone else to stay put. Once that was decided, it took Cheryl 18 months to plan the wedding, via long distance.

We hear variations of Cheryl's story all the time: brides who have relocated themselves across the country after school; brides whose friends, family, or even fiancés are constantly on the move; brides who choose, for whatever reason, to marry abroad. It is not an easy situation, but it can be handled successfully with good communication and a little sensitivity to those far away.

If yours is to be a long-distance wedding, take a cue from Cheryl and allow yourselves, and everyone involved, plenty of time for the extra planning you'll need to go those extra miles.

Tips for the Long-Distance Wedding

- Set a date and determine a location right away. The sooner you do, the easier it will be for everyone else to plan their participation.
- Budget for phone calls, photocopying, faxing, and travel costs during the planning period. All those expenses will be significantly higher than usual.
- Plan your planning. You may have to use vacations and holidays, even piggyback business trips to see people and make arrangements.
- Consider hiring a wedding consultant, not only to handle details, but to act as a liaison in all the long-distance communicating.
- Contact the clergy or civil officiant early, and investigate religious, local, and state marriage requirements in the place you will have the ceremony. Some locations have residency requirements.

- Shop early for attendants' attire. No doubt you will have to send swatches, dresses, and shoes through the mail.
- Provide whatever transportation information you can for those who must travel. Many carriers (rail, air, and bus) offer discounted fares for groups of people traveling together.
- Secure a block of hotel rooms at discounted rates for out-of-towners. Check into complimentary shuttle service to and from airports, rail stations, and so on.
- Try to keep costs down for those participating, and be understanding of any family members or friends who feel they cannot bear the expense of being with you.
- Think about holding the wedding where you two or most of your friends live, then have subsequent receptions in your and/or his hometowns at a later date. You might display wedding pictures or show a video of the ceremony, have another wedding cake, or even wear your wedding dress. Do whatever you can to make those guests feel a part of your happiness.

Marrying Abroad

"Couples should think very carefully before just blithely deciding to get married in a foreign country because they think it would be fun," advises Tambra Riggs, founder and president of Weddings Around the World, a Dallas firm that makes arrangements for marriages and wedding celebrations in foreign locations. "Not only do the marriage laws of every country differ, but the rules and regulations often differ in every city and town in every country. Securing the proper paperwork from the proper authorities for a valid marriage can be very, very difficult and involved."

If, for a serious reason, you must be married abroad, you can begin by contacting that nation's consulate here in the United States. They will be able to give you a general outline of what will be required. And it is vitally important that all requirements be met if you want your marriage to be legally recognized here at home, because *U.S. law recognizes only the marriages that are valid in the country in which they take place.*

"Bear in mind that foreign consulates are not in the marriage business," cautions Riggs. "The information you get may be outdated, incomplete, or not entirely accurate for the specific town or province in which you plan to be married. Everything has to be verified with local authorities and, if you don't reach the right official or you don't speak the language, you can be in for some nasty surprises."

All member nations of the United Nations have foreign consulates in New York City, of course, and most also have embassies in Washington, D.C. Some nations also have offices in other major cities throughout the United States. The U.S. State Department publishes a directory, called "Foreign Consular Offices in the U.S.," available in large public libraries, through which you may find the appropriate foreign consulate nearest you.

With rare exception, marriage abroad is not as easy as it is here in the United States. Most countries, for instance, have strict separation of church and state, so that only civil authorities are empowered to perform a legal marriage. Such authorities may be hard to locate and, in some cases, the wedding may have to take place in a less than elegant setting, perhaps in a busy town hall or a crowded civil office.

While it's almost impossible to generalize about the various legal requirements you might face, here are some common ones:

• A waiting period or residency requirement (some as long as 30 days)
• The filing of an official petition or application for marriage
• Authentic personal documents (U.S. passport, birth certificate, health records, proof of economic solvency, etc.); sometimes, these documents must be presented "in translation" in the language used by that nation

• A medical examination, including X-rays, blood tests, or physical exams, conducted in the country itself
• Fees for processing and filing
• Publishing of banns (local announcements of your intention to marry)
• An authenticated (sometimes translated) divorce decree for those who are marrying again; there may be a special waiting period required from the date of divorce to the date of remarriage

Once married, you'll need a copy of the marriage certificate, and it is recommended that you have it authenticated by the American consular office in that country, mainly to verify the signature(s) of the civil officials involved.

Marrying a Foreign National

Marrying a foreigner usually complicates the whole process, and U.S. immigration laws come into play if the two of you intend to return to the United States and/or your foreign spouse plans to become a U.S. citizen. A foreigner must be married to and residing with a U.S. citizen for three years before the naturalization process can begin. (Check with the United States Immigration and Naturalization Service for more specific information.)

Some nations seem arbitrary in their attitudes. An American woman seeking to marry a Mexican male, for instance, is easier to effect than an American man who wishes to marry a Mexican woman. Nations are understandably concerned about their own immigration patterns, as well as the security and well-being of their own citizens, so that they will often exact compelling reasons for the marriage. Even an American who has lived in a country for a long time will face the rigors of trying to marry a citizen whom he has met there.

If you are marrying on a U.S. military base abroad, there's no real problem since military bases are under U.S. domain. Marrying in a U.S. territory or commonwealth (the U.S. Virgin Islands, Puerto Rico, American Samoa, or one of several other Pacific islands) will require compliance with their particular regulations, but the process is considerably less complicated, even routine. A local tourist bureau can probably give you basic information and tell you how to submit a marriage application (see "Honeymoon Weddings" in Chapter 17).

Finally, American consular offices abroad are not empowered to perform marriages, nor is permission given for marriages to take place on the premises of a U.S. embassy in a foreign land. Officials there may validate your marriage certificate, offer information and assistance for the emigration of a foreign spouse to America, or be able to answer questions about local marriage laws and arrangements, but you would be wise to begin your preparations for marrying abroad while here in the United States.

Dealing with Illness and Disabilities

The subject of illness and disability comes up more often than you might think in our discussions with couples planning to marry. Sometimes, questions pertain to the couple themselves, sometimes to members of the wedding party or the immediate family. Whatever the condition or situation, though, questions almost always reflect a concern about the feelings and reactions of others, and almost always begin, "How do we handle . . . ?"

If you, your fiancé, or someone close to you has a serious medical condition or a physical or mental disability, here are some things to keep in mind:

• In general, people with disabilities and disorders do not want to be singled out or considered "handicapped" by others; a little thoughtful planning on your part, such as ramps for wheelchair accessibility, sign language interpreters for the hearing impaired, or glow tape, contrasting lighting, or other environmental landmarks for the visually impaired, can minimize awkwardness and inconvenience for everyone.

• If one of you has an obvious physical disability or a chronic health condition, make sure the other's family knows and is prepared before you announce your engagement; people do not always react well, or even reasonably, when such situations come as a surprise.

• Should you invite an ill or disabled friend or relative to be a member of your wedding party, be understanding of his or her decision to accept or decline; one is the best judge of his or her own health condition and limitations.

• If you, a member of your wedding party, or someone in your family has special needs, consider them when choosing the location(s) for your wedding and when making decisions regarding the ceremony and reception: escorts can be assigned to those who need assistance, attendants can walk in two by two, people can enter through side doors and be seated earlier or later, sections or space can be reserved for those in wheelchairs, etc. Whatever adaptations you make to accommodate those you love will be proper and appreciated.

• In the unfortunate event that one of your attendants, close friends, or family members passes away before your wedding, you might want to remember them with a special prayer or tribute in your ceremony or printed program, especially if that person had shared in the excitement of your forthcoming wedding. Someone who loved you would certainly want you to go ahead with your plans for happiness.

The Pregnant Bride

"I hugged the doctor, jumped up and down, and laughed out loud all the way home when I found out I was pregnant," Carol recalls. "After my serious illness, it was the most welcome, wonderful, life-affirming news I could have imagined, even if I wasn't married. I hated to tell Frank something like this over the phone, but I couldn't help myself. I called him at work."

"Thank God," he said, "maybe now we can set a wedding date!"

"At first we thought well, gee, maybe we should just have a small wedding, something simple, because both our families are very traditional and very well-known in the community. It wasn't that I was ashamed—far from it—but I had no intention of lying or making excuses a few months after we were married by claiming that the baby was premature or anything like that."

But the couple's families surprised them, especially Carol's future mother-in-law. "Why not have the wedding you want?" she asked. "You would have had it sooner or later anyway, so what difference does it make? You're happy, we're happy, and anybody who really cares about us should be happy too."

Exactly. Pregnancy is not a reason, in and of itself, to get married, but it is often the impetus a long-standing couple needs to set a date. Planning a wedding in three months the size of Frank and Carol's, for 300 guests, was certainly a challenge, but for them it was a happy challenge. In retrospect, Carol even sees some advantages.

"I didn't have time to fool around, to hem and haw, or to get confused by everyone else's opinions," she says. "We just got on the phone, got busy, and made decisions like clockwork—one-two-three!"

Whether you're pregnant or you have some other compelling reason to plan a wedding with a minimal amount of lead time, here's how to accomplish it.

Wedding Planning Tips for Couples in a Hurry

1. Get to the clergy or officiant right away, and be honest about your situation. With good reason, exceptions to the usual time frame can be made, paperwork facilitated, and premarital programs compressed.

2. Do all of your preliminary legwork by phone. State that you have pressing time constraints (you need not explain why in detail) and eliminate any site, caterer, or vendor who is not willing to quote prices or availability without a personal visit.

3. Choose a less-popular weekday or Sunday evening for your celebration when bookings tend to be light.

4. Look for reception packages that offer everything under one roof, and through one negotiation, or consider hiring a wedding consultant to handle the coordination of separate details for you.

5. Use photographers, florists, and musicians who are already familiar with the ceremony and reception sites, perhaps those whom the locations recommend.

6. Have only one or two bridesmaids and let them find their own dresses in a color and degree of formality you suggest. Have as many ushers as you need.

7. Be up front with your bridal retailer about how soon you will need your gown and why. If that retailer has reservations about meeting your timeline, go somewhere else. A pregnant bride can benefit from an experienced consultant's advice regarding style and adaptability for her condition, and probably arrange to have her final fitting done the week before the wedding.

8. Anticipate some additional expenses because of special favors or the inability to shop around.

9. Understand if someone close to you is unable to participate in your celebration because of prior commitments, and forgive those who are too prudish or prim to want to share in your happiness.

10. Plan a honeymoon, even if it's only a weekend. You deserve it.

Cohabiting Couples

The U.S. Bureau of the Census reports that an estimated 2.6 million households are composed of unmarried couples living together. For some, cohabitation is a prelude to marriage; for others, the arrangement is akin to marriage in terms of the relationship, but a substitution for the supposed legal entanglements of an official marriage.

Technically, unwed cohabitation is still illegal in some states, though criminal prosecution is rare. Yet, the increasingly common phenomenon of unwed couples living together is having a profound effect on society, and on the interpretation of marriage and family laws everywhere.

For cohabiting couples planning a wedding, difficulties will arise from family and friends who have objected, on moral grounds, to the arrangement all along. Many believe that those who have already assumed the privileges of married life have thereby abrogated the privileges, namely the gifts and parties, afforded engaged couples who have not yet established a life, and a household, together.

Some will even see the public pronouncement of a cohabiting couple's commitment in a big wedding as a scandalous affront to decent moral values. On the other hand, often families are so relieved that their daughter or son is finally "doing the right thing" that they will muster a surprising amount of enthusiasm for a big wedding.

There's no arguing with people's beliefs or moral standards. If you have been cohabiting for quite some time and have been open and honest about your relationship, no doubt you have already endured questions and criticism. You can expect more when you announce your wedding plans, though more may be said behind your back than to your face.

That's the reality and, if you didn't share some insistence on the value of marriage yourselves, you probably wouldn't be bothering to make your relationship official now. If people have serious objections to participating in your wedding, you'll have to understand and accept their position. If your families refuse to contribute to the expense of your celebration, you'll have to be prepared to host the wedding yourselves.

The reasons you decided to cohabit, and the reasons you have for getting married now, are entirely personal and between the two of you. Those who can separate who you are from what you do and love you accordingly will share your happiness.

Age Differences

"I had a lot of trouble when I first met my daughter's fiancé," confesses a father of the bride. "How do you treat a son-in-law who's almost your own age?"

Age differences between brides and grooms seem to follow a pattern of inverse correlation; that is, older men (77 percent of those over 35) marry women six or more years their junior, and older women (40 percent of those over 35) marry men seven or more years younger than they. Only when couples are marrying each other in their early twenties do they tend to be close in age.

Beyond the private issues a couple might face because of a significant age difference, they may also have to deal with the questions and concerns of their families. Parents typically worry about future grandchildren, about whether or not there will be any, and about the health and longevity of the older partner. Parents may also experience some awkwardness in trying to determine what their roles should be with a son-in-law or daughter-in-law who is a contemporary of their own.

Finally, there are the societal pressures and presumptions. The older man with a much younger woman has become a cliché and is greeted with indulgent smiles, while the older woman with even a slightly younger man is still a cause for raised eyebrows. "He's only five years younger than I am," says a 34-year-old professional woman, "but I feel somehow guilty and apologetic every time we have to fill out an application together or state our ages."

We've all heard oldsters say that age is a state of mind. Maybe so, but it's a state that not everybody has come to terms with yet.

Socioeconomic Disparities

It happens occasionally that someone of great wealth, position, or promise will choose to marry someone with nothing other than a good heart to share. We say occasionally because such a situation is not usual; families tend to preserve and perpetuate their wealth and influence by marrying within the same social class. In fact, less exalted, ordinary families essentially do the same thing.

Families of great wealth and social position often question the motives of someone of lesser advantages seeking to marry into the family, sometimes with good reason, sometimes not. If you are in this situation, try to remember that the cold-hearted skepticism stems from good intentions: parents simply don't want their child taken advantage of.

A premarital contract may help ease suspicion in these circumstances, but not always. Sometimes there are deeper issues at work, a very real prejudice or snobbery, that a practical, legal solution cannot mitigate. In this case, your only hope is to prove your love and loyalty, and your worth, over time through a lasting, successful marriage.

CHAPTER 8
Preparing for Marriage

For many couples, the period of engagement is synonymous with the wedding planning. There are so many happy choices to make, so many important details to remember in order to turn the vision of a wonderful wedding day into a reality. It's understandable that joyous anticipation about such a major rite of passage would dominate a couple's consciousness.

If we examine the history of courtship, however, we find that the period of engagement, or "betrothal," has been traditionally devoted to less romantic matters, to the transfer of property and the practical preparations for married life. Even today, couples who focus their attention only on romance and neglect such practical needs as employment, housing, income, home furnishings, family, and community obligations would be considered shortsighted.

It is said that "what goes around, comes around," and so it seems to be with social attitudes. Being older, more established, and better educated, today's couples have rediscovered the importance of preparing for their lives together in a pragmatic way. Formal marriage preparation sessions, in many different areas, are the result.

Religious Preparation

Even couples who share the same faith might be surprised to learn of specific requirements for their religious wedding ceremony, so we emphasize, again, that the clergy should be contacted as soon as your decision to marry has been made. Every major religion has its own rituals and traditions that must be honored, and most also have some restrictions regarding when and how the marriage ceremony takes place.

Some faiths strongly oppose divorce, for instance, so that if one of you has been married before, time will be needed to resolve your eligibility to marry. Some require waiting periods, official membership in that church or congregation, or public or published proclamation of your intention to marry. Some have premarital conferences or programs to be attended, paperwork to be processed, or specific liturgical guidelines to be followed and planned for in the ceremony itself. And, most have at least a few holy days or sacred seasons in the year when marriages cannot be performed.

But meeting with the clergy is more than just a matter of deciphering rules and regulations. The religious wedding ceremony brings another dimension to a routine civil procedure, and couples who want that obviously value their faith and expect to share their spiritual, as well as their temporal, lives together. The clergy of virtually every faith is appreciative of that, and most will be willing to do whatever they can, not only to help you create a loving, personal ceremony, but also to provide you with the spiritual guidance to support you in your new marital roles.

Some clergy will keep meetings casual and informal, especially if they know you well. Some may recommend your participation in one of the many values-oriented marriage preparation programs, such as the Engaged Encounter Weekends. Still others might have formal, required premarital programs of their own, such as the Pre-Cana Conferences run through the Family Life offices of each Roman Catholic diocese.

Whether it's a series of informal chats or more structured programs with other couples (usually conducted by experienced, married lay people), such sessions can be helpful and inspiring. They will lead you to identify and explore the spiritual values you share, and also will address many of the day-to-day issues of married life. Through them, you can strengthen the commitment and communication between you.

Interfaith Preparation

The basic problem in interfaith marriage stems from the premise that, if two people don't share the same religious values and beliefs, how can they enter a valid religious contract of marriage? "How can I, who am not empowered under Judaic law over nonbelievers, perform a valid marriage between a Christian and a Jew?" asks a Conservative rabbi.

The question is a logical one, and one that many clerics are forced to ask. Even among Christian denominations, wherein a few consider marriage a sacrament (Episcopal, Roman Catholic, and Eastern Orthodox) and others don't, or some profess a belief in the Holy Trinity (most mainline Christian faiths)

and others don't (Unitarian), the issue of a priest's or minister's authority might be raised.

Some faiths have resolved their ideological difficulties, others have not. Some will require that certain conditions be met and promises be made before an interfaith ceremony is performed, others will not. Some will agree to co-officiate with the clergy of another faith or to conduct the ceremony in a neutral location where no religious symbols are present, others will not.

If you're an interfaith couple, you probably have some idea already of what you're likely to face. If not, a brief description of the positions on marriage of the world's major religions appears on the following page.

Interfaith Ministries

Many churches, synagogues, and community religious and cultural organizations, especially those on college campuses, have undertaken a special ministry to reach out to interfaith couples and to support them through formal premarital programs and informal self-help groups. The Prepare/Enrich, Inc., programs are entirely nondenominational (see Appendix), and even the Catholic Pre-Cana sessions in most areas have become decidedly ecumenical. Sometimes couples who have been unable to resolve their religious dilemmas on their own can come to terms with the issues through interfaith counseling.

Such was the case for Simon, who is Jewish, and Lee Ann, who is Catholic. Even though they had known each other for a long time, their decision to marry threw their families into turmoil—"yelling, crying, and for a while, not speaking to us." Nagging questions about religious traditions, family, and children brought them to a series of meetings with five different rabbis and priests in search of answers. Their problems seemed insurmountable and so, with much sadness, they finally broke their engagement.

But the personal soul-searching continued. Simon joined an interfaith counseling group through a Reform synagogue in Boston, where he lived, and Lee Ann began regular meetings with the parish priest

INTERFAITH GUIDELINES

Buddhism: Marriage is a civil matter not outlined in Buddhist scripture. The monk traditionally gives a blessing for the couple before or after the marriage ceremony, but interfaith unions are not a religious issue.

Catholicism (Roman): Dispensations are routinely granted by the Church for a Catholic to marry a non-Catholic (Christian or not), provided there are no "impediments" to marriage. Determination of impediments and "freedom to marry" are made on a case-by-case basis through the priest and the local diocese. Non-Catholic partners will be asked to respect the religious traditions of the Catholic Church and to consider raising the children of the marriage as Catholics. Some dioceses do not permit a Catholic marriage to take place outside of a church. Priests routinely co-officiate marriage ceremonies with other clergy and, today, "mixed-marriage" couples may even have a Nuptial Mass.

Eastern Orthodox (including **Russian, Greek, Serbian, Slovak**): Interfaith marriage is not encouraged, but a dispensation may be granted provided the non-Orthodox party is a Christian baptized in the name of the Holy Trinity. Divorce is also a "freedom to marry" issue in Orthodox churches. See a priest for an assessment of individual cases.

Hinduism: Interfaith marriage is not advocated, but it does take place under special circumstances. Check with the Hindu priest for a case evaluation.

Islam: *The Koran*, the book of Islamic law, classifies Muslims, Christians, and Jews as believers in the true God and, therefore, as acceptable for intermarriage. By extension, a Muslim may also marry a practicing Buddhist or Hindu.

Judaism: Strict Judaic law does not recognize the validity of a contract between a Jew and a non-Jew. Some Reform rabbis, however, will perform an interfaith ceremony.

Mormonism: Mormons may marry outside the faith, but if they do, they may not have a wedding in a Mormon temple. Divorce is a real concern, since marriage is forever, into eternity, in the Mormon Church.

Protestantism: Some conservative Protestant groups will not perform a marriage between a Protestant and a non-Christian, and the Episcopal Church has strictures against divorce and remarriage. Check with the minister of your denomination.

---

in her hometown church in Connecticut. In time, they came to some personal decisions, got back together, and were married six months later by both a rabbi and a priest.

"I think it's fair to say that had we not each gotten the help and guidance we needed to clarify the religious issues, our love alone might not have been enough to get us back together," says Lee Ann. "There was certainly no support from our families. We weren't even sure until the day of the wedding who would actually attend."

But the families did attend, and the priest, who had recently made a trip to Jerusalem, presented the couple with their first wedding gift: a ceremonial dish inscribed with Hebrew blessings. "You both come from the same place. It's your homeland," the priest said. "I hope you visit it together one day."

Simon and Lee Ann hope so, too.

Premarital Therapy

All too often, people don't see the need for professional counseling until a real crisis occurs. Unfortunately, then it may be too late.

"Marriage tends to separate 'the men from the boys,' so to speak," says Dr. Paul Dasher, a New Jersey psychologist who works with engaged couples in his family practice. "Relationships are idealized during the dating stage but, once the engagement solidifies the commitment to marry, unfamiliar feelings and ingrained family patterns start to surface. Partners don't always understand themselves or what's happening between them, and so they may break up [the engagement or the marriage], often unnecessarily, I think."

Professionals, including Dasher, feel that spiritually motivated marriage preparation programs are excellent, but not always sufficient for those who have deeply rooted conflicts and/or the need to explore their own personalities.

"The couple is striving for intimacy during the engagement," Dasher explains. "Yet, the pressures of wedding planning—the demands of time and money, the unreasonable expectations of in-laws, the concerns about careers and lifestyles, and the issues of control—can all work against developing that intimacy. One partner complains that the other has suddenly changed but, in reality, there has been no change, only a new situation which has triggered pre-existing patterns of behavior and unresolved personal conflicts."

The kinds of problems that surface, over family, money, marital roles, etc., and the manner in which they are handled preview the kinds of issues and the kind of communication skills the couple will have in marriage. Whatever can't be negotiated successfully now will probably not get any better later on.

Who Needs Therapy?

If you have serious reservations about the viability of your future as a couple and unresolved conflicts have already erupted between you, you'd be wise to seek professional counseling. The following questions, if answered honestly, could be an indication of that need:

1. How do we deal with conflict? Does one of us consistently refuse to bend, lack sympathy for another point of view, or resort to violence or hysteria to win an argument?
2. Do we handle our problems by not addressing them? Does one of us want peace at any cost, gained by avoiding all conflicts, by refusing to admit or discuss any controversy, or by consistently giving in?
3. Does either of us show signs of substance abuse or dependency (drugs, alcohol, eating disorders)?
4. Does either of us exhibit compulsive behavior that is threatening to our future (gambling, shopping, workaholism)?
5. Are we reasonable in our expectations of each other and the life that we intend to share? Is there any hidden competition, jealousy, or manipulation going on between us?

Premarital therapy with a mental-health professional cannot guarantee your success as a couple, but it is a positive step toward removing some of the obstacles and developing some of the tools for building your lives together.

Financial Planning

Rare is the couple whose attitudes about money are exactly the same. One of you relies on credit, the other is strictly cash 'n carry; you keep your checkbook current down to the last penny, he doesn't know what his balance is until the statement comes in; one of you lives to spend and enjoy, the other lives in fear of a rainy day.

Such variations in attitude are perfectly normal because they emanate from one's family background and personal financial experience. Patterns in spending and saving are also habituated; that is, we handle our money in a certain way because we have always done so, or because we simply aren't aware of other alternatives.

Reasonable, solvent couples can learn to negotiate the minor differences between them, and to balance their attitudes, as well as their checkbooks, through financial honesty before marriage and a serious discussion of their short- and long-term financial goals. In the process of setting up a household budget and estimating income and expenses, for instance, you will undoubtedly talk about each partner's financial contribution and responsibility, and determine the kinds of tools you will need (checking and savings accounts, credit cards, insurance policies, investment plans, wills, etc.) to manage your marital partnership.

For most, an evening or two should be sufficient to get your combined affairs in order. If one of you is already employing the services of a financial planner or accountant, you might want to verify any decisions you make with him or her before actually changing names, opening new accounts, etc. Also, keep in mind the various tasks a professional can help you accomplish:

• Formulate a budget and organize your cash flow;
• Consolidate debt and structure a reduction plan;
• Prepare for income taxes and set up a system of record keeping;
• Plan ahead for major purchases (home, car, education);
• Set long-term goals and institute a savings/investment program;
• Evaluate your assets including insurance policies, profit-sharing/retirement plans, stock portfolios, trust funds, etc.;
• Form a contingency plan for risk management (accident, casualty, and disability);
• Create an estate plan.

Some couples may find a financial discussion awkward, or even downright difficult to have. "Putting your money matters out on the table is, for many people, akin to getting undressed in public," says Andrew Flagg, a Certified Financial Planner and a partner in American Financial Consultants, Inc. "There may be some nervousness in such a frank conversation, even with one's own fiancé, never mind a

very real reluctance that comes when somebody suggests including a third party."

Even so, while most professionals understand a couple's reluctance to seek help, Flagg points out certain conditions that clearly signal that expert financial advice is needed:

• If either party is bringing significant debt to the marriage (consumer credit, education loans, alimony/child support);
• If either has had significant credit difficulties (personal bankruptcy, foreclosures, poor credit rating);
• If either has experienced tax problems, has past-due tax bills, or has failed to file returns;
• If either party is clearly unwilling to make a full and complete financial disclosure to the other.

Such liabilities, both fiscal and psychological, can threaten the solvency of your partnership, impede your growth as a family, and endanger your achieving future goals many years from now. Finally, and not incidentally, under many state and federal laws, the innocent partner can be held responsible for the sins of the offender from the moment the marriage takes place. (See Appendix and next section on prenuptial agreements.)

Financial planning is a process, not a product. The professional can help you understand where you are and where you're going, and what strategies you need to employ to get there. Look for a Certified Financial Planner or a Certified Public Accountant with financial planning expertise through local banks, investment houses, brokerage firms, or in independent practice, or contact the financial planning division of the American Institute of Certified Public Accountants or the Institute of Certified Financial Planners (see Appendix).

Premarital Agreements

Premarital contracts, also called prenuptial or antenuptial agreements, are legal agreements entered into

CONTEMPORARY SOLUTIONS

FAMILY, SOCIOECONOMIC

❦ *You and your fiancé want to buy a condominium, and your parents have offered to lend you the down payment. Is that a good idea?*

It is if *all* of you agree that it is. You should, however, formalize the terms of your agreement in writing, because this is a loan, not a gift. Be sure to include details regarding interest, liabilities, and repayment schedules, have everyone sign the agreement, and make copies of it for all involved to keep. You don't necessarily need an attorney for this kind of private contractual arrangement.

❦ *Your wedding is three months away, and your fiancé has just lost his job. While he's actively looking for another, the industry he's in is depressed and the outlook for gaining a new position by the time you're married is not good. His parents have offered to let you move in with them after the marriage until he gets back on his feet. Should you do that, or should you postpone the wedding?*

It all depends. Living with in-laws is not the best or easiest way to start a marriage; on the other hand, if you stand to lose a sizeable amount of money by postponing the wedding, it might make more sense to go ahead with your plans.

You and your fiancé have to give this decision serious thought and be totally honest with each other about how you feel. People at all ages and stages of their careers find themselves out of work every day and, unfortunately, this may not be the only time you'll ever face this kind of problem.

If you do decide to accept your in-laws' offer, talk candidly with them before you take up residence there. Clarify the nature of your financial contributions, domestic obligations, and any other "house rules." It helps if the two of you can ensure some privacy from other family members while you're living there, and if you can set a deadline, for yourselves and for them, for when you expect to move out.

PERSONAL, SOCIOECONOMIC

❦ *You don't have enormous assets, but you do have enormous bills. Your credit cards are "maxed out," you're over-extended in your living expenses, and your record keeping is a mess. You don't dare sit down with your fiancé to discuss money until you've gotten some order and control over your own affairs, but you don't think you can afford expensive professional advice.*

Assuming that this is an atypical situation for you, and that you're not talking about monumental sums of money and chronic credit problems, you can go to any one of over 600 Consumer Credit Counseling Services located around the country (look in the telephone book or see the Appendix). There is no charge for basic budget counseling, and charges for debt-management programs and other services are very low. (You and your fiancé might even want them to help you set up a household budget for married life.)

Also, professional financial planners are not always expensive. Most will give you an initial consultation (of 30 minutes to an hour) without charge or for a nominal fee. Call to find out. Whatever you do, though, you're right to want to "get your own house in order" before moving in with someone else.

before the marriage that become effective once the marriage takes place. They are designed to anticipate areas of possible dispute between people (and families) about to marry and to settle them in advance.

Such contracts are most useful in prearranging financial matters and safeguarding inheritance rights, but they may also be used to specify rights and privileges within the marriage or to provide for the division of property or the custody of children in case of divorce. In theory, anything that does not violate the law or reduce the dignity of marriage can be included in a prenuptial agreement, though minor provisions, such as who does the dishes or who walks the dog, will carry the weight of your convictions more than the weight of the law. Practically speaking, the terms of a premarital contract become legally enforceable only when a couple is seeking a divorce or when one of them dies.

Many people find the idea of premarital agreements inconsistent with the relationship of trust that should exist between two people before marriage. After all, no one marries with the presumption of divorce. Yet, the process of working out the terms of such an agreement often improves the couple's communication and clarifies their expectations of each other. Furthermore, a prenuptial agreement will almost always quell the objections of families and children to a marriage where significant wealth and inheritance rights are involved.

Family law practitioners generally agree that very young couples with few assets and no real prospects for a sizeable inheritance don't need the safeguards that a formal agreement is intended to provide. But older, better-established couples should definitely consider an agreement if they are:

- Professionals who bring significant assets to their marriage: cars, real estate, businesses, stock options, investment portfolios, or rights of inheritance;
- Those who have been married before and who have the rights of children from a previous marriage to protect;
- Those who come to a marriage with a disproportionate share of the wealth;

- Those who stand to inherit family businesses, homes, trust funds, etc.;
- Those who have significant personal debt or other financial obligations and liabilities not involving the new partner.

Because premarital contracts have come under closer scrutiny, and because a greater number of them are being upheld in the court system, attorneys are now better able to advise clients on recommended safeguards to insure the validity of their contracts.

Seven Safeguards for a Prenuptial Agreement

Both parties must be fully informed of their rights under existing state law in the event of death or divorce. Only then can the parties agree to amend or waive those rights.

- There must be no evidence of coercion. Both partners must sign the agreement voluntarily and with full acceptance of its provisions. What's more, the contract should be executed well in advance of the wedding (two to four weeks is recommended) to avoid charges of hasty, ill-conceived decisions.
- Lest there be future claims of complicity or unfair advantage, it is best if each party is represented by his or her *own* counsel. In some states, this is a requirement.
- There must be full financial disclosure on both sides. Sworn financial affidavits are usually attached to the prenuptial contract.
- In many states, the agreement must be deemed "fair and reasonable" under the law and not considered "unconscionable" at the time of enforcement. There may be limits as to what rights to alimony or child support can be waived.
- The language of the contract has to be clear and precise so that both parties understand what is expected of them. A court may void a contract provision that seems vague or incomprehensible.

Quiz

How Much Do You Know?

See how much the two of you know about love and the law by taking this quiz together. Mark each answer either true or false.★

	True	False

1. Marriage is an entirely personal matter between two individuals.

2. The requirements for a marriage license are the same in every state.

3. A woman must assume her husband's name after marriage to ensure the legitimacy of children.

4. Husbands are legally responsible for the support of their wives.

5. There is no such thing as "separate" property after marriage.

6. In order to get credit, a woman will need her husband to cosign the loan/application.

7. According to the IRS, when you file joint tax returns you are each responsible for half the tax bill.

8. Remarriage never alters the terms of a divorce settlement.

9. A will drafted in one state will be automatically valid in another.

10. Legally, a woman cannot use contraception or have a child without the express consent of her husband.

Answers: All are false. The section on Practical Preparations explains why.

★ Quiz based on information contained in *Your Legal Guide to Marriage*, published by the American Bar Association Public Education Division.

- There should be a "severability clause" to insure that if any one provision of the contract is held invalid by a court, the whole contract won't be invalidated.
- After the marriage: If you want your agreement to remain useful and valid, don't intentionally violate any of its provisions. If circumstances change, rewrite or terminate the agreement.

To find out more about marriage law and prenuptial agreements, or to locate an attorney in your area, contact the American Bar Association (see Appendix).

Practical Preparations

Marriage may be an act of free choice and personal commitment between two adults, but it is also a social institution. As such, the state has a vested interest in the success of your partnership as a basic unit of society.

In the weeks and days before your wedding, or very shortly thereafter, you will have to take care of some of the following practical matters.

- Find out how to apply for a marriage license (in the city or county where the ceremony is to be performed) and meet whatever requirements exist there. (These vary from place to place and state to state: waiting periods, blood tests, evidence of vaccinations, a general physical exam, or in Illinois, an AIDS test.) Ask your officiant about the licensing requirements, or call the county clerk's office.
- Make appointments for any medical check-ups or procedures you want to have completed before marriage (see next section).
- Change beneficiaries and/or include your spouse on any pre-existing health/disability/life insurance policies or investment plans. (Most people have these plans through their employer, so talk to your benefits adviser at work to find out how your marriage will affect whatever policies and plans you have.)

- Compare the benefit and protection plans each of you holds and determine what else you may need. Contact your independent insurance agent for changes and additions on car and homeowner's insurance, as well as on any other coverage.
- Add your spouse's name/signature to any bank accounts, car registrations, investment accounts, or credit cards you intend to share. (Note: The little words *and* and *or* make a difference. A joint savings account for Mary Doe "and" John Doe means that both signatures are required for a transaction; "or" means either signature will do.) You should understand that, if you hold bank accounts and/or credit accounts in both names, you will each have free access to those accounts and each be legally responsible for any bills incurred by the other.

You would be wise to thoroughly investigate the legal and tax ramifications, under the laws of your state, of placing any previously owned private property into joint ownership. The state does not automatically assume that a husband and wife are one entity, and sometimes, even if only in the interest of marital harmony, it makes sense to retain some "separate" property rights on significant holdings. Get professional advice.

- If you will change your name after marriage (or if he will be combining his surname with yours), you each need to effect that change on driver's licenses, employment records, Social Security cards, bank accounts, credit cards, etc. (No other "official" procedure exists; ordinary usage changes one's name after marriage.) A married woman does *not* have to change her name at all, and failure to do so will *not* affect the legitimacy of children born of the marriage.

Furthermore, under the Equal Credit Opportunity Act (ECOA), a woman is entitled, and encouraged, to maintain her own separate credit rating. Even if she has no outside employment, she can establish a personal credit rating by simply using her name, not her husband's (Mrs. Mary Doe, not Mrs. John Doe) on any credit accounts. Also, under the

ECOA, one may not be denied a credit application or refused a loan because of marital status. Contact a local Consumer Credit Counseling Service office for more information.

- If you have a will, you might want to review its provisions in light of your new status with an attorney *in the state in which you will be residing* after marriage. Rights of survivorship vary from state to state, and a will executed in one location is not automatically upheld in another.

If there are any assets at all between you and any concern for the welfare and convenience of your spouse should something happen, you should each have a will. Nobody likes to think about such things, but the time to do it is now when you are both healthy and happy. Contact an attorney.

- If either of you has been married before and is receiving alimony, that will stop once you are remarried. Other aspects of the divorce settlement could be affected, as well. You will need to inform your former spouse about your marriage plans, and one, or both, of you may need to see an attorney.

- If either of you owns a business, or if you plan to own and operate a business together, seek legal and professional advice. There are special considerations for husbands and wives as business partners under the law.

- Review your tax situation. If you will be married on or before December 31, you may legally file joint returns for that calendar year. In spite of all the publicity to the contrary, most married couples still find filing jointly to be the easiest, most advantageous method. But that may not be true for you. Note that if you do file jointly, you will each be responsible for the full total of the tax bill.

- Now is also the time to talk about family planning, marital roles, and existing obligations to other family members. While the vast majority of today's couples are dual income and, out of necessity, also share domestic burdens at home, some still prefer a more "traditional arrangement" (though it may well be the husband who stays at home while the wife works). What you decide about rights and duties in your marriage is not important; whether or not you agree is.

Marriage and family laws are constantly changing to reflect new patterns of living among modern couples and families. Now, eschewing stereotypes and gender roles, the law generally considers both spouses mutually responsible for each other's support, financial and otherwise, regardless of how individuals decide to combine their efforts and lend that support.

Yet, married partners are also considered separate entities: each is guaranteed equal protection under the law (from abuse, endangerment, rape, etc.); one spouse may testify against the other in court; one may make independent contracts and hold separate property without the other; and one may make personal health choices, including the woman's right to make decisions regarding her own body (contraception, childbearing, abortion) without the consent of her husband.

Overall, society has a stake in the peace, harmony, and profitability of your marriage, but practically speaking, the law will not intrude into the private agreements and arrangements between you unless called upon to do so (as in the case of crime or divorce). Like the two of you, government and society want to believe that your marriage will succeed. And it will, provided you are both committed to working at it and that you keep the lines of communication open between you.

Health Testing

State laws vary regarding the kinds of medical testing required for a marriage license. In some, couples will have to show evidence of rubella immunity or vaccination; many require blood tests for venereal disease; a few demand a general physical; and one state, Illinois, has enacted an AIDS test requirement. If either partner is found to have a sexually transmitted disease, some states will deny the marriage license until effective treatment has been obtained.

Variations from state to state may make such requirements seem arbitrary; yet, all are generated by a concern for the physical welfare of citizens and the protection of any future offspring. Premarital health testing also prompts disclosure of medical and sexual histories between the couple, hardly an unreasonable expectation of two people who are about to embark upon a lifetime of intimacy. The important point to remember here is that all sexually transmitted diseases, except AIDS, can be treated, provided one first knows he or she is suffering from it.

Today, when couples are older and may have long personal histories, and when they might be intimate with each other before marriage, it seems prudent to expect a disclosure of medical and sexual histories before that intimacy occurs. Otherwise, disease will have already been transmitted by the time testing for the marriage license takes place.

No one is suggesting that you should recount every previous sexual encounter by name, date, and place, but if you are responsible, and if you truly love each other, then you have an obligation to be honest. Sexually transmitted disease is rampant, and syphilis is approaching epidemic proportions. There is simply no reason to withhold information or endanger another when such conditions can be treated and, in most cases, cured.

AIDS, of course, is another matter, and there is much controversy regarding the Illinois testing requirement. Those in high-risk categories (the sexually active, former drug users, or members of the healthcare professions) are understandably alarmed at the prospect of testing HIV positive when there is no known cure. On the other hand, doesn't the prospective spouse have a right to know?

One hospital doctor put it succinctly: "The bottom line on AIDS, or any other incurable disease, is would you still marry the person if you knew? And nobody can make that decision for anybody else."

The same dilemma presents itself to those with genetic disorders or adverse family histories (cystic fibrosis, pulmonary disease, Tay-Sachs, sickle-cell anemia, etc.). Heredity becomes an issue in family planning, and couples who suspect that their offspring would be at risk are wise to seek testing and advice before deciding to have children of their own.

Yet, we have to remember that science is fallible and that much remains unknown about the exact nature of genetic transmission. Do members of a family suffer from the same complication because they have inherited it or because they are all exposed to the same physical and environmental influences? And, here again, will knowing your partner carries a "genetic marker" for a particular disease reverse your decision to marry?

Ultimately, the best advice is for each of you to be honest with the other about your medical conditions and concerns, and for each of you to have a complete physical before marriage to ensure that health goes along with happiness on your wedding day. Women should have a gynecological exam and discuss methods of contraception with their doctors, as well as with their fiancés. This is also a good time to have dental check-ups, eye exams, and any other preventative health procedures you've been postponing.

Handling Stress

"Now listen," the young professional woman said earnestly to her wedding consultant. "I don't want any of those silly traditions, like throwing the garter belt and stuff."

People do and say funny things when they're excited and under stress. There was the groom who forgot his bride's name while reciting the vows in front of the altar, and the bride who, amid a standing ovation at the reception and with all eyes on her, went to sit down and missed the chair.

If you can laugh about the things that happen, or make jokes even about the most frustrating moments, you'll get through your wedding, and your life, in much better shape. After all, most events that trigger stress are neutral; it's how we interpret them and react to them that gives them a positive or negative effect.

Prolonged periods of negative stress, like that experienced by some couples with lots of prewedding problems, can actually begin to take a physical toll. As bodily defenses wear down and mental exhaustion sets in, people are more susceptible to illness and more prone to accidents. Their energy wanes, they become chronically tired, and they say and do things, even hurtful things, that they wouldn't ordinarily do.

Negative stress most often results from feeling overwhelmed and out of control. The myriad details and unusual demands of wedding planning make engaged couples prime candidates for stress-related complications. Don't let them get you down.

Wedding Stress Reducers

- Discover what helps to relax each other and make sure your intended takes the time to indulge: a massage for her, an afternoon of fishing for him.

- Clear your calendar of unnecessary nonwedding chores that take up time: meetings, volunteer work, social obligations.
- Exercise regularly, eat well, and get plenty of sleep.
- Call on others who have offered to help with specific tasks; once the chore is delegated, quit worrying about it.
- Take time out to do something you enjoy for at least a few minutes every day: reading, sewing, having a bubble bath, etc.
- Keep your perspective; ask yourselves what's the worst that can happen if a specific problem doesn't go your way.
- Spend time with each other, and with friends, in activities you enjoy that have nothing to do with wedding planning: going to the movies, dinners out, sports, picnics, art galleries, etc.
- Don't be a martyr; share your problems and frustrations with your fiancé. Look for the humor in all that's happening and laugh a lot!

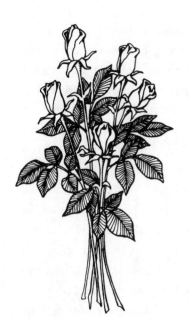

CHAPTER 9
Marrying Again

National polls indicate that between 60 and 70 percent of those divorced or widowed remarry within five years, and the nation's vital statistics indicate that 46 percent of the 2.4 million marriages each year are remarriages for one or both parties. Remarriage is truly a cause for celebration because the decision to marry again is an affirmation of one's faith in couplehood.

Age and experience make a big difference in that decision, too, not only in terms of a couple's confidence about their future together, but also in terms of the confidence with which they exercise their own wedding style. Couples marrying again usually plan and pay for their own celebrations, and the choices they make reflect the certainty, sophistication, and maturity of people in control of what they want.

The Challenge of a Second Marriage

In many ways, the pleasures and pitfalls in a second marriage are just like those in a first. There will be the excitement of being newlyweds, of planning a new life together and discovering new secrets about each other. There will also be priorities to set, habits to adjust, and needs to juggle.

In other ways, however, second marriages often involve issues more common to couples who have been married several years. Most young people just starting out have few material assets and liabilities, no dependents, and no well-set family and social patterns. In contrast, older couples may have to reevaluate lifestyle decisions, career goals, financial arrangements, and family and social obligations in order to successfully merge two independent lives and two established households into one.

"People marrying again with established families have to accept the facts, and maybe the limitations, of their situations," says Sharon, who recently married Walter and is the mother of a six-year-old. "There's more than just the two of us involved here. Between us, we have three children, two ex-spouses, and four sets of grandparents, all of whom are very much a part of our lives. For this marriage to succeed, it will have to be a group effort."

Everyone has a past, but people marrying again tend to bring a more complicated personal, family, and financial past with them to the present. Any problems that exist in those backgrounds have to be solved before a viable future with someone else can be established.

Yet, while the extended or blended family can present special difficulties, it can also create the potential for a richer, fuller life for everyone concerned. Remarriage becomes part of a whole life cycle of coupling, a concept that places high value on personal growth and fulfillment and that allows individuals to strive for better relationships. It is a concept that reaffirms the ideals on which every successful marriage is built.

Doing It Your Way

It is your prerogative to have the kind of wedding that suits your age, lifestyle, and social circle. If you eloped the first time, you may now want to have the formal wedding of your dreams. If your previous wedding was an extravaganza, you may now opt for something simpler. If friends or family offer to help with certain expenses or planning efforts, you're certainly free to accept their offers. Or, you can "have it your way" and do everything yourselves.

We've attended second weddings that we didn't know were going to be weddings until we got to the party and the couple announced, "Surprise! We're getting married—right now." We've attended affairs of such regal formality that no one would have guessed that the bride had been married before, except for the fact that her children were in the wedding party. And we have attended, or heard about, virtually every type of second wedding celebration in between these two extremes. In short, regardless of your marital history, or his, you may have whatever kind of wedding celebration, large or small, formal or informal, traditional or avant-garde, civil or religious, that you feel is appropriate.

No doubt most of your guests will be mutual friends and family members. Ex-spouses are usually not invited to the wedding, though you may want to inform them of the remarriage. If you have remained close to former in-laws, as is often the case when widowed, there is no reason to exclude them from your present happiness. Children from a former marriage should be included in the festivities to the extent that their ages and attitudes allow.

Guidelines contained elsewhere in this book on all aspects of wedding planning also apply when coordinating your remarriage ceremony and reception: attire, location, decorations, music, food, and fare should all be in keeping with the style and tone you want to set. When the two of you are hosting your own wedding, wording on the invitations should reflect that (see Chapter 11).

Parties and Gift Giving

Old rules of etiquette maintain that gifts are optional for a couple marrying again but, in reality, that's nonsense. Most of your friends and family will want to celebrate your happiness by giving you some token of their good wishes. Some may even want to honor you with a prenuptial party or shower, and there is nothing wrong with graciously accepting the offer.

Gift giving will involve helping the two of you replace and coordinate what you already own. To this end, the bridal gift registry can be a welcome convenience. Major department stores report that a sizeable portion of their gift-registry business is being generated by older, second-time brides, so there is no need for you to feel uncomfortable in utilizing this service.

Unfortunately, there may be some among your family and friends who still believe that a second marriage should take place almost in secret, or certainly without fanfare. To be blunt, don't let them rain on your parade. No one should be forced to participate in your wedding plans but, by the same token, no one should be allowed to dissuade you from having the kind of wedding you want.

Adaptations for Remarriage

You may want to adapt some wedding formalities and traditions to accommodate your special circumstances. Consider:

- Retaining your former name for business or professional reasons, or in order to eliminate confusion regarding the surnames of your children;
- Walking down the aisle by yourself, or with the groom, or with your son if you have one;
- Having your children as honor attendants (legally, one must be 18 to be an official witness to the marriage, but you can always let a youngster play the part and ask another adult to actually sign the document);
- Making a special presentation to your children during the ceremony or somehow including them in the program to acknowledge the "marriage of family" that is taking place (You might light a community candle, share a cup, or present them with special "family medallions," featuring three entwined rings that are available for such a purpose. Contact: Clergy Services, 706 W. 42nd St., Kansas City, MO 64111);
- Circulating the word that you'd prefer donations to charitable organizations as wedding gifts when you just really want your friends to celebrate your happiness with you.

Marrying with Children

If either of you has children from a previous marriage, as six out of ten remarrying couples do, you should inform them of your plans to marry before you tell anyone else. Again, unless you've appeared with a total stranger in tow, the news shouldn't come as a big surprise to the kids. No doubt you have a good idea of what their reactions will be, so you can judge whether to inform them alone or together. In any case, be prepared to answer all the questions about what your marriage will mean for them.

Children are always most concerned about the immediate impact of new living arrangements. They'll want to know if they have to move, change schools, or otherwise alter their lifestyles. If they are close to your former spouse and those grandparents, they may worry about what the new stepparent will expect of them, what he or she will want to be called, or what new rules and restrictions he or she might try to impose. And, if they are still dealing with the insecurities of loss or divorce, or harboring secret hopes of their natural parents getting back together, they may resent the claim on your affections by someone new.

The objections of children from a former marriage present a real difficulty. Small children generally take the news of the remarriage of one of their parents better than children of teenage or college age do. Scars from a tragic loss or a bitter divorce can take years to heal, and anger and resentment in children can flare up even after you thought it was long put to rest.

If you are marrying someone with children, as well as have children of your own, don't assume that everything will work out like a television sit-com. Competition for attention and battles over territorial rights can ensue when one family physically moves in with another. The need for space and privacy will be more important than ever, and you as parents will have to be particularly sensitive to the very real adjustments being demanded of everyone involved.

The choice between your children's happiness or your own is not an easy one to make because the two can hardly exist independently of each other. Don't allow problems to force you into an either-or situation. Get help from a stepfamily support group or a certified family therapist now *before* the wedding. Unresolved issues between blending families won't solve themselves, and they could get much worse after the marriage takes place, especially if and when the new couple has more children of their own. (See Appendix.)

If you have joint custody of the children, you'll also have to inform your former spouse, particularly if your marriage will affect alimony, residency restrictions, visitation rights, or other legal arrangements. If a former spouse is deceased and you still have a warm relationship with those in-laws, it is a kindness to share your news with them and to assure them, and your children, that their relationships will not be severed because of a new husband or wife.

Reaffirmation

Years ago, the only time a couple got married to each other again was when they wanted, or were able to finally get, the religious sanction of a civil marriage that already existed. But times have changed! These days, couples are choosing to reaffirm their marriage vows more and more often, at five years or fifty, and for many different reasons. Sometimes it is the religious ceremony they didn't have the first time, and sometimes it's so they can finally have the kind of wedding party they couldn't afford before. We've even heard of a reaffirmation as a sort of "second take" because the first wedding turned into a disaster.

Reaffirmations often coincide with other special life events, such as the birth of a child, the defeat of an illness, or a landmark wedding anniversary, but they

CONTEMPORARY SOLUTIONS

PERSONAL, FAMILY

❦ *Both you and he live in homes with furnishings associated with a former life with a former spouse. Neither of you feels entirely comfortable moving into the other's house. What kind of changes can you make to allay the discomfort?*

You can change everything, and you probably should. Sell or rent both houses, have a gigantic garage sale to get rid of all furnishings acquired with a former spouse, and start fresh in a new residence with all new furniture, dishes, linens, accessories, etc. Memories provide enough ghosts in a new relationship without being haunted by tangible reminders of someone else every day.

FAMILY

❦ *Your children don't want to move, but neither your place nor his is big enough to accommodate the other spouse's children and the needs of your new blended family. What can you do?*

The children have to understand that they, too, will be inconvenienced and cramped for space once everyone moves in together. Provided their objections to moving are motivated purely by concerns about changing schools or losing friends rather than something deeper, the kids can probably be caught up in the excitement of a new house if you and your fiancé will take them with you when house hunting. Offer them the additional enticements of picking out new furnishings or colors for their rooms in the new house, and try your best to find a residence in the same school district not too far away from old neighborhood friends.

If that's not possible, call the school district and see if an "out-of-district" exception can be made, at least for the remainder of the year, to allow your children to continue to attend their same school. (Schools are increasingly sensitive to special requests for changing families.) Also, make an extra effort to arrange for your children to continue to see their old neighborhood friends, at least until they've made new ones where they live.

may also simply celebrate the blessings of being in love and staying together. You may host your own reaffirmation celebration, as most couples do, or your children, family, or friends may give it for you. A big part of the fun, of course, is planning it all.

Choosing a Style

The style of celebration you choose will reflect your reasons for deciding to renew your marriage vows at this particular time. Generally, the reenactment of wedding vows has religious, or at least spiritual, overtones, but not always. Couples might also ask a family patriarch, a community leader, a civil official, or a trusted friend to do the honors, or they might write their own vows and recite them before their guests themselves. Since there's no legality involved this time, it doesn't really matter who officiates.

Reaffirmation ceremonies often take place in a church or synagogue, sometimes as part of a regular service in front of the regular congregation and invited guests. They may also take place privately, in a house of worship, at home, or anywhere else you'd like. Many couples like to have the same officiant who originally performed the marriage conduct the renewal, if that's possible, and members of their original wedding party present, as well. This time, though, the couple's children will have a place of prominence in the ceremony, too.

If you're having a religious reaffirmation, the clergy will again bless the rings, either your original ones or new anniversary rings; you'll again be asked to pledge your love; and the two of you will receive a marital blessing. You'll certainly want to consider personalizing your vows this time, perhaps with references to children or moments you've shared. If yours is a private ceremony, you might also like to have programs printed with important dates and personal messages that your family and friends would appreciate. Talk to the clergy to see what he or she suggests, and don't forget to arrange for the music and the flowers.

What to Wear

You don't dare ask your old bridesmaids to don their original matching taffeta dresses again, and you may not be able to fit into your wedding gown either, but everyone can still go all out with attire appropriate for the occasion. The degree of formality is your choice, just as it was the first time, but now everybody is likely to be better able to afford the choice.

You probably won't choose to wear full bridal regalia yourself, but you can wear white if you like and capture the look of a bride with flowers and fabrics, even a simple headpiece with a touch of veil. Your husband can wear a tuxedo if it's appropriate to the time of day, certainly a boutonniere, and your children can also be specially outfitted for the occasion. Flowers and boutonnieres will make them feel festive too. All other guests, including the wedding party, wear clothes suitable to the type of affair you're having.

If your reaffirmation celebration is to be small or informal, handwritten, telephoned, or printed invitations will be perfectly fine; if larger and more formal in tone, you will want to have invitations printed in a style and color to reflect that. Wording for a very formal invitation would be as follows:

The honour of your presence (if religious)

or

The pleasure of your company (if not)
is requested at the reaffirmation
of the wedding vows of
Mr. and Mrs. John Doe
on Saturday, the tenth of June
nineteen hundred and ninety-___
at six o'clock
Saint Joseph Church
Newport, Rhode Island
Reception
immediately following the ceremony
Candlewood Country Club
124 Foxwood Road
Newport

R.S.V.P.   *Black Tie*

Wording for a less formal affair would be adjusted accordingly. If your children are hosting, the wording would read:

The family of
John and Mary Doe
request the honour of your presence . . .

Reaffirmation Receptions

You'll certainly want to celebrate with old friends and new after the ceremony, and there's no better excuse for a party. Again, the choices are the same as those for a wedding reception. It all depends on your style and your budget.

Many couples have reaffirmation parties, even quite formal ones, at home, and that seems especially appropriate to a celebration of married life. If you choose to do so, however, get help with the food and service. You want to be able to enjoy this event. After all, you're more than the host and hostess, you're the guests of honor!

You also want to remember it, so consider hiring a professional photographer to capture the moments, and don't forget to have a guest book for all your friends and family to sign. Music, flowers, and a special "reaffirmation cake" will complete the scene and set the mood.

Gifts are not expected for a reaffirmation, but most guests will probably bring them to your reception as a token of their affection and good wishes toward you. If you really don't want personal gifts, then circulate the word that you would prefer gifts of charity to be made in your name. The fact is, though, there is joy in giving and people always want to do

something. In return, you might also want to think about some sort of memento of this happy event for your guests to take home.

Reaffirmation Ideas

- Consider having your reaffirmation party at the place where you two met, if that's at all possible.
- Let your children invite some of their friends, too; they are also a part of the celebration.
- Go out for a "rehearsal dinner" the night before with any old friends attending your celebration from out of town.
- Decorate using your original wedding colors.
- Display your bridal portrait, wedding album, wedding guest book, or other keepsakes from that special day.
- Construct a pictoral time line of children, family members, and major events over the years that illustrates the story of your marriage.
- Use your wedding cake top on your reaffirmation cake.
- Have your original wedding cake replicated.
- Have "your song" as part of the ceremonial music, and be sure to have your first dance to it at your reception.
- Play music at your party that was popular when you got married.
- Take posed photographs with your original bridal party.
- Go back to your original destination for a second honeymoon, or at least plan some getaway just for the two of you.

CHAPTER 10
People, Parties, and Things

The months before a wedding involve many people, many plans, and many things. Those who love you will be eager to show you how much they care and anxious to do whatever they can to enhance your happiness at this exciting time. Dealing with well-wishers, though, can sometimes demand as much diplomacy as dealing with adversaries. A little sensitivity and consideration on your part will help everyone remember what is really important and minimize any misunderstandings that might inadvertently occur.

Selecting Your Attendants

The invitation to be a bridesmaid, usher, or honor attendant is the recognition of a very special relationship, and that relationship should be one of affection, not of obligation. You *do not* have to have people in your wedding party simply because you are related to them, or because your fiancé is, or because you were in their wedding. The decision about honor attendants is entirely personal and up

to each of you. While you may feel an explanation is in order to a close friend, sibling, or relative whom you did not invite to participate, you should resist any family or social pressures to have more attendants than you need or want.

You will probably want at least a best man and a maid or matron of honor to act as official witnesses for your ceremony, but legally, any two adults can sign for you. The choice of who they are and what role they play is entirely up to you. A sibling is not the automatic choice for the honor position, because a friend can be much closer to you than a relative. Likewise, an early childhood friend may be chosen, by virtue of a long-standing history, over a current best friend with whom you spend time every day. Such are the complexities of love and friendship; you'll have to handle them as graciously as you can.

The general rule of thumb for ushers in a formal wedding is one per fifty guests. Couples usually want an equal number of female attendants, but the number of male and female attendants does not have to be the same. (When more men are involved than women, some couples make the distinction between groomsmen, who actually act as escorts for bridesmaids, and ushers, who only seat guests.) If you can't decide between two close friends or relatives, you may have two maids or matrons of honor, or one of each, and divide the duties between them.

As often happens, "wedding fever" spreads among a circle of friends, and one can find himself or herself being asked to participate in several weddings over a period of a few short months. Be cognizant of that when selecting your own attendants, and don't feel hurt if someone admits frankly that he or she cannot afford to participate in yours. Even if you offer to assume the expense of their attire, that may not be enough to offset the other obligations they will feel by being an attendant, so don't insist if they continue to decline.

Attendants' Duties

Maid or Matron of Honor: She should help before the wedding day if asked. Perhaps she will assist in selecting attendants' dresses or in addressing invitations. She may also want to give a wedding shower for the bride, or to select a special gift from her and all the attendants. Mostly, the maid or matron is a source of support before the wedding. She and all the attendants pay for their own attire and travel expenses.

On the wedding day itself, the maid or matron of honor will arrive early to help the bride dress and to finish packing. During the ceremony, she holds the groom's ring and the bride's bouquet, adjusts the veil and train, and signs the marriage license as an official witness. She stands next to the groom in the receiving line at the reception, and she mingles with guests and offers a toast to the couple.

Bridesmaids: Bridesmaids may offer to help the bride with any errands, including addressing wedding invitations. They will pay for their own attire, attend fittings, and participate in prewedding parties and showers. They may collectively host a shower.

On the wedding day, bridesmaids are expected to be charming in the receiving line and to mingle with guests.

The Best Man: The best man makes the arrangements for the bachelor dinner and selects the gift for the groom. He might also help with honeymoon and travel arrangements for out-of-town guests and ushers, including tuxedo rentals.

On the wedding day, he arrives early to help the groom dress, to offer support and friendship, and to take care of any last-minute details. At the ceremony, he holds the bride's ring. Afterwards, he signs the marriage license as a witness and gives the offering to the clergy. At the reception, he offers the first toast to the couple, dances with the bride and her attendants, and reads any telegrams or special messages that have been received.

Ushers: Ushers offer any assistance they can to the groom, get fitted for their attire, help with the bachelor party, and review the seating lists.

On the wedding day, they arrive early and are in place to escort the guests to their seats—traditionally left side for the bride, right side for the groom, although some couples now mix the guests, especially if one side has a much larger share of guests than the other. At the reception, they dance with bridesmaids and mingle with guests.

Inviting Guests

Time for the truth: even when your wedding guest list was sincerely estimated from the very beginning and everyone, supposedly, agreed on the number that would be invited, the list will still start to get out of hand when you actually begin putting names down. You forgot about the people at the office, this one can't be invited without that one, so-and-so just got engaged, and so on.

As we said earlier, first priority for guests goes to relatives and friends closest to the two of you.

CONTEMPORARY SOLUTIONS

FAMILY

❦ *You feel bad. The groom has invited your two brothers to be ushers, but you just can't ask your fiancé's three sisters to be attendants because you already have four close friends in mind. At this point, you're only close to one of your future sisters-in-law anyway, but you would feel funny asking just her. What should you do?*

There's a big difference between four and seven bridesmaids, and it probably isn't advisable to single out one of your fiancé's sisters anyway, especially at this early stage of your family relationships. Talk to your fiancé. He will understand your predicament better than you think.

If you want to make your future sisters-in-law feel special, or any other family members for that matter, honor them with corsages or boutonnieres to wear and seat them in places of prominence at the ceremony. Keep them up to date on all your plans, and include them in all prewedding festivities.

FAMILY, SOCIAL

❦ *Ask friends and relatives you wish to honor to be members of the houseparty, a popular tradition in some parts of the country, especially where stand-up receptions of coffee, cake, and tea sandwiches are the rule.*

The houseparty is composed of female relatives and friends who have a special, almost familial, relationship to the bride. The women are stationed at key serving areas, identified by matching corsages in wedding colors, and often help by pouring coffee or tea or serving cake. Photographs of them are included in the wedding photo album, and their names are also listed in newspaper accounts of the wedding.

Invite another to sit at the bride's book to greet and register guests; younger girls may be charged with distributing rice bags and/or favors at a stand-up reception. They, too, could be given a small identifying corsage, and their names might also appear in newspaper accounts of the wedding.

❦ *Choose others to be liturgical assistants.*

Religious wedding ceremonies often require the services of readers, lectors, soloists, cantors, deacons, altar servers, and special ministers. When friends or relatives are invited to perform these duties at your wedding, it becomes a special honor. You might suggest special attire for them, in coordinated wedding or liturgical colors, or present them with a corsage or boutonniere.

Note: Some ethnic celebrations prescribe the participation of relatives and/or close family friends as part of the wedding ceremony, such as the family procession in the Jewish ceremony or the *padrinos* in the Spanish nuptial Mass. See more under "Ethnic Weddings" (Chapter 16).

Whatever is left over can be divided between the families. If your location or your budget won't allow for last-minute expansion, then some cold, hard decisions will have to be made—probably by your parents.

If you're really organized and on top of things, however, you might soothe some headaches by having both an "A" and a "B" guest list. Briefly, this is how it works:

"A" list wedding invitations are sent out earlier than usual, eight weeks before the wedding. As a regret comes in, that place is filled by issuing an invitation to a name from the "B" list. You can continue this process as long as you're sure invitations sent to names on the "B" list will arrive at least a month before the wedding. Of course, if you get no regrets, or you get them too late, your problems remain.

Here are other ways to reign in a burgeoning guest list:

- In large families, cut off the list at aunts and uncles or first cousins; consider having an informal family reception for uninvited relatives later, after the wedding.
- Decide on "no dates" for single guests. (Spouses and fiancés of guests, however, must be included.)
- Don't include children under age 18. (Make sure the word is circulated, and address the invitations accordingly. Should anyone respond that their children will be attending, call them up and explain that there will be no other children present and that you simply cannot accommodate them.)
- Eliminate all professional friends and keep the wedding strictly personal.

Parents may wail that it isn't possible to pare down their lists, or that your wedding must be either very large or very small, that there's simply no in between. Don't you believe it. Where there's a will, there's always a way, and this wedding belongs to you. Your families have no right to look for reciprocation for all the gifts they've given and all the affairs they've attended over the years, nor should they use your wedding to fulfill their own social needs and obligations.

Even so, there are limits on how you can limit. Here's what you *cannot* do to trim the guest list:

- Fail to invite the clergy or officiant and spouse to the reception.
- Invite some guests to the ceremony only and not to the reception; you may, however, do it the other way around if the location for your ceremony is too small to accommodate everyone.
- Fail to invite anyone who has been invited to a prewedding party or shower, unless your wedding is a strictly private family affair; however, coworkers who held an office shower, if not personal social friends, would not expect an invitation.
- Fail to include the parents of flower girls and ring bearers or the spouses or fiancés of anyone in your wedding party.

Consideration, Please!

Your wedding can be an expensive proposition for your relatives and friends. Multiple parties mean multiple gifts, as well as the suitable attire and the transportation to attend them all. Furthermore, an invitation to a large, formal wedding almost always makes a guest feel obligated to give an appropriately large, formal wedding present. Consider the following:

- If someone gave you an engagement gift upon initially hearing the good news, don't expect another gift at any formal engagement party.
- If you're having several prewedding parties and showers, invite different groups of guests to different events; that way, no one gets overburdened.
- If someone hosts a shower or party for you, don't expect anything more than a small token gift from that person at the event itself.

- If someone hosts a large, expensive prewedding party for you, consider this their wedding gift, or expect any wedding gift they present to be proportionately small.
- If a friend who is also a wedding professional (florist, musician, photographer, etc.) offers his or her wedding services to you for nothing, then assume that is the wedding gift.
- If you have a large party or shower right before the wedding, realize that any significant gifts brought to that event might be intended as wedding gifts, as well.
- Don't expect large wedding gifts from anyone who must also bear the cost of being a member of your wedding party, or from any guests who will incur significant travel expenses in order to be with you.
- Realize that friends or relatives who spend a lot of time helping you with wedding chores and details may be doing so, at least in part, because they can't afford an expensive gift. Be sensitive to that and take the burden of explanation off them by stating how much you appreciate their efforts and how you consider the gift of time to be the most valuable you could receive.

Prewedding Parties

Depending on the size of your wedding and the number of friends and family members who reside in the immediate area, you're likely to be feted with a number of showers and other prewedding parties. Sometimes, brides who no longer consider themselves ingénues, or those marrying for the second time, feel reluctant to accept offers of parties in their honor, but they shouldn't. No one is ever too old, or too sophisticated, to have a good time, and wedding parties for modern couples are much less traditional, much more imaginative, and much more fun than they used to be.

Usually, someone offering to host a special event for you will tell you what they have in mind

in terms of time, fare, and number of guests, and ask you what kind of shower or party you would like it to be. Feel free to be honest in your response. If you would prefer a "his-and-her" shower to a "ladies only" affair, state that preference. If you would rather have a backyard barbecue than a sit-down luncheon, say so. If you really, honestly would rather not have the party at all, or have too many on your calendar already, explain that, too. While it's nice to be popular, enough really is enough, and there are only so many guests to go around for so many affairs before it becomes a hardship.

Technically speaking, a member of your immediate family (parent, sibling, aunt, or uncle) should not host a gift-giving event (other than an engagement party) for you. If you have a particular need for a particular type of activity, such as a get-together with older relatives or future in-laws, or even an entertainment for out-of-town guests right before the wedding, there is nothing wrong with suggesting that someone who has offered to have a party for you host one of these events. Once the time, date, location, type, and size of the party have been determined, be sure you provide a complete, legible guest list, with all addresses including zip codes and phone numbers (for those who fail to R.S.V.P.) to the host or hostess. The larger the affair, the more time they'll need to prepare invitations, so be considerate about getting the list to them well in advance. After the event has taken place, promptly send a handwritten thank-you note to your host or hostess. You might also wish to send flowers or deliver a small gift with your note.

Wedding Shower Ideas

You may have a wedding shower a couple of weeks before the wedding, or several showers beginning a few months before the wedding. It is traditional to make a "bridal bouquet" out of the bows from the gifts (for your wedding rehearsal); it is also traditional to open the gifts while all guests are present.

Make sure someone is in charge of recording who gives you what so you can write thank-you notes later. Someone should also take photos of the fun.

For women only:
- *Types*: kitchen, lingerie, linens, recipe/cookbooks, bed and bath, personal fitness/beauty, general household
- *Forms*: breakfast, brunch, lunch, tea, dinner, afternoon or evening informal get-together

For couples:
- *Types*: patio/gardening, kitchen/appliances, household maintenance, entertainment, general household
- *Forms*: picnic, dance, barbecue, keg party, buffet brunch, lunch, or dinner

Themes:

Holiday: gifts are the decorations the couple will need for holiday celebrations

International: gifts representing various nations

Time of Day: each guest brings a gift to be used at an assigned time of day

A Labor of Love: guests don't bring gifts; instead they come prepared to paint, wallpaper, or otherwise help the couple spruce up their new "old" home

Honeymoon: using the decorative motif of the couple's honeymoon destination, guests bring travel items likely to be needed for the honeymoon trip

Nontraditional gift ideas:

Paper products, tools, wine and spirits, tickets to sporting or cultural events, gourmet foods, plants, luggage, magazine and newspaper subscriptions, ordinary household products (cleansers, detergent, etc.), office supplies, gift certificates, picnic items, reference books, photo albums, film and photography equipment, blank tapes (video or audio), "maid for a day" service

Besides the engagement parties and showers already discussed, other parties that are an integral part of the prewedding festivities are:

Bridesmaids' Party—The traditional luncheon has given way to other options: breakfast, brunch, or dinner out, or just an informal get-together. The bridesmaids' party is hosted by the bride and/or her mother, often in the bride's home, a few days before the wedding. It is a special way to get "the girls" in the wedding party together and to say thank you for their friendship and support. As noted earlier, close female relatives and future in-laws may also be included. If there will not be a rehearsal dinner, the bride might present her attendants with their gifts on this occasion.

Bachelorette Party—The equivalent of a bachelor party for women only, this event is usually hosted by the maid or matron of honor and/or other female attendants, and guests include the bride's closest friends. The party may take the form of an adult slumber party, a dinner out, or a last night on the town through all the old singles' haunts.

Bachelor Party—Designed to be the "last bash" of bachelorhood for the husband-to-be, this party is given by the best man and/or another close friend or brother of the groom and includes the groom's closest male friends and relatives. This event is not usually as rowdy as most men would like the women to believe, though a fair amount of drinking and toasting, and the traditional smashing of the glasses after a toast to the bride is made, are commonly considered part of the expected festivities. For this reason, bachelor parties held in the evening are now more often held a week and no less than three or four days before the wedding, rather than the night before. If there is not to be a rehearsal dinner, the groom might present his attendants with their gifts at this event.

Since this is the one time during the wedding when the groom is the sole focus of attention, those giving the bachelor party really should consider the style and personality of the guest of honor and not let the fun get out of hand. Many grooms are made very uncomfortable by some of the rites of initiation their friends put them through; still others can't even remember what went on. While they might not admit it, most men would probably prefer a classy dinner out, a sporting event, or a weekend camping trip as a bachelor party, rather than the usual routine.

Brides often have a curiosity about their fiancé's bachelor party, and if you don't, you probably should feign one, because the "big secrets" of all-night revelry are part of the mystique of the whole event. In truth, though, most bachelor-party activities are little more than slighty risqué. If you are unduly concerned about his night out with the guys, or if you adamantly oppose his having a bachelor party, you might ask yourself if there are deeper issues in your relationship that make you feel that way.

Rehearsal Dinner—Usually held the day or evening before the wedding and after the wedding rehearsal, this event is often hosted by the groom's parents, at home or out. It may also be hosted by the bride's parents, a close friend or relative, or the couple themselves.

The rehearsal dinner may be as formal or as informal as you and the hosts like, and will include all members of the wedding party and their spouses, as well as the clergy, parents, and grandparents. Out-of-town wedding guests should also be invited.

If you haven't already done so, you and your fiancé will present your gifts to your wedding attendants at this event, as well as any gifts you may wish to give your parents or others who are special to you. It is customary for the best man to propose a toast to the couple at the rehearsal dinner, and for the couple to toast their parents. Others may also join in the toasting. If you do not host this event yourselves, be sure to write a special thank-you note to those who did after the wedding.

Entertaining Out-of-Town Guests—From informal get-togethers in a club or restaurant, to a wedding-day or day-after brunch in a friend or relative's home, to a well-stocked hospitality suite in your guests' hotel, thoughtful couples come up with all sorts of ways to make their out-of-town guests feel welcome and important. Gift baskets with maps and a schedule of events will help keep them informed, and activities just for them, such as shopping excursions, golf, or sight-seeing tours (arranged through the hotel), will help them get to know each other and to feel more at home in an unfamiliar place.

You don't have to plan for every minute of your guests' stay, nor do you have to attend every event you plan for them. But since the typical Saturday wedding will bring most out-of-towners to your locale for an entire weekend, whatever you can do to minimize their expenses, facilitate their convenience, and make them feel a part of your celebration will surely be appreciated.

Wedding Weekends—When *everyone* is from out of town, including the bride and groom, and the wedding becomes an occasion for a reunion of family and old friends, pre- and postwedding parties are clustered around the main event.

Typically, a wedding weekend happens over a long, three-day holiday, and may take place at a resort or other special location. Guests arrive to a welcoming dinner or reception Friday night, have a prewedding party, rehearsal, or other social activity on Saturday, attend the wedding and reception on Sunday, and enjoy a farewell brunch on Monday morning. The bride and groom attend all events, maybe even the postwedding brunch. (Or, this may be a Thursday night through Sunday event where out-of-towners take a Friday off.)

The difference between the wedding weekend and other types of planned entertainments for out-of-town guests is that everyone participates in everything, and all parties are organized around a central wedding theme. Guests are given a complete "schedule of events" in advance of their arrival.

You may host these parties and events yourselves, or close friends or family members may offer to host, and pay for, any one of them. You and/or your wedding consultant will have to work closely with the special events coordinator at whatever

location you've chosen to make the wedding weekend a success.

Gifts for the Attendants and Families—and Each Other

Throughout history, the presentation of gifts has
been symbolic of honor and respect among nations,
families, friends, and lovers. Over time, the act of
gift giving has come to have more than just ceremonial significance. Chosen with care for a particular individual, it comes to represent the taste, style,
and affections of the giver as much as it does the
message of the moment.

The months before your wedding will be filled
with giving and receiving. That's part of the wedding tradition. You'll have to keep track of the gifts
you get, so you can properly thank the givers, and
you'll have to shop for the gifts you plan to give to
those who mean so much.

For the Attendants

Your wedding attendants are special people, and
each of them should be recognized with a special
gift from the two of you. The gifts may be large or
small, whatever you feel is appropriate and can
afford, but all should be of roughly the same monetary value. Presents for attendants, however,
should be something lasting, memorable, or sentimental that will reflect the way you feel and the
importance of the occasion.

You may choose to single out your honor attendants (best man and maid or matron of honor) with
gifts that are different from the other men's and
other women's, which are all alike, or you may
choose a different gift for each and every member
of your wedding party. Wrap attendants' gifts in
wedding colors, each with an enclosure card containing a personal message just for him or her, and
present them at your rehearsal dinner or at one of
your other prewedding parties.

Gift Ideas

President John F. Kennedy, then Senator, gave his
ushers umbrellas, but you might prefer some other
ideas, especially if you live in a sunny clime.

For the men: Blazer buttons, brandy snifter,
pewter mug, fountain pen, desk set, wallet or
leather goods, writing portfolio, silver key chain,
ice bucket, decanter, cuff links, watch or other
timepiece, grooming set, paperweight, dresser
caddy, a book, gloves, gift certificate, anything that
might be worn in the wedding (such as a tuxedo
shirt and/or studs), anything that can be monogrammed with initials or inscribed with a message.

For the women: Dressing-table set, perfume
atomizer, picture frame, cachepot, Victorian stor-
age box, jewelry, jewelry box, leather goods, fountain pen, desk set, paperweight, vase, personalized
stationery, decanter, tea set, book, diary or journal,
anything that might be worn in the wedding (such
as gloves, headpieces, or pearls), anything that can
be monogrammed with initials or inscribed with a
message.

For flower girls or ring bearers: Child-size
cups and dishes, combs and brushes, banks, stuffed
toys, tiny boxes, cachepots, figurines, lockets, jewelry, glass or crystal sun-catchers, books, games.

For Each Other

Even though couples exchange wedding rings and
treat each other to mementoes on their fabulous
honeymoon, and even though the car, condo, or
new furniture they buy may be considered gifts to
themselves for their new lives together, most couples still want to remember each other, and their
special day, with a memorable wedding gift.

The item doesn't have to be expensive, but it
should be valuable in a sentimental way, something
you know your fiancé would really love, and would
love you for giving. Gifts between the couple are
usually exchanged in a private moment just before,
or just after, the wedding, unless offered as a surprise.

Gift Ideas

Anything monogrammed or inscribed, jewelry, leather goods, luggage, desk set, book, camera or video recorder, something for hobby or home.

For Your Families

It's easy to rely on those you love—your families. Let them know how much you appreciate them and all they've done to make your wedding a success with a special gift that says thank you. Sign the card from the two of you, and present the gift at the rehearsal dinner or at some private family moment before the wedding, or wait until after you get back from your honeymoon.

Gift Ideas

For parents: China, crystal, or sterling silver serving pieces, vases, candlesticks, picture frames, porcelain collectibles, limited edition works of art, clocks, jewelry for him and for her, fine tablecloth or linens, luggage, tickets to the theater or sporting events, dinner out, anything for home or hobby.

For other special relatives: Miniature wedding portrait in a cameo frame, crystal vase or bowl, a book, travel clock, bon-bon dish.

For Others

Acts of generosity can come from anyone: a considerate neighbor, a concerned cleric, or someone else involved in orchestrating your wedding day. Let them know you're aware of the extra effort they've made by remembering them with "a little something." Gifts need not be expensive; it really is the thought that counts.

Have these unexpected gifts delivered soon after the wedding, perhaps even while on your honeymoon. A simple "thank you for . . ." on the enclosure card will do.

Gift Ideas

Bowls, bud vases, cameo picture frames, desk accessories, pens, goblets or mugs, trays, flowers, and plants.

The Bridal Gift Registry

Legend has it that the bridal gift registry service dates back to 1902 when a Minnesota china store clerk began listing the names of brides and the patterns they picked on index cards. The custom spread to jewelry stores in the 1930s and the rest, as they say, is history.

Today, with the average wedding gift costing $75 to $100, department and specialty stores aren't the only ones to see the advantage of providing gift registration services for wedding couples. You can register your selections at gourmet food emporiums, antique shops, art galleries, health spas, travel agencies, even The Metropolitan Museum Store!

The fact is that people are going to want to give you gifts. If your wedding is to be very small and your friends and relatives all live close by, then you can probably let them all know what you need and want by informal word of mouth. But when your wedding is large, some of your guests live far away, or you have several prewedding parties and showers planned, the bridal gift registry is a sensible service for everyone to use.

Here's how it works: you and your fiancé go to your favorite store that has a bridal gift registry and you decide, with the help of a trained gift registrar, on the basics you need and the extras you would like to have for your new home. Selections include fine china, crystal, silver flatware, informal china, everyday flatware and glassware (serving pieces and accessories), linens, bedding, small appliances, cookware, electronics, or other equipment.

You'll want to make selections in various price ranges so guests will be able to find a gift that fits their budget. (To give you one of your more expensive choices, two or more guests may pool their resources.) Once you have made your choice of patterns, colors, and individual pieces, your selections will be on record in the store's computer under your name and wedding date. Those who wish to purchase a gift for you simply go to the store and make a selection from the list of items you have chosen. There's no duplication because with each purchase the computer updates your registry list; there's no fear of exchange because every giver knows his or her gift will be something you want.

The location of stores where you are registered can be noted on informal invitations (for showers), but not on formal invitations (for the wedding). When guests ask what you would like, however, it is perfectly all right to tell them where you are registered and suggest that they look there. Of course, many people still enjoy shopping, making their own unique gift choice, and wrapping it up themselves, and that is certainly their privilege as gift givers.

Large department stores with branches throughout the country can coordinate their computer listings, which is a real plus when your friends and relatives are scattered. Stores can even ship the gifts to the address on your registration—a convenience for everyone. You may register at more than one specialty store for particular items carried only there (hardware, fitness, garden supply, etc.), or you may register for different items at different stores in different areas of the country where your friends and families live. But don't register the same items at more than one retailer; that will create confusion and defeat one of the purposes of gift registry.

Bridal gift registration costs you nothing and offers a real convenience to your friends and family. But there are also advantages to you. First of all, making your selections together, all at the same time, will ensure a coordinated look for your home. You and your fiancé will have the fun of shopping together, of choosing items and accoutrements you

will both enjoy, and of determining your style as a couple. If you each have households and furnishings already, your gift registrar will be able to help you adapt what you have by blending new selections with the old for a more uniform decorative appearance.

Secondly, your wedding is likely to be the only time in your lives, except for maybe your silver or golden anniversary, when others will be so generous and when you will receive so many new things all at once. So this is the time to select that fine china, crystal, or silver that you've always dreamed of owning. Later, as children come, household repairs are needed, and other priorities emerge in your lives, you will feel guilty splurging on such items. But, if you make these selections now and begin to build your service sets, relatives and friends will continue to present you with these items on future anniversaries and special occasions until your service is complete.

Unusual Gift Ideas

While tableware, linens, and kitchen equipment continue to top the gift list for most couples, changing lifestyles and unusual interests have made some wedding gifts decidedly difficult to wrap:

- Services: cleaning, decorating, consultations, home renovations, lawn care.
- Travel items: pocket translators, camping and boating equipment, designer luggage, video camcorder.
- Lessons: scuba diving, dancing, sky diving, cooking.
- Garden: lawn mowers, patio furniture, planters, garbage cans, sprinkler systems, outdoor lighting, power tools.
- Business: computer, printer, computer supplies, facsimile machine, cordless phone, bookcases.
- Sports: season's tickets, equipment, club memberships.

CONTEMPORARY SOLUTIONS

PERSONAL

❦ *You've been married before and are not exactly a blushing young bride. Won't you feel a little silly going into a department store to register a china pattern?*

You may, but if family and friends want to give you a gift (and most will), it's good judgment because money spent on useless gifts is wasted. You don't have to limit your registry to china, crystal, silver, or any home furnishings. Consider registering at a sports, record, or hobby store, a book shop, a computer center, or anywhere else that the two of you window shop with a big wish list in mind.

PERSONAL, FAMILY

❦ *Your mother is insisting that you register china, crystal, and silver because "it's a bridal tradition." You can't imagine ever entertaining that formally, and besides, that stuff is expensive. Frankly, you'd rather get money as wedding presents anyway. What can you do?*

Times change, and so do people. One day you might feel differently about owning some of the finer things in life. In the meantime, though, make your mother happy with a compromise: register less-expensive glassware, informal dinnerware, and household appliances and accessories.

As for the kind of wedding gifts you'd like to receive, that choice is really up to the giver. It simply isn't polite to tell people you want money.

❦ *Your grandmother is offering you her set of china as a wedding gift. While it is very old and very fine, and it does sort of appeal to you, you're afraid it may be a bit too traditional and old-fashioned for your new home. But you wouldn't hurt her feelings for the world.*

Take a place setting with you to the registry at your favorite store and let a trained sales specialist show you how to coordinate the old with the new for a distinctive, eclectic look. Part of the charm of heirloom pieces is the character they bring, even to the most contemporary tablesettings. Chances are you'll discover how timeless good design really is.

• Entertainment: subscriptions, televisions, VCRs, tickets to theater, opera, etc., dinners out (or catered gourmet dinners in), flowers or food-of-the-month plans, cases of wine.

Monetary Gifts

In some communities, ethnic groups, and areas of the country, monetary gifts, given at the wedding, are customary. These gifts may take the form of cash or checks, stocks or bonds, or a gift certificate to a favorite store. The bride may even carry a little white silk bag or purse to put them in.

Checks and certificates will be made out to Mr. and Mrs., so you will have to either leave them with trusted family while you're away on your honeymoon, or endorse them before you go and have someone deposit them for you into your account.

The Bridal Gift Registry

Here is a sample checklist for your use. You obviously do not have to select everything on the list, but it will help you to think about your choices.

Register at least six months before your wedding so that guests will know what you like and need.

FORMAL DINNERWARE

Qty.	Mfr.	Pattern
	Dinner plates	
	Salad/dessert plates	
	Bread/butter plates	
	Soup bowls	
	Fruit bowls	
	Coffee cups/saucers	
	Teacups/saucers	
	Demitasse cups/saucers	
	Coffee server	
	Teapot	
	Sugar bowl/creamer	
	Vegetable dishes	
	Covered casseroles	
	Platters	
	Serving bowls	
	Gravy boat	
	Salt/pepper shakers	

FLATWARE: STERLING/SILVERPLATE

Qty.	Mfr.	Pattern
	Knives	
	Forks	
	Salad Forks	
	Soup spoons	
	Teaspoons	
	Iced-beverage spoons	
	Individual butter spreaders	
	Butter serving knife	
	Pierced tablespoon	
	Serving spoons	
	Serving fork	
	Cheese serving knife	
	Salad servers	
	Gravy ladle	
	Pie/cake server	
	Carving set	
	Pickle/lemon fork	

Qty.	Mfr.	Pattern
	Sugar spoon	
	Silver chest	

FINE CRYSTAL

Qty.	Mfr.	Pattern
	Goblets	
	Champagne flutes	
	Champagne sherbets	
	Wines (red/white)	
	Hoch wines	
	Cordials	
	Brandy snifters	
	Decanters	
	Pitchers	
	Vases/bowls	

BARWARE/EQUIPMENT

Qty.	Mfr.	Pattern
	Tumblers	
	Brandy snifters	
	Highballs	
	Double old-fashioneds	
	Irish coffee glasses	
	Pilsner/beer glasses	
	Ice bucket/tongs	
	Wine/champagne cooler	
	Wine rack	
	Decanters	
	Decanter labels	
	Cocktail shaker	
	Trays	
	Bar utensils	

CASUAL GLASSWARE

Qty.	Mfr.	
	Iced beverage	
	Juice	

CASUAL DINNERWARE

Qty.	Mfr.	Pattern
	Dinner plates	

Qty.	Mfr.	Pattern
	Salad/dessert plates	
	Bread/butter plates	
	Soup/cereal bowls	
	Fruit bowls	
	Cups/saucers	
	Sugar bowl/creamer	
	Vegetable dishes	
	Covered casseroles	
	Platters	
	Serving bowls	
	Covered butter dish	
	Gravy boat	

FLATWARE: STAINLESS

Qty.	Mfr.	Pattern
	Knives	
	Forks	
	Salad forks	
	Soup spoons	
	Teaspoons	
	Iced-beverage spoons	
	Individual butter spreaders	
	Butter serving knife	
	Pierced tablespoon	
	Serving spoons	
	Serving fork	
	Gravy ladle	
	Cake/pie server	

COOKING EQUIPMENT

Qty.	Mfr.
	Saucepans
	Saucepots
	Skillets
	Covered casseroles
	Omelet pan
	Double boiler
	Dutch oven
	Stockpot

Qty.	Mfr.
	Microwave cookware
	Roaster and rack
	Cookie sheets
	Pie plate
	Wok
	Muffin tins
	Cake pans
	Lasagna pan
	Quiche dish
	Soufflé dish
	Fondue pot

KITCHENWARE

Qty.	Mfr.
	Canister set
	Cutlery
	Steak knives
	Cutting boards
	Teakettle
	Utensil set
	Timer
	Mixing bowls
	Storage containers
	Kitchen clock
	Spice rack
	Kitchen shears
	Food scale

ELECTRICAL APPLIANCES

Mfr.	Model #
	Toaster oven
	Toaster
	Mixer
	Blender
	Food processor
	Coffee maker
	Coffee grinder
	Fry pan/skillet
	Waffle iron/griddle
	Can opener
	Electric knife/food slicer
	Teakettle
	Knife sharpener

Qty.	Model #
	Warming tray
	Slow cooker
	Corn popper
	Ice-cream maker
	Espresso/cappuccino machine
	Pasta maker
	Juicer
	Steamer
	Wok
	Yogurt maker
	Rotisserie/broiler
	Microwave/convection oven

HOME ELECTRONICS

Mfr.	Model #
	Television
	Radio/clock radio
	Stereo components
	Cassette recorder
	Video cassette recorder
	Telephone/answering machine

DECORATIVE ACCESSORIES

Mfr.	Model #
	Perfume bottles/atomizers
	Crystal/silver picture frames
	Lamps
	Frames
	Vanity items
	Decanter with glasses
	Crystal/silver candlesticks
	Crystal/silver bud vases
	Porcelain/crystal figurines
	Crystal/silver/porcelain tree decorations
	Collector plates, bowls
	Silver/porcelain decanter labels
	Desk sets

HOME CARE

Mfr.	Model #
	Vacuum cleaner
	Cordless vacuum
	Iron/ironing board
	Smoke alarm

Qty.	Model #
	Sewing machine

QTY.	LINENS/BEDROOM:	
Mfr.	Color	Size
Flat sheets		
Fitted sheets		
Pillowcases/shams		
Pillows		
Blanket, lightweight		
Blanket, woollen		
Electric blanket		
Bedspread		
Comforter/quilt		
Duvet		
Mattress and foundation pads/protectors		
Pillow protectors		

QTY.	LINENS/BATH:	
Mfr.	Color	Size
Bath sheets		
Bath towels		
Hand towels		
Washcloths		
Guest towels		
Bath mat/rug		
Shower curtain		
Shower massager		
Electric toothbrush		
Scale		
Hamper		
Shelf unit		

QTY.	LINENS/TABLE:	
Mfr.	Color	Size
Tablecloths		
Runners		
Napkins		
Place mats		
Napkin rings		

QTY.	LINENS/KITCHEN:
Mfr.	Pattern
Dish towels/cloths	
Pot holders/mitts	
Aprons	

Monetary gifts are the only wedding gifts that may be brought to the wedding itself. (Though many guests persist in bringing wrapped presents to the affair, and many brides have given in and set aside a decorated table in anticipation of that reality, the practice is not recommended because it is inconvenient and especially because the gifts could be misplaced, lost, or stolen.) Thank-you notes for monetary gifts should be written promptly upon return from your honeymoon. The exact amount of money should not be mentioned in the note, but your intended use for it should be.

In other circles, however, and in some regions of the country, monetary gifts are considered gauche, especially when brought to the wedding. Only immediate family members or very close family friends might present a monetary gift or certificates, and then it is usually presented in private, and in person, to the couple well before the wedding.

As discussed earlier in the section on personal finance, money carries cultural, social, even psychological connotations. To some, cash or a check seems cold and impersonal, a careless way to give a gift. To others, it is a sign of shared wealth and shared happiness, and a practical way to show it. Monetary gifts are not a matter of prescribed etiquette so much as they are of local custom. Keep that in mind if you and your fiancé, and your families and friends, are from different backgrounds or different regions of the country. (Remember it, too, when deciding on your own gift for someone else's wedding.)

Gift Expectations

What *is* a matter of etiquette is the blatant expectation of money as a gift, or the implication that guests should offer approximately what it cost to feed and entertain them at the wedding. If guests are being counted on to defray the expenses of the affair, then one may just as well sell tickets! "No one lives in anyone else's pocket," or so the saying goes, and no

guest should ever be told, by you or anyone close to you, that a monetary gift is expected or preferred.

By the same token, a gift should not be judged in proportion to the lavishness of the celebration. The decision about the size and style of the wedding belongs to you; the decision about the kind of gift one can afford and wishes to give belongs to the giver.

Every gift, large or small, should be recorded and handwritten thank-you notes should be sent as the gifts arrive. As the wedding approaches, you may fall behind, but within two months of return from your honeymoon, all gifts should be acknowledged. Your fiancé can help, of course.

Those who do not attend the wedding are not obligated to send a gift, nor are those who receive only announcements of the wedding.

You may return or exchange gifts that you don't like, but be discreet about doing it. Never ask a giver about where a gift was purchased, and don't mention duplication or exchange in your thank-you note. If a gift is damaged, call the store and try to return it; again, it is considerate not to involve the giver if possible.

You'll need some sort of record book to keep track of gifts received and notes sent, or you can make your own using the Gift Record or photocopying the page.

Displaying Wedding Gifts

Long ago when ladies and gentlemen of leisure made social calls on each other in the afternoons, it was customary for the bride to display her wedding gifts, usually on the dining room table, in her parents' home for all to see. These days if anyone were to be found at home in the afternoon, it would probably be a burglar.

Nevertheless, even though the bride is out working, and so is her mother, it is still customary in some communities to display bridal gifts. For large expensive weddings garnering large expensive gifts,

Gift Record

Indicate in the appropriate box: E—Engagement Gift, S—Shower Gift, W—Wedding Gift,

NAME(S)	ADDRESS	GIFT & DESC.	STORE NAME	DATES		E S W
				GIFT REC'D	NOTE SENT	

families even go so far as to arrange an elaborately decorated display, to take out additional insurance coverage for the presents, or to hire security guards to protect them when no one's at home. Whether or not you do any of this is entirely up to you.

Bear in mind that wedding gifts are sent to the return address on the wedding invitation. If that address is your parents' home and you don't live there or nearby, you'll have to make arrangements to transport the gifts to your own home. That alone could preclude a gift display if you have to ship them clear across the country.

If you do have a home gift display, use your common sense. Arrange items attractively, taking care not to put lavish gifts next to modest ones or to display multiples of an item. (Don't stack china; set out one place setting.) You may or may not display enclosure cards with the presents. A check is acknowledged with a card or envelope indicating "check" (no amount) and the name of the giver.

CHAPTER 11
The Honour of Your Presence

Issuing invitations, keeping up with thank-you notes, and taking care of other wedding-related correspondence can be a formidable task, especially for a large affair. Luckily, there are ways to facilitate the process, provided you keep accurate records and plan ahead for everything you'll need. Your fiancé can help, of course.

Selecting Wedding Invitations

As soon as the date has been set and your guest list is complete, at least three months before the wedding (earlier if your guest list is large), go to a stationer, jeweler, department store, or specialty shop to place your orders. You may also order wedding stationery by mail (see advertisers in the pages of bridal magazines and write for their samples). A consultant will show you a wide range of paper choices, colors, and styles, and will be able to assist you with proper wording for special needs and/or unique family situations (see

samples later in this chapter). You'll need to appreciate the subtle implications of process, wording, and design to make appropriate selections.

The wedding invitation is the first important indication of the style and tone of your wedding. Formal invitations, whatever their size, are engraved or thermographed on the front side of a single or folded sheet of heavy white or off-white paper. They are very plain, having perhaps only a raised border or panel, and using a legible, classic typestyle in black ink. The more variation on this basic model, the more informal the invitation becomes.

Should your celebration be within a close-knit ethnic community, you should know that your invitations may be written in Spanish, Hebrew, French, or any one of several languages. The degree of formality is still determined by the overall style of the invitation, but the customs of your particular community may indicate different wording and placement, for example, the inclusion of both sets of parents or the names of the wedding party. Write the form out and bring it with you when you order in case your stationer is unfamiliar with it.

It's best if you select all stationery at the same time you choose your wedding invitations. That way, everything will reflect a uniform style and taste. Be sure to order enough invitations, and everything else, when you order initially, because getting more later will take time and may mean an additional expense. Ask about getting the envelopes in advance, so you can get an early start on addressing them, and also find out how many extra envelopes will be included with your order, in anticipation of making mistakes. It's a good idea to order some extra invitations, too, in case you need a few more, and for mementoes.

Beside the invitation, there are other enclosures you might need:

Reception Cards: Even if you're inviting everyone to both the ceremony and the reception, you might want a separate enclosure with the wording, "The pleasure of your company is requested at the reception . . ." It is equally proper, however, to put the reception information on the wedding invitation with the words "Reception immediately following at . . ."

Printed Directions/Maps: Sometimes these are provided by your reception coordinator for enclosure with your invitations; if not, you'll have to order them. Maps and directions should be printed or clearly photocopied for inclusion with a formal invitation.

Ceremony Cards: These are needed when more people are invited to the reception than to the ceremony. The main invitation is to the reception, and the enclosure is for the ceremony. Formats are essentially reversed.

Response Cards: These days, when many are careless about responding promptly, and when many are no longer aware of the old rule of etiquette that mandated a written response to wedding invitations, modern brides save themselves aggravation by including R.S.V.P. cards with stamped, self-addressed envelopes. Guests simply check whether or not they will attend, and mail them back. Sometimes, when a choice of several entrees at a sit-down dinner is being offered, those choices will also appear for selection on

INVITATION TERMS YOU NEED TO KNOW

Engraved invitations are the most elegant, and the most expensive. The words are cut into the paper with copper plates, so that the lettering can be felt on both sides. Engraving is generally chosen for formal, traditional invitations on white or off-white stock. These are appropriate for formal daytime or evening weddings.

Thermographed invitations are less expensive, but their raised lettering, achieved through the application of a powder compound, approximates the look and the feel of engraving. When used on white or off-white stock in a very plain style, they, too, are appropriate for formal weddings. More fanciful, informal designs for less-formal affairs may also be thermographed.

Printed (on a press, by photo-offset, or laser printer) invitations are generally less expensive, and less formal. The style and color of paper used may affect the degree of formality, of course, but printed invitations are usually best suited to less-formal affairs.

Handwritten or **calligraphied** invitations are lovely. If your wedding is small, you might consider handwriting each invitation on beautiful stationery, or hiring a calligrapher to do them. For a larger number of invitations, a calligraphied look can also be achieved by computer graphics.

Decorative details, including laser cuts, embossed designs, lithographs, photographs, ribbon, and other trims are considered informal invitations, though they are not always "informal" in price.

Typeface is the style of lettering, and there are literally hundreds of styles from which to choose. Most are available in either **serif**, which has elaborate curls and can be harder to read, and **sans serif**, which is without curls and more legible.

the response card. (Remember postal size restrictions, and make sure your response card envelopes aren't too small to mail.)

Pew Cards: Should you be rich and famous, or planning such an elaborate affair that guests would need to prove that they were actually invited, a pew card would read, "Please present this card at St. Patrick's Cathedral on Saturday, the fifth of June."

If your invitations contain several enclosures, the proper order of placement is:

1. Response cards are placed inside their own envelopes.
2. Tissue paper is placed over the invitation to ensure against smudging.
3. The invitation is placed fold-side down in the ungummed inside envelope.
4. All enclosures are placed inside that envelope with the invitation.
5. The inside envelope is placed in the outer mailing envelope face-side up toward the flap.

Wording for Wedding Invitations

The formal invitation follows certain conventions in wording and order of presentation of information. Obviously, the more formal your wedding, the more you'll want to observe these conventions. Here they are:

• Names are always written in full using first, middle, and possibly last; never nicknames, never initials.
• Family order is written out, "Junior," or indicated by Roman numerals, "III."
• The word "and" is always written out.
• The words "honour" (honour of your presence) and "favour" (the favour of a reply) take the English spelling.
• "The honour of your presence" is used to invite one to the ceremony; "the pleasure of your company" is used to invite one to the reception; the latter may also be used for a civil ceremony.

• Days, dates, and times are always written out.
• Only "Mr." and "Mrs." and "Dr." are abbreviated, and punctuation is used only after such abbreviations; a comma appears after the day of the week and the city.
• The address of the ceremony location is not included when everyone knows it; the name of the state may be omitted when the city is well known, as in New York City.
• The year is not necessary on the invitations, only on announcements; when it is included, it is spelled out.
• A wedding invitation may include the reception information in the corner: Reception immediately following/location/R.S.V.P., or that may be printed on a separate enclosure card.

Note the order and wording of the standard, formal wedding invitation:

> *Mr. and Mrs. John David Gale*
> *request the honour of your presence*
> *at the marriage of their daughter*
> *Anne Marie*
> *to*
> *Mr. Robert Anthony Cole*
> *on Saturday, the fifth of June*
> *at half after six o'clock in the evening*
> *Saint Joseph's Roman Catholic Church*
> *112 West Palm Street*
> *Clearwater, Florida*

If everyone is to be invited to the reception, the following might be added:

> *and afterwards at the reception*
> *Clearview Country Club*
> *31 Water Road*
> *R.S.V.P.*

Adaptations

Modern situations, of course, require modern adaptations of the traditional forms. Use these samples to help you, and rely on your stationer's advice.

The Hosts

If the bride's parents are:
    married
> Mr. and Mrs. John David Gale

    separated, but amicable
> Mr. and Mrs. John David Gale

    divorced, but hosting together
> Mrs. Mary Ann Gale
>
> and
>
> Mr. John David Gale

    divorced mother alone
> Mrs. Mary Ann Gale

    widowed mother alone
> Mrs. John David Gale

    divorced or widowed father alone
> Mr. John David Gale

    remarried mother and stepfather hosting
> Mr. and Mrs. Marc Roy Hammer
>
> at the marriage of her daughter
>
> Anne Marie Gale

    remarried mother and natural father hosting
> Mrs. Marc Roy Hammer
>
> and
>
> Mr. John David Gale
>
> at the marriage of their daughter
>
> Anne Marie Gale

    both remarried, all hosting
> Mr. and Mrs. Marc Roy Hammer
>
> and
>
> Mr. and Mrs. John David Gale
>
> (omit "their"; say "at the marriage of")
>
> Anne Marie Gale

    divorced, one remarried, all hosting
> Mrs. Mary Ann Gale
>
> and
>
> Mr. and Mrs. John David Gale
>
> (as above, omit "their" daughter)
>
> or
>
> Mr. and Mrs. Marc Roy Hammer
>
> and
>
> Mr. John David Gale

If the groom's parents are hosting:
> Mr. and Mrs. Robert Jay Cook
>
> request the honour of your presence
>
> at the marriage of
>
> Miss Anne Marie Gale
>
> to their son
>
> Michael Andrew Cook

If the bride's and groom's parents are co-hosting:
> Mr. and Mrs. John David Gale
>
> and
>
> Mr. and Mrs. Robert Jay Cook
>
> request the honour of your presence
>
> at the marriage of
>
> Anne Marie Gale
>
> and
>
> Michael Andrew Cook

To include the groom's parents:
> Mr. and Mrs. John David Gale
>
> request the honour of your presence
>
> at the marriage of their daughter
>
> Anne Marie
>
> to
>
> Michael Andrew Cook
>
> son of
>
> Mr. and Mrs. Robert Jay Cook

When the couple, themselves, host:
> The honour of your presence
>
> is requested
>
> at the marriage of
>
> Anne Marie Gale
>
> to
>
> Michael Andrew Cook

When the bride is widowed or divorced but her parents, or his, are hosting, the invitation is worded without regard to her marital history but with her maiden and married name, if she has retained both:
> Anne Marie Gale Preston

Another relative hosting:
> Mr. and Mrs. Albert Patrick Kelley
>
> request the honour of your presence
>
> at the marriage of their granddaughter (niece, etc.)
>
> Miss Anne Marie Gale

A friend hosting:

Mr. and Mrs. George Tulley
request the honour of your presence
at the marriage of
Miss Anne Marie Gale

Other Situations

A double wedding (eldest daughter's name first):

Mr. and Mrs. John David Gale
request the honour of your presence
at the marriage of their daughters
Anne Marie
to
Mr. Michael Andrew Cook
and
Janice Elizabeth
to
Mr. Walter Kenneth Banks

When the bride and/or groom are on active duty in the military:

at the marriage of their daughter
Captain Anne Marie Gale
United States Air Force
to
Major Michael Andrew Cook
United States Air Force

About Titles

There is much discussion today about the propriety of women using titles, if they have them, on formal invitations and social correspondence. Some women feel very strongly about this and insist on it; others abide by the more traditional rules of etiquette, which tend to ignore a woman's professional status in deference to her marital status, at least on formal, social occasions.

You'll have to make your own decision about this if you are titled or hold a doctoral degree. Just keep in mind that the wording can get pretty cumbersome if your parents are both doctors, and his are both judges, and the two of you hold titles, as well. An invitation, after all, is not a resume.

TITLE TERMS YOU SHOULD KNOW

Professional titles:

The Honorable (judge, governor, mayor, U.S. senators, members of congress, cabinet members, ambassadors); The Reverend or The Rabbi (clergy); Dr. (for medical doctor, dentist, veterinarian, and the academically degreed who use that title)

Military titles, according to rank:

enlisted personnel and noncommissioned officers:

James Henry Tucker
United States Army

senior officers (above captain in the army and lieutenant senior grade in the navy):

Lieutenant Colonel John Daniel Gray
United States Air Force

junior officers (title appears on second line):

Scott David Siegel
Second Lieutenant, United States Air Force

Grooms and brides on active military duty use their rank and/or branch of service on the wedding invitation. A groom who has a title uses it in lieu of "Mr.," but a bride who has a title would not use it unless she would otherwise be using "Miss." Married couples traditionally reflect the title of the husband only, as in "Dr. and Mrs. James Smith," even though Mrs. Smith may be a doctor, too.

Contemporary variations of these rules include (note that the woman's name is always first):

Dr. Jane Smith and Mr. Harry Smith

Dr. Jane Smith and Dr. Harry Smith

The Doctors Smith

Keeping Track

You'll need a system to keep track of invitations and responses. You can purchase planning or record keeping books for this purpose at a stationer's or through the pages of bridal magazines, but a plain spiral notebook (for gift records) and a file of 3x5 index cards (for invitations) will do just as well. Computer buffs will find database programs ideal for this purpose.

You and your families should compile your guest lists with complete names, addresses, zip codes, and telephone numbers, and code them according to the following categories:

> "A" or "B" list, if using
> invitation to ceremony and reception
> invitation to reception only
> wedding announcement only (if using)

Check the cards for complete information when you first receive them, then categorize them and file each category alphabetically. A card might look something like the one below.

Note: On a computer program, each line of information would be entered into the appropriate "field" for sorting. See the instruction manual for the particular program you're using..

As responses come in, pull the card, make the proper annotations, and place it with other confirmations. Eventually, you'll be down to the few remaining cards for which a response is still outstanding.

| Name: |
| Address: |
| City/State: |
| Phone: |
| Date mailed: |
| Response rec'd: yes/no |
| Gift item: |
| Thank you sent: |

Addressing and Mailing

Unless you are using the "A" list–"B" list method (see previous chapter), invitations should be mailed four to six weeks before the wedding date to allow plenty of time for everyone to make their plans and respond so that you can give sufficient notice to your caterer/reception manager. All wedding invitations should be mailed at the same time (with the exception of the "A-B" list method).

Outer envelopes are hand-addressed in black ink; names (except for the titles Mr., Mrs., and Dr.) and addresses are not abbreviated:

> *Mr. and Mrs. John Walker Smith*
> *124 Browning Street*
> *Jackson, Mississippi 08742*

Some other particulars of propriety:

Cohabiting couples: receive one invitation with names written on separate lines in alphabetical order

Children over age eighteen: each should receive his or her own invitation

Other adult relatives who reside in the household: each should receive his or her own invitation

Inside, ungummed envelopes containing the invitation should read simply "Mr. and Mrs. Walker." If minor children are included in the invitation, their names should appear underneath their parents': "Sarah and Mark." Note that if minor children's names *do not* appear, that means they are not invited to the wedding. (The words "and family" are never used on wedding invitations.) If a single guest is welcome to bring a date, then the words "and Guest" appear after his or her name on the inner envelope. Obviously, if those words don't appear, the single individual is not supposed to bring a date.

There may be those among your families and friends who are not aware of these fine points of etiquette. They may return response cards with the indication that their children or a date will be attending also, even when they weren't invited. In such cases, you will have to call them and tell them that children or a guest cannot be accommodated. You will have to be diplomatic, but firm.

Finally, there is the common situation of those who simply fail to respond at all, even with an R.S.V.P. enclosure. If you haven't heard by the date requested, call them to determine if they plan to attend. It is possible that a response card has been lost in the mail, and that is probably the best way to approach your query.

Wedding Announcements

Wedding announcements are an appropriate way to notify those whom you did not invite to your wedding, professional associates, distant relatives, and friends who live far away, but who have reason to be interested in your nuptial news. Since receipt of a wedding announcement carries no obligation of a gift, you need not feel awkward about sending them.

The announcement may be issued by the two of you, your parents, or his. The wording is similar to that on a wedding invitation, except that "have the pleasure to announce" appears in place of "requests the pleasure of your company." Announcements are chosen to reflect the same style and degree of formality as your wedding invitations, and are usually ordered at the same time. Announcements are put in the mail on the day of the wedding or soon after, but never before.

You may also wish to enclose "at home" cards with your announcements. These indicate your new address after marriage, the date you will be in residence and, if you have chosen to do so, an indication that you will continue to use your own name after the marriage, an important piece of information for professional colleagues. At-home cards may also be ordered at your stationer's, and they would be worded as follows:

Mr. and Mrs. Thomas Allan Hartsdale

or

Cathy Sue Avery

and

Thomas Allan Hartsdale

After the first of January

53 Morningside Drive

Philadelphia, Pennsylvania 19104

Thank-You Notes

Today's bride can select a thank-you card or folded note paper that carries out the style and theme of the wedding and reflects the couple's personal tastes. Called "informals" by stationers, thank-you note stationery may be printed across the front with your names, "Mr. and Mrs. Thomas Allan Hartsdale," or with combined initials (surname goes in the middle, your first initial on left, his on right), or you may each have your own notecards.

To keep up with thank-you notes for shower gifts and wedding gifts that arrive before the wedding, use printed informals with your name or initials. Plain informals are appropriate, too. The secret to managing thank-you notes is to keep good records and to acknowledge all gifts promptly.

Traditionally, the bride is responsible for all thank-you notes (except for personal gifts to the groom), but contemporary couples often share this responsibility. Don't hesitate to enlist your fiancé's help, especially for notes to his own family and friends. Before the wedding, each of you would mention the other but sign your own name; after the wedding, the signature may be from both of you.

Writing Rules

All thank-you notes must be personal and handwritten. In the case of a very large wedding for which many gifts are sent from far away, printed acknowledgment cards may be sent to let the giver know that the present did arrive and that a personal note will follow. There is *no* substitution for the formal, handwritten note that must follow.

Notes can be short and sweet, but they should be warm and personal. Each one includes:

- A date
- A salutation (addressed exactly as it appears on the gift enclosure card)
- A message, which expresses appreciation, mentions the gift itself, and actually says "thank you"; a statement of how the gift will be used, and the inclusion of your fiancé's name (or yours in his note) are also nice touches
- A closing, using the terms "Love, Fondly, Sincerely, Affectionately," etc.

Sample formal:

July 16, 19___

Dear Mr. & Mrs. Frank,

    The silver platter is gorgeous! Your thoughtful wedding gift is sure to give Tom and me years of entertaining pleasure and pride.

    Thank you so much.

Sincerely,
Jane

Sample informal:

July 16, 19___

Dear Joe,

    What a buddy you are. Besides traveling to our wedding, you still present Jane and me with a check. We appreciate it, Joe. We'll buy something extra special with it for our new condo, and I hope you'll come visit us there soon.

Sincerely,
Tom

Notes for showers and gifts are similar, except that they usually mention the event and are more personal in tone.

For a gift:

June 12, 19___

Dear Susan,

    It was such fun to see you at the shower last week, and the juicer is an ideal gift. Tom and I will think of you each morning as we start our day, happy and healthy.

    Thank you, Susan. You always seem to know exactly what I would choose myself.

Fondly,
Jane

For a hostess:

June 12, 19___

Dear Judy,

    How can I thank you for such a memorable afternoon? The shower was just lovely, and the honeymoon travel diary you gave me will be a source of happy recollections for years to come.

    I hope you know how much I appreciate all your time and trouble; most of all, though, I hope you know how much I appreciate having a dear friend like you.

Love,
Jane

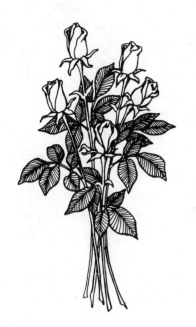

CHAPTER 12
Ceremonies and Protocol

Anthropologists tell us that marriage is one of the oldest customs of mankind, and that rites of marriage dating back thousands of years have been found in virtually every known society. Marriage rites have evolved from both secular and religious traditions and have generally incorporated visible signs and symbols of a couple's emerging social status: instruction, preparation, decoration, sacred ornaments, distinctive dress, dramatic ritual, and celebration. Historically, all have proclaimed the bonds between husband and wife and their kin, and all have stressed the importance of the marital union as a means of ensuring an orderly society.

Many wedding customs in the United States are Anglo-Saxon in origin. The word "wed," in fact, dates back to the early custom of wife purchase. The "wed" meant the money, cattle, or property that the groom pledged as security to purchase the bride from her father. From this we have derived the English word "wedding" and the notion of a public proclamation of the marriage contract. Even the civil cere-

mony we use is a legal adaptation of our Protestant ancestors' *Book of Common Prayer*.

But the real beauty of weddings in the United States today is the diversity with which they are celebrated, as each new generation adapts and incorporates the customs and beliefs of the previous generation into American life. Many religious rituals, in particular, have endured for centuries, even though they may be enacted in modern dress, in modern homes, or in the company of a modern, heterogeneous community of family and friends. The blending, and in some cases the bending, of traditional practices preserves individual heritage while, at the same time, forges new bonds based on the values we share.

No other ritual, religious or secular, is as universal in meaning and intent as a wedding. All of us, regardless of our differing religious or cultural backgrounds, have a common respect for the institution of marriage, and that explains why all of us go to the trouble we do to celebrate it.

Religious Ceremonies

It would take volumes to describe in detail the many religious rituals and cultural traditions that govern and define weddings as they are celebrated in this country today. The major religions, defined as those claiming the largest numbers of Americans as members (Roman Catholic and the mainstream Protestant faiths), have been through so many centuries of missionary conversion in all nations, and so many generations of intermarriage in this country that they have lost most of whatever original ethnic identity they might have had.

But other religions, such as Orthodox Judaism, Eastern Orthodoxy, Hinduism, and some expressions of Christianity (Mormon, Quaker, Seventh Day Adventists), struggle to retain their ethnic heritage and ideological identity in the midst of an increasingly pluralistic society. The values, customs, and beliefs of these faiths are still closely entwined with their native origins, so that it often becomes difficult to separate the religious from the cultural in a discussion of their wedding rituals.

In spite of all the differences, however, some generalized statements can be made:

• All religions consider marriage a joyous occasion.
• All religious marriage ceremonies assume a certain dignity and seriousness.
• Mainstream religions are generally more accepting of interfaith marriage than are smaller, culturally close-knit religious communities.
• The more elaborate the ritual and the more an ethnic heritage defines the ceremony, the less it will allow for adaptation and personalization in form.
• Local customs and attitudes of individual celebrants usually prevail; within the same religion, what is acceptable, even common, in one community will not always be so in another.
• Even among those groups that do not require membership in their community for marriage, the clergy or governing members of that community will want

to know why a religious ceremony in their faith is being requested by the couple.

In the interest of fostering understanding and respect for religious differences, a brief description of several religious ceremonies follows. This is by no means the definitive source for information on these marriage practices. All couples seeking a religious wedding ceremony, even those who are regularly practicing members of a religious community, should consult the local clergy or official representatives regarding the requirements for marriage in that faith and specific directives about the ceremony itself. Interfaith couples or those who are not observing, practicing members of a faith will have to think carefully about why they want a religious ceremony and take the time to investigate their options.

The Roman Catholic Church (Western Rite)

Though it doesn't have to be, the marriage ceremony in the Catholic Church is often performed within the context of the Holy Sacrifice of the Mass, called a Nuptial Mass for weddings. The bride, preceded by her attendants, forms the processional at the beginning of the service. The priest waits for her at the altar with the groom by his side. Met by the groom, or handed over to him by her father, the bride and groom remain in front of the altar, kneeling, sitting, or standing, throughout the ceremony. Introductory remarks and the priest's Homily reflect the occasion and address the couple.

The actual marriage rite takes place after the Homily and before the Offertory. The priest asks if the couple has come to marry freely, to which they answer "I do," and then they join hands and exchange marriage vows. The priest blesses the ring(s), the bride and groom place them on each other's fingers, and the nuptial blessing is given. The Mass continues into the Offertory, Consecration, and Communion, with music and readings at appropriate intervals. (In the past, a Nuptial Mass took place only when both bride and groom were Catholic. Today, there are Nuptial Masses when only one is Roman Catholic; the other simply does not receive Holy Communion.)

The Catholic ceremony allows for personalization and participation by members of the family in various roles. The bride may, for instance, place her flowers in front of a statue of the Virgin Mary, patroness of the family. Friends or family members may be invited to sing or read passages. Attendants may flank the couple at the altar or be positioned in front pews. Altar boys, lectors, deacons, and special ministers of the Eucharist may all be especially chosen. Some dioceses require that the marriage be performed in a church, others do not. Interfaith marriage is common, and priests often co-officiate with the clergy of other faiths.

Within the context of the Nuptial Mass, the whole ceremony takes about an hour; the wedding ceremony alone takes roughly 20 minutes. Marriage is a sacrament in the Catholic Church, so regardless of where it takes place or what adaptations in form are made, the dignity and solemnity of the occasion must always be upheld. The language of the Catholic Church in America is English, though weddings and Masses will often be performed in the dominant language of the local community (Spanish, Italian, etc.). A date for marriage must be made at least six months in advance and, in some parishes, a year's notice is required.

The Byzantine Catholic Church (Eastern Rite)

Few people realize that the Catholic Church in America includes over a million Eastern Rite Catholics, who are under the jurisdiction of the Holy See in Rome and who practice their faith under Catholic Canon Law, but whose customs and traditions are quite different from those practiced in the Western or Roman Rite. The Byzantine Church encompasses Ukrainian, Maronite, Melkite, Roma-

nian, Slovakian, Armenian, Chaldean, and Assyrian Catholics.

Emanating from the same Eastern European and Mediterranean cultures as the Eastern Orthodox Churches (Greek, Russian, etc., who do not recognize the Pope as the head of the Church and who are therefore not Catholic), the wedding ritual of the Eastern Rite Catholic is similar in form and pageantry to the rituals of the Eastern Orthodox Churches (description of Eastern Orthodox ceremonies follows). The nuptial liturgy has its own ritual and is generally not performed within the context of a Mass. The ceremony is very prescribed and ornate, involves processions, crowns, and icons, and takes approximately one hour. Music is choral, not organ, and the language of the service is generally the language of the community (Ukrainian, Romanian, etc.).

Eastern Orthodox Churches (Non-Catholic)

Orthodox congregations in America include Greek, Russian, Polish, Yugoslavian, Serbian, and Syrian, among others. Eastern Orthodox Churches adhere to strict dogma and ancient traditions, and marriage is considered a sacrament.

The wedding ceremony begins with the Betrothal outside the church doors. Here, the rings are blessed and exchanged. Then the couple is led by the priest into the church and onto a white rug or cloth in front of the wedding platform. A wedding icon is carried in the processional, and the couple receives lighted candles to hold throughout the service.

The most solemn part of the ceremony is the Crowning. Metal crowns or floral wreaths, sometimes attached with ribbon, are placed on the heads of the bride and groom to symbolize their roles as king and queen of a heavenly kingdom on earth. This is followed by scriptural readings, the sharing of a common cup of wine, and a ceremonial walk three times around the Holy Things on the altar or platform.

Then, the priest gives the final blessing and the recessional ends the ceremony.

Many of the rituals are performed three times to signify the Holy Trinity, a convention common to all Eastern Churches. Particulars regarding music, attire, language, and details of the liturgy will differ according to the various ethnic customs honored in Orthodox traditions. Intermarriage with non-Orthodox baptized Christians is allowed, but not encouraged.

The Episcopal Church of the Anglican Communion (Protestant)

Though admitting to some variation among regional communities, the Episcopal wedding ceremony is prescribed by *The Book of Common Prayer* and has essentially five parts. Following a traditional bridal processional, the priest opens with an introduction, the familiar "Dearly Beloved, we are gathered . . . ." Then there is the declaration of consent, the "Will you have . . ." public witness of the marriage. Next is the ministry of the Word, using one or more Scriptural passages (usually one from the Old and one from the New Testament, a Gospel or an Epistle). After the readings, the exchange of vows takes place, the priest blesses the rings, and the Lord's Prayer and others may be recited. Finally, the couple kneels for the Trinitarian blessing of the marriage.

Holy Eucharist is central to the service of the Episcopal Church, so most consider it proper to continue from the marriage ceremony into the communion liturgy. Altogether, with appropriate music, the wedding and communion service take about 45 minutes. Marriage is considered a sacrament in the Episcopal Church, so at least one partner must be baptized in the name of the Trinity, and the ceremony must reflect the seriousness of a Christian commitment.

Interfaith marriage is fairly common, and Episcopal priests often co-officiate with other clergy. A divorced person, however, will have to obtain a dispensation from the local bishop to marry in the Church.

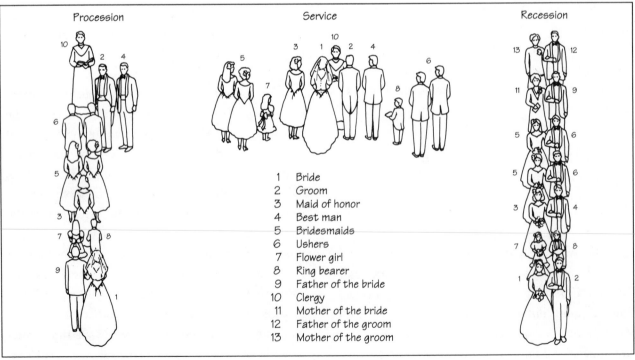

Procession	Service	Recession

1   Bride
2   Groom
3   Maid of honor
4   Best man
5   Bridesmaids
6   Ushers
7   Flower girl
8   Ring bearer
9   Father of the bride
10   Clergy
11   Mother of the bride
12   Father of the groom
13   Mother of the groom

Christian Ceremony

Mainstream Protestant (Baptist, Lutheran, Methodist, and Presbyterian)

The wedding ceremonies of all major Christian denominations have special significance because the relationship of Christ to the church is considered analogous to the relationship between husband and wife. Major Protestant ceremonies have much in common. They all include a traditional processional and recessional, they all use passages from the Old and New Testaments as the cornerstones of the ritual, and they all basically consist of three parts: the introduction by the celebrant, the exchange of vows and rings, and the final blessing. The Protestant ceremony is the most familiar one, the one most often depicted in film and on television.

Protestant ceremonies can be extremely brief, unless embellished with music, readings, or other additions. Some faiths offer Holy Communion, at the request of the couple, and when they do, they append that liturgy to the wedding ceremony much as the Episcopalians do.

Marriage is not considered a sacrament in these churches; nevertheless, it is considered a holy and desirable union. While most allow considerable latitude in personalizing the ceremonies and adapting them to interfaith situations, none will allow any practices that contradict or detract from Christian principles. Ministers often conduct wedding ceremonies outside of their respective houses of worship, but many have reservations about performing a marriage for a Christian/non-Christian couple. Attitudes and restrictions will vary with the liberalism or conservatism of a particular community, even within the same faith.

The Church of Jesus Christ of Latter Day Saints (Mormon)

The marriage ceremony in the Mormon faith is called a "sealing ordinance" because the husband and wife are "sealed" for all eternity, as opposed to "until death do you part." The ceremony takes place between two Mormons who are deemed worthy of marriage by members of the Holy Priesthood, and is conducted in one of the 44 Mormon temples around the world. The couple, dressed in white for purity, kneel before the altar as the officiant performs the sealing; it is a sacred, serene ceremony, one toward which all Mormon couples aspire.

The Church also recognizes civil marriages, however, performed by bishops of the Church or other proper authorities. Many couples marry this way first, and then have a temple wedding ceremony later. A Mormon marrying a non-Mormon may be wed only in a civil ceremony.

Jehovah's Witnesses (Watch Tower Bible and Tract Society)

Though the Jehovah's Witnesses is a Christian faith, there is no ministerial clergy among them, only several elders in each congregation. Couples seeking to marry in the "kingdom hall" (the meeting place for worship) should apply for a date to do so through one of the elders.

Weddings in the kingdom hall are simple in format, though they may be embellished with music, flowers, and attendants for a traditional processional and recessional. The ceremony, conducted by one of the church elders, begins with a Bible talk. Then the couple exchanges their vows, after which more Scripture is read. The whole ceremony takes about 45 minutes.

Guidance for couples wishing to marry among the Jehovah's Witnesses can be found in *The Watch Tower*, the official publication of the faith. Intermarriage is not common, nor is it encouraged. Wedding guests, however, need not be members of the faith to attend the ceremony in a kingdom hall.

Religious Society of Friends (Quaker)

Though some congregations have appointed "pastors," the Quakers are a Christian faith without a clergy. Their belief is that every individual is his own minister; thus, in a Quaker wedding, the couple is in charge of the marriage and effect it upon themselves.

Couples wishing to be married in "a meeting house" during a worship service should apply to the Committee for Ministry and Council at a monthly business meeting. That committee, in turn, appoints a "clearance committee," which will, through a series of interviews with the couple, determine the "clarity of their intention" and freedom to marry, and then grant approval for the marriage to take place. Once permission is granted, "overseers" are appointed to supervise the arrangements. Application for marriage should be made two to three months in advance.

In keeping with the simplicity of Quaker tradition, the bride and groom enter the meeting house and take places among the circle of Friends already present for worship. Today, some brides may emulate a modified processional by entering with their parents, honor attendants, and sponsors, but there is probably no music. The congregation meditates in silence "awaiting upon the Lord." When the couple is ready, they rise, join hands, and make their vows. The groom speaks his promise first, then the bride. Vows may be personalized and original, or they may follow a traditional formula.

After the vows are spoken, the marriage certificate is signed by the couple, the witnesses, and/or the overseers or clerk. Silent worship may continue until the couple feels ready to leave. Before departing, all present also sign the marriage certificate.

Externals are irrelevant to the Society of Friends, so that rings, bridal gowns, attendants, flowers, music, etc., are not necessary or, strictly speaking, in keeping with their tradition. Some congregations, however, may have adopted more popular customs. Interfaith marriage is not an issue because couples seeking to marry in the Quaker tradition tend to do so for valid reasons; at least one of them is likely to be a committed member of the Quaker community.

Unitarian-Universalist Society

Unitarians joined with Universalists in 1961 to form a "non-creedal" community. Though its roots are Judeo-Christian, the Unitarian-Universalist is not a Christian faith; rather, it is a pluralistic religion in which each congregation determines its own affairs and operates within local custom.

A wedding in the Unitarian-Universalist Society is a highly individualized ceremony. Marriage is viewed as a holy union, but couples are encouraged to construct a service that is meaningful to them out of whatever spiritual, religious, or humanistic traditions they share. This is not a church, per se, and the minister/officiant does not sanctify the marriage, but merely officiates. Most ceremonies take about 20 minutes, and marriages between couples of all, any, or no particular faith are common.

Judaism (Orthodox, Conservative, and Reform)

The roots of Judaism are ancient and are of both a civil and a religious nature. Thus, the Jewish wedding ceremony evolves from both Jewish law and cultural tradition, and it is rich in symbolic meaning.

Escorted in procession by their parents, the bride and groom, their attendants, and families gather under the *chuppah* (canopy), which represents the tent home in which newlyweds dwelt in ancient times. The couple takes a sip of ceremonial wine (symbolic of the commitment of the betrothal) and receives a blessing from the rabbi. The bride then receives a gold wedding ring from the groom (plain, so as not to be misled by his wealth). The *ketubah*, or marriage contract, is read aloud and presented by the groom to the bride.

The Seven Blessings are then given, usually by a special guest or member of the family, followed by another ceremonial sip of wine (symbolizing the commitment of the marriage). The ceremony ends with the groom stomping a glass (evocative of the destruction of the Temple in Jerusalem) amid happy cries of "*Mazel tov!*" from those gathered. The recessional is led by the bride and groom.

The wedding ceremony usually takes about 20 minutes, after which, traditionally, the bride and

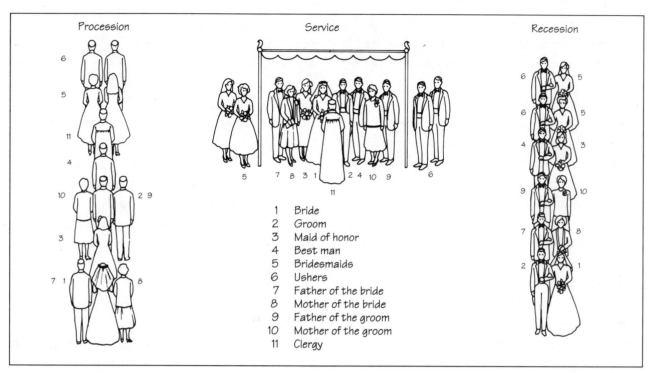

1   Bride
2   Groom
3   Maid of honor
4   Best man
5   Bridesmaids
6   Ushers
7   Father of the bride
8   Mother of the bride
9   Father of the groom
10   Mother of the groom
11   Clergy

Jewish Ceremony

groom retire to a private room for a few minutes before the reception (symbolic of the consummation of the marriage). It is also traditional to begin the wedding feast with a blessing of the *challah*, a loaf of braided bread, to signify the sharing of families and friends.

Joy and symbolism characterize every Jewish wedding ceremony, but the particulars of the service vary from Orthodox to Conservative to Reform branches of the faith, and even from community to community. Though Jewish weddings do not have to take place in a temple, and many don't, rabbis and synagogues often have their own interpretations and directives regarding what is appropriate in attire, music, flowers, etc. Couples wishing to have a double-ring ceremony, for instance, or hoping to have traditional wedding-march music, or to add the words "Do you take this man/woman . . . I do" from the American civil ceremony will have to consult the rabbi. The Jewish ceremony is typically conducted in both Hebrew and English.

Intermarriage is not encouraged in the Jewish faith, but it is becoming increasingly common none-theless. As a rule, Orthodox and Conservative rabbis will not perform interfaith ceremonies; some Reform rabbis will, and some will even co-officiate with other clergy. Also, in Orthodox and Conservative communities, and even some Reform circles, a divorced woman cannot be remarried without a "get," the official rabbinical document of divorce.

Jewish weddings are not performed on the Sabbath, on certain holy days, or in some seasons of the year. There may also be special requirements of witnesses for the wedding, and of guests at the ceremony. (They may have to have their heads covered, particularly when the wedding is held in a temple.)

Hinduism

Hinduism is an ancient collection of socio-religious practices and beliefs dating back to the Indo-European peoples who settled in India (and the adjacent areas today known as Pakistan, Bangladesh, Sri Lanka, and Nepal) two thousand years before Christ. Marriage is not merely a contract to the Hindus, but a *samskara* (sacred trust), so the wedding ceremony is presided over by a priest and conducted in accordance with rites prescribed in the *Veda* (Holy Scripture). It is an elaborate and lengthy ritual; in India, it can last all day.

Here in America the ceremony has been amended to roughly an hour and a half, though cultural pre- and postwedding customs can extend the celebration over several days. The wedding is characterized by symbolic rituals intended to instruct the couple in the lessons for married life, and by the chanting of *mantras* (prayers in the Sanskrit language) to invoke blessings on their union. Though it is a rich and holy ceremony, a Hindu wedding need not be performed in a temple.

The ceremony begins when a beautifully adorned bride (she usually wears a red and gold sari and is decorated with jewels) welcomes her groom and the two exchange floral garlands. Blessings are sought, protective amulets are tied to the wrists of the couple, family lineage is recited, and the father of the bride offers his daughter in marriage. The groom accepts by tying a pendant around the bride's neck as a symbol of happiness and fidelity.

Further prayers are chanted as the couple makes offerings to each other and sacrifices into the ceremonial fire. Then, bound together with a sash, they lead each other around the fire seven times (called *Sapta Padi*) to signify their vow to walk through life's challenges together. The groom applies vermilion powder to the part in the bride's hair as a mark of her new status as a married woman, the priest pronounces a benediction, and the couple is showered with tumeric rice.

The Hindu faith is not dogmatic; it acknowledges that every religion is true or a path to truth. Thus, interfaith marriage is not an issue from a religious standpoint, though the loss of a cultural identity and a way of life through intermarriage may be.

Sikhism

Emanating from the Hindu tradition, but not a part of that religion, Sikhism was founded in 1469 by Guru Nank Dev Ji. The Holy Book, the *Guru Granth Sahib Ji*, contains the teachings and hymns of the religion whose basic philosophy is the belief in one God and the equality of all people.

Sikhism originated in Punjab, India, and while the faith has spread to other regions of the world, the language of prayer remains Punjabi and the dominant culture of its traditions is Indian. The Sikh wedding ceremony, appropriately called *Arnand Karaj* (the ceremony of bliss), seals the religious, moral, and legal obligations of the couple and solemnizes the union of souls. In some ways, it is similar in tone and appearance to the Hindu wedding ceremony, but in other ways, it is very different.

A Sikh marriage may be performed in a *guardwara* (Sikh temple) or not. Regardless, the ceremony is characterized by the central platform on which The Holy Book is displayed, by the *granthi* (official reader/priest) who conducts the ceremony, and by the *raagis* (professional singers) who play the harmonium and sing the poetic hymns from the *Granth*. Guests are seated on the floor around the central area, men to the right of The Holy Book, women to the left.

Before the actual ceremony begins, the parents of the bride welcome the groom and his parents and garland them with flowers. Then the bride is brought in by her friends to greet the groom. She garlands him, and receives a garland in return. The *raagis* play as guests enter and the couple take their places before the priest and The Holy Book. The bride's father hands one end of a sash to the groom and the other end to the bride to signify giving her away.

The wedding ceremony consists of four holy verses from the *Granth* that explain the obligations of married life. Each verse is read, then sung. During the singing, the groom leads the bride in a ceremonial walk around The Holy Book for a total of four circumambulations called *lavaans*. The ceremony concludes with a short hymn and a final prayer and the sharing of a sweet food, *karah parshad*. Guests may then garland the couple or throw flower petals as symbols of happiness.

The Sikh ceremony takes about an hour and is almost always held before noon, the morning being the happy time of day. Brides wear traditional Indian dress, in red, pink, or white, depending on their regional custom, and grooms wear white brocade suits and carry swords. As in the Hindu faith, intermarriage is not a religious issue, but more of a cultural one.

Islam (Muslim)

The world's second largest religion (after Christianity), Islam was founded by the Prophet Muhammad in the seventh century A.D. It remains the dominant expression of faith in all of Arabia and much of the Middle East. But Islam is more than a religion; its emphasis on the temporal community makes it, in a Western sense, law. In Muslim states, Islam provides the guiding principles of political, economic, and social life, as well as of religious belief and practices.

The word Islam means "surrender." All Muslims accept surrender to the will of Allah, the one supreme God, and His will is made known through the *Koran* (Islamic scriptures). Consequently, tenets for every aspect of spiritual and temporal life can be found there, including the rules governing marriage and family.

Marriage is a holy and desirable union under Islamic law and, contrary to popular perceptions, monogamy is largely the rule of practice. Women have preemptive rights over home and children, and their husbands are bound to protect them and to provide for them.

For this reason, the actual "wedding" is a private civil and religious contract. It does not take place in a mosque, but in an office. The agreement having been negotiated beforehand by the groom and the bride's closest male relative (but not without her consent), the couple comes before a religious sheikh (an Islamic magistrate) with three male witnesses to effect the marriage. The magistrate will ask what the groom is giving the bride (a dower). The dower must include enough money, gold, and gifts to serve as her "insur-ance" for the future. (Thus, the popular Arabic saying that "The father of many daughters is a wealthy man.")

Once all is agreed, the papers are signed. Under Islamic law, the couple are now legally and spiritually wed, though usually, the bride returns to her parents' home to finalize plans for the "wedding" celebration. A week or two later, the public celebration of the marriage takes place with a series of parties and rituals. There is no wedding, in a Western sense, only the receptions. The festivities may be held at the bride's home, or out (at a hotel or club), but the groom or his family bears the cost.

The first night is for women only, as the bride is dressed in a ceremonial caftan and her hands and feet are patterned with henna. On the second and, sometimes, third nights, banquets are held (one for the bride, one for the groom), often for several hundred relatives and friends. These celebrations are characterized by Arabic *oud* music, singing, dancing, and the traditional "wedding wail" of the women.

At the end of the last evening's banquet, the couple (the bride often wearing a white wedding dress) appears and ascends to a throne or place of honor. Traditionally, after this public appearance, they will go to their own home to consummate the marriage (though legally they already may have done so).

The traditional celebration of a Muslim marriage translates easily to the United States, but the marriage itself must be arranged through a local Islamic community leader. Interfaith union is not an issue, since Christians, Jews, and Hindus are regarded as "people of the Book," but intercultural marriage and equal protection under Islamic law may be.

Buddhist

Founded in India in the fifth century B.C., Buddhism is a religion and a philosophy that informs much of the spiritual, cultural, and social life of the Eastern world. The central focus of Buddhism is a person's quest for *nirvana* (salvation) through the inner spiritual journey toward perfection; in practical terms, then, the only reality is an inner entity. All else is fleeting and temporary.

Weddings in Buddhist temples or shrines in America are rare since, strictly speaking, there is no prescribed Buddhist wedding ceremony. A Buddhist priest may be asked to bless a nuptial union, in which case the ceremony is constructed individually to reflect the couple's cultural traditions. It usually includes some adaptation of the American civil form of marriage.

Shinto

Shinto (meaning the way of *kami*, the mystical or divine) is the name given to the religious beliefs and social customs indigenous to Japan. Shinto was founded in the sixth century A.D. to distinguish Japanese beliefs from those of Buddhism. Thus, Shinto is not Buddhism, though belief in the social customs and spiritual practices of Shinto does not preclude being Buddhist or any other religion.

The Shinto wedding ceremony is an elaborate ritual interwoven with Japanese culture and tradition.

Usually, the ceremony itself is small and private, held among close family and friends. Before it begins, the Shinto priest cleanses and blesses the four corners of the room, and the floor is covered with rice paper. Then, the couple enters. They sit or kneel before the priest who recites Shinto prayers. If held in a Shinto shrine, there may be Imperial Japanese music to accompany the ceremony.

The high point of the ceremony is the *sansankudo*, meaning "three, three, nine times," in which the bride and groom share sips of sake (rice wine) from each of three lacquered cups. This three-times-three ritual symbolizes luck and happiness and solemnizes the marriage.

Afterward, the marriage is celebrated with a larger group of family and friends at a banquet. Typically, respected guests (relatives and close friends) make toasts and tell stories about the couple. The bride will have changed from her wedding robe into a colorful gown or kimono. At the end of the banquet, she may even change again—this time into a white Western-style wedding dress!

CONTEMPORARY SOLUTIONS

The integration of religious and cultural traditions into modern American life can be a challenge, especially when all your families and friends don't share the same origins, practices, and beliefs. Here are some things you can do to facilitate understanding and to help everyone feel a part of your wedding celebration, no matter how diverse your group of guests might be.

Respecting Rituals

CULTURAL,
RELIGIOUS

❦ *Respect comes from understanding.* If your ceremony is to be a very prescribed ritual that may be unfamiliar to some of your guests, ask the clergy to help you write a wedding program that briefly outlines the parts of the ceremony and the symbolic meaning of each. That way, guests can follow along. If the service is in a foreign language, have the programs printed with that language on one side and the English translation on the other.

The distribution of wedding programs to guests is becoming increasingly popular, even when the ceremony is not all that unusual or difficult to understand. Programs can be designed with decorative covers and printed with your names and wedding date; they can list the members of your wedding party and contain a personal message from the two of you to your guests; and they can serve as meaningful mementoes of your special day, as well as handbooks to the service.

❦ *Even though your faith may have no strictures against interfaith marriage, a ceremony that is very ritualistic and prescribed may not be able to be configured for a co-officiant or for the integration of another religious tradition.* In that case, consider having dual ceremonies, one following right after the other. This is especially easy to do when the wedding will be held in a hotel or home; you can simply move everyone to an adjacent room.

RELIGIOUS

❦ *For an interfaith marriage but not an interfaith ceremony, acknowledge the other religious tradition at the reception.* One Christian-Jewish couple, for instance, had a Protestant wedding ceremony, but then commenced their reception with the cutting of the *challah* and a Rabbinical blessing. The groom stomped the glass and the festivities got underway with *"Mazel tov!"*

Considering Your Guests

CULTURAL

❦ *If attendance at the ceremony requires your guests to have their heads covered, see to it that appropriate coverings are provided.* A Sikh bride we know made gifts of beautiful silk scarves, purchased in Delhi, to all female guests.

❦ *If wedding guests are supposed to sit in certain places (such as women on one side, men on the other), be sure to have ushers on hand to inform arriving guests of the protocol and to help them get properly situated.*

❦ *Try to anticipate the comfort and convenience of your guests.* Long periods of kneeling, for example, or sitting on the floor could be a hardship for some. Ask your officiant about alternatives. Guests could be informed during the ceremony when they might be allowed to sit or stand; some could be seated near the doorway so they might step out, unobtrusively, if necessary.

Likewise, be aware that some people are extremely sensitive to heat and odors (such as incense). If your ceremony is being held outdoors or in an un-air-conditioned place, particularly in the warmer months, take a cue from a caterer we know: place small, pretty fans on each guest seat.

Preparing Yourselves

PERSONAL

❦ *If yours will be an elaborate, prescribed wedding ritual, make sure you know what to do.* Rehearse with the officiant until you are sure that you can perform your roles and duties without embarrassment, even when experiencing normal wedding-day nervousness.

CULTURAL, RELIGIOUS, FAMILY

❦ *If the rituals and customs of the ceremony you've chosen are totally foreign to one of you, try to secure a videotape of the ceremony you're having so you can study it and prepare together.* Books, photographs, and recordings will help. Often, the "outsider's" performance and attention to protocol and custom during the wedding can engender new respect for him or her among the older generations and allay any misgivings they might have about the intermarriage.

PERSONAL, CULTURAL

❦ *When your ceremonial attire is restrictive and cumbersome, change clothes for the reception.* (This is, in fact, a routine custom in many cultures.) You might have something specially made that reflects your heritage (in fabric, color, or ornamentation), but that is designed for comfort in a more Western style. If the groom has worn ceremonial dress, he, too, may want to change into a suit or tuxedo for the reception.

Special Ceremonies

Some types of wedding ceremonies, whether they are religious or civil, have a protocol all their own. They will probably take additional planning time, so start early if you want one of these special celebrations.

The Military Wedding

The regalia of uniforms and the flash of swords (Army, Coast Guard, Maritime) or sabers (Marines, Navy, Air Force) give the military wedding a special drama and dignity. Any enlisted man or woman on active duty, any officer, or any cadet at any of the academies may have a military wedding. That is a privilege of being in the armed forces.

All military weddings are formal, regardless of time of day, and that means full dress uniform (blue in winter, white in summer). Guests dress as they would for any other formal wedding at that time and in that season. Often, the father of the bride is the only male member of the wedding party in civilian attire, unless he is on active duty or retired military, in which case he might wear his uniform as well. Other male attendants not in the military wear civilian formal attire. A bride who is in the military may wear either her dress uniform or, more than likely, a wedding gown. (If she will be in uniform, then it is appropriate to mention her rank on the wedding invitation. See Chapter 11.) Men in uniform do not wear boutonnieres. Bridesmaids generally wear formal civilian attire, though they may wear dress uniforms if they are on active duty.

Military weddings often take place at chapels on bases, posts, or academy campuses, but they may be held elsewhere. In addition to flowers, decorations for both the ceremony and the reception should reflect a patriotic motif by including the American flag and the standard of the groom's and/or the bride's unit(s).

The processional into the ceremony is the traditional one, but the recessional is characterized by the nuptial couple's exit under an arch of drawn swords or sabers formed outside of the church or chapel or on the steps. The senior officer gives the commands to form two facing lines and to hoist the swords or sabers point to point. Part of the tradition is for pairs of swordsmen to cross their weapons in front of the couple, allowing them to pass only after they've kissed. As the couple exits the arch, the last swordsman on the bride's side introduces the couple as husband and wife. To be effective, there should be four to twelve sword or saber bearers, who also serve as wedding ushers.

Protocol at the reception follows military procedure, with officers of the highest rank being seated first. Of course, the most honored tradition of the military reception is the cutting of the wedding cake with the groom's sword or saber. The chaplain's office, chief of protocol, or club manager on the base or post can give you specific information for your particular branch of service.

Should you or your fiancé be a cadet or an alumnus of one of the military academies, remember that weddings on those campuses are popular, particularly around graduation time. Plan ahead. At least a year's notice will probably be needed to make arrangements to be married there, and there may be restrictions. For this information, write directly to:

United States Naval Academy
Annapolis, MD 21402

United States Air Force Academy
Colorado Springs, CO 80907

United States Military Academy
West Point, NY 10996

United States Coast Guard Academy
Groton, CT 06340

United States Maritime Academy
Kings Point, NY 11021

The Wedding of Clergy

When the groom is a clergyman, the wedding usually takes place in the bride's congregation with her minister, rabbi, or pastor officiating. If the bride is a member of the groom's congregation, another officiant, of equal or higher rank, is invited to perform the ceremony. If the bride is a member of the clergy, the ceremony usually takes place in her church or denomination, with an officiant of her choice.

Either the bride or the groom may wear clerical attire or attire appropriate to the style of the wedding. Often, at weddings of a member of the clergy, his or her entire congregation is invited to attend. If any parent of the couple is a cleric, he or she may officiate at the ceremony, may co-officiate, or may assume a strictly parental role.

The Double Wedding

Double the pleasure, double the fun, and double the planning time, because there are that many more people to be considered. About the only thing that doesn't double is the cost, which is why families with two siblings getting married at the same time may choose to have a double wedding.

The double wedding is not seen very often anymore and, when it is, it usually involves members of the same family. Very close friends might decide to have a double wedding, but that's rarer still, since the agreement of four people and four families on every single detail of a wedding seems more than most people can imagine.

At any rate, if you are considering a double wedding, here is what you'll have to do:

- Issue the invitations together; one invitation if siblings, two invitations sent together, or separately but simultaneously, if friends.
- Invite the same number of attendants for each couple, and have them dressed alike or in complementary fashion.
- Decide on the same degree of formality, time of day, food, fare, and locations.
- Assume that the guest list will be proportionately larger, though not necessarily doubled.
- Work out detailed arrangements for the distribution of costs and the organization of responsibilities.

At the ceremony itself, the two bridal parties may enter simultaneously if you have two aisles at your location, or one party proceeds down the aisle first (usually the elder bride), followed by the other. The officiant can help you work out standing and seating arrangements for your attendants and your parents. Just make sure that whatever location you choose is large enough to allow for an attractive, comfortable presentation of two complete wedding parties. The recitation of the ceremony and the exchange of vows may also be sequenced or simultaneous. Brides and grooms leave first in the recessional.

The logistics of a double wedding have to be worked out with considerations for space and common sense. Two sisters might choose, for instance, to let their wedding parties precede each of them, maybe even two-by-two together (both bridesmaids, both maids of honor, etc.), and then both brides enter on the arms of their father. But the aisle might not be wide enough for three people and two wedding gowns. Each might walk down alone, then meet her father or parents at the altar and be "handed over" to respective grooms there. Another possibility is to let the father escort one bride and the mother escort the other.

At the reception, there is one receiving line if one hosting family, two if two hosting families. You may have two bridal tables, two wedding cakes, and two separate enactments of reception traditions. Or you may have one large, simultaneous everything! When brides or grooms are siblings, expect wedding gifts to both couples; when all are just friends being married at the same time, expect gifts only from guests invited by that particular couple.

The Candlelight Ceremony

The candlelight ceremony is exactly what it says it is: the reliance on the drama of candlelight through the use of a profusion of candlelit pedestals, candelabra, hurricane lamps, and lanterns at dusk or in the evening. Artificial lighting is kept to a minimum, and the ceremonial lighting of candles at altars or shrines, or the transference of lighted candles among couples and families may add to the symbolic significance of the ceremony. Often these symbolic acts are devised by the couple and are accompanied by special prayers, readings, music, or poetry.

Couples often visualize members of the wedding party proceeding down the aisles with lighted candles, or guests at the ceremony participating in some way with the lighting of candles, but fire regulations may prohibit all or some of these ideas. The same dramatic effects can be achieved with sheer numbers of stationary candles used throughout the location. Whatever you envision, check on the fire codes for your facility before making your plans.

If you have a candlelight ceremony, it is also a nice touch to follow through with it at the reception. Fea-ture candles with the centerpieces on each table (just make sure the flame won't come too close to the flowers), and situate large, decorative candelabra around the room. Remember, everyone looks better by candlelight, and everyone feels more romantic.

Personalizing Your Vows

Many couples today want to personalize their vows, to give special recognition to their families, or to include favorite friends and family members in their wedding rituals. Wishes for personalization are signs of affection and respect, and most officiants will honor them and integrate them into the wedding ceremony whenever they can.

Even with traditional vows, most mainstream ceremonies today no longer include the phrase "to honor and obey." Catholic and Protestant services routinely incorporate individually chosen Scriptural passages, inspirational readings, or spiritual poems and hymns. Most ministers and priests have several selections from which the couple can choose, and some religions even expect the couple to construct a service that is uniquely meaningful to them, their families, and friends.

Check with the officiant first. Then, depending on just how personal you want to get, you may have to do some research. Look to the Bible and different translations of it, inspirational poetry, famous quotations, and leading philosophers for sources. Think about your own attitudes toward marriage, and your feelings for your fiancé and your families. Don't be afraid to add your own humble words to those of famous writers and thinkers. You may have to "script" what you want to say, and practice the script before the ceremony so that it sounds natural and sincere.

You'll want to make sure that the music, decor, and tone of your wedding celebration are in keeping with your ceremony and with whatever personalized touches you've made. There are books available, some included in the Appendix and some advertised in

Modern Bride, to help you create the ceremony that expresses what you feel.

QUESTIONS TO ASK

1. Are there any specific restrictions or directions regarding flowers, decorations, music, or attire for the ceremony?

2. What is your policy or preference regarding photography and videography?

3. What resources are available to me in the way of equipment (sound, lighting, aisle runner, carpets, decorative accessories) and personnel (choral director, lectors, readers, servers)?

4. Are fees to servers, custodians, or other personnel customary? If so, are there guidelines?

5. Will there be other services or ceremonies held on the same day as my wedding? If so, how do we avoid conflicts?

6. Is a rehearsal necessary for the ceremony? If so, when will we hold it and how long will it take?

7. Through whom do we arrange for floral deliveries, musical set-up, cameras, etc.?

Note: If you have booked the date of your ceremony very far in advance, you'll want to arrange a visit to answer these and any other last-minute questions about eight weeks before the wedding. In any case, call to confirm final arrangements about a week before the ceremony.

Fees for Officiants

If there is no set fee stated by the officiant, it is customary to present some payment for his or her services, quite aside from any routine charges for the use of the site. Usually, the money is placed in an envelope, with a short note of thanks, and given to the officiant privately by the best man right after the ceremony or the rehearsal. The problem with the practice of voluntary offerings, however, is that many couples have no idea what amount is expected or appropriate.

Ask around. Lay members of your congregation may have an idea, or other recently married couples might tell you what they offered. From what we've heard, fees are not at all uniform; they range from as little as $50 to as much as $300 or $400.

Consider the lavishness of your celebration, how much the officiant has done for you (counseling, paperwork, rehearsal, etc.), and what the local economy and social custom seem to be. You should be able to determine an equitable compensation by thinking about what you're paying for other services and fairly allocating something reasonable to the person performing the most significant act of the day.

A close personal friend acting as officiant would not expect a monetary fee, but it would be a nice gesture on your part to present him or her with a special gift. Also, remember to issue invitations to the officiant and spouse to both the rehearsal dinner and the wedding reception.

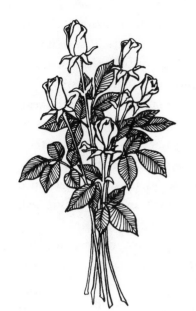

CHAPTER 13

Flowers: The Language of Love

What would a wedding be without flowers—their dewy freshness, their fragrant aroma, their natural beauty and significance? Flowers and herbs always have been a part of wedding celebrations. Their universal appeal transcends time and cultures, and speaks, in various forms, the language of love.

Choosing a Florist

To employ nature's beauty for maximum effect, choose a florist or designer who understands you and the message you are trying to deliver, and who can translate that understanding with flair and imagination. It helps, too, if the florist has a realistic appreciation of your budget limitations.

There are two facts to keep in mind when discussing wedding flowers: (1) florists are artists; (2) flowers are expensive. Money and art can be an uneasy alliance unless someone is firmly in charge. And, for your wedding, that someone has to be you.

The first thing to decide is whether you need the basic service of a competent florist or the more comprehensive services of a floral designer. A good florist does everything with flowers: bouquets, corsages, arrangements, and spatial decorations. He or she does weddings, banquets, proms, and other parties. A florist has a shop with stock for walk-in customers and talented employees who know flowers and know what can be done with them.

If yours is a traditional wedding with traditional needs, a reputable full-service florist is for you. Ask around among family and friends in your community, particularly among those who have had weddings or other parties at which the flowers have been especially lovely. Take pictures (of your gown, bridesmaids' dresses, the sites) with you to the florist and ask to see his or her album of wedding selections. Be prepared to discuss your own wedding in detail (degree of formality, colors, themes, floral needs), and to explore the possibilities, and the costs.

Choosing a Floral Designer

If you are having a theme wedding, an authentic ethnic wedding, or a wedding in a characterless, nondescript location where you need to create a festive atmosphere, then you may need the services of a floral designer. These people are magicians; they can create worlds and transform environments. They work with flowers, and anything else at hand, to fabricate a fantastic space in which you can be married. Yes, they will do the bouquets, corsages, and boutonnieres, but they also will install lighting, lower ceilings, cover walls, etc.

Often, a floral designer doesn't have a shop, but he or she does have many resources and a talented staff. The approach to weddings, or any other special occasion, is much the same as that of a set designer. Flowers may be the mainstay, but whatever else is needed to create the appropriate ambiance will be employed.

Many well-known floral designers have become, in effect, wedding consultants, and vice versa. If yours is to be a gala event with a multiplicity of needs, find a designer through someone you know, or contact the artist whose work you have admired when attending one of his or her other events. Corporate party planners or those involved with organizing charity events may also provide leads to designers they have used.

Making Floral Selections

You should plan to visit florists three to four months before the wedding, earlier if you have extraordinary needs. Before you go, have the answers to the following questions:

- Are there any restrictions on the kinds of decorations I may use at my ceremony and reception sites (candles—fire laws, colors—liturgical seasons, delivery and set-up—conflicts with other services or parties)?

- Are there any necessary limitations on my choices of flowers (bridesmaids' gowns, available table linens, the decor of the site(s), lighting or the lack of it, seasonal availability, or budget considerations)?
- Given my locations, time of day, season of the year, and planned reception activities, do I need flowers that are particularly hardy, which will retain their appearance under less than ideal conditions?
- What wedding tone or mood am I trying to enhance with flowers: casual, country, formal, sophisticated, dramatic, etc.?
- Do I have any specific needs that may be out of the ordinary: a floral *chuppah,* garlands, symbolic blossoms, herb wreaths, etc.?
- Have I made a preliminary list of what I think I'll need in numbers of bouquets, arrangements, boutonnieres, etc.?

If possible, try to interview several florists and compare their ideas and estimated costs before making your final decision. Once you're ready to make a commitment, expect to sign a written agreement. Be sure adequate descriptions of every bouquet and arrangement are included (noting the shape, size, number, and type of blossoms and the amount of filler or greenery). Also, have delivery and payment schedules, as well as cancellation policies, clearly expressed and understood.

QUESTIONS TO ASK

1. Are you familiar with the site(s)? If not, will you visit the site(s) with me?
2. May I see photographs of your work, sketches, or sample wedding albums?
3. What suggestions do you have given my needs and budget?
4. When will the flowers be delivered? Who is to receive them?
5. What are your guarantees regarding freshness, availability, and substitutions?
6. Can you also provide aisle runners, stanchions, candelabra, or any other needs I have that the site cannot provide?

7. What is the estimated total cost of all my selections?

8. What is your payment and cancellation policy?

Note: Though the groom often pays for the bridal bouquet, mothers' corsages, men's boutonnieres, and rehearsal dinner flowers, it is wise, for both coordination and economy, to make all floral selections at the same time from the same vendor. The two of you should visit the florist together.

The Bridal Bouquet

Nothing bespeaks a bride more than the flowers she carries or wears. Your bouquet should complement your bridal attire, be in harmony with the style and tone of your wedding (and the other wedding flowers), and be configured in a shape and size that are proportionate to you.

The four basic types of bridal bouquets are shown below. Instead of one of the traditional bouquets, a bride might also choose:

- A single long-stemmed blossom
- Flowers attached to a prayer book, fan, or other object
- A wrist corsage
- A corsage worn on the dress

The bride's flowers are traditionally white, or mostly white, with some filler or greenery. Often,

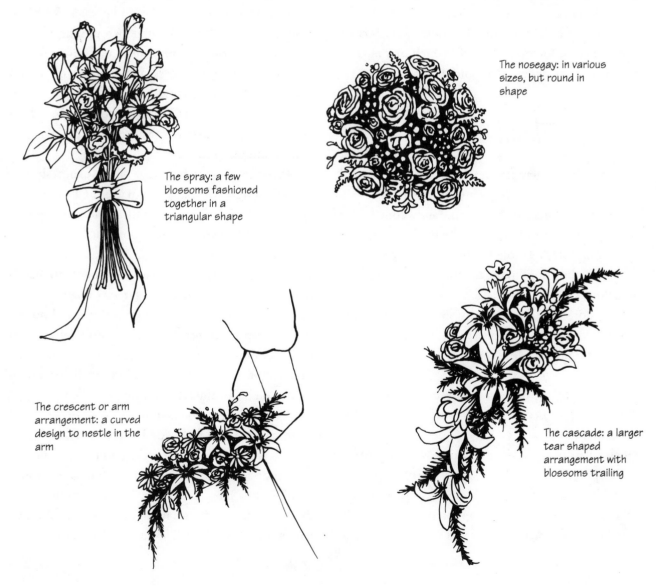

The spray: a few blossoms fashioned together in a triangular shape

The nosegay: in various sizes, but round in shape

The crescent or arm arrangement: a curved design to nestle in the arm

The cascade: a larger tear shaped arrangement with blossoms trailing

though, her flowers will echo wedding colors, either through the incorporation of colored flowers or with the addition of colored ribbon, lace, or other decorative accents. Bridal bouquets may also incorporate silk or dried flowers.

You may have your bouquet designed with a "break-away" section (for tossing) or with a detachable corsage (for going away). Also, by tradition, the groom's boutonniere is a flower plucked from the bridal bouquet; in reality, though, most florists simply fashion his boutonniere from a matching white blossom.

The most popular choices for bridal bouquets are roses (the number one choice), orchids, lilies, and stephanotis, but you certainly don't have to limit yourself to those. You can take a cue from Mother Nature's design by using flowers of the season or take advantage of holiday periods by using characteristic flowers and decorations, some of which may already be in place at your ceremony and reception sites.

Floral Trends

For everything there is a season—and a style—and flowers are no exception. The nineties have seen a rebirth of an appreciation for nature and a concern for ecology. This, according to Rocky Pollitz, vice president of industry relations for Telaflora, has prompted some new directions in floral design, including wedding flowers.

Telaflora's 18,000 members report the following wedding trends that promise to be more than trends by the time the decade's done:

- Roses are still the number one wedding choice, but they're being used open and in full bloom, rather than as buds.
- Regardless of the season, a natural "spring garden" look prevails for weddings; this means bountiful containers full of fragrant blooms, large, lush cascades, and lots of color, as opposed to the studied, architectural designs of years past.

- Line flowers (those with several blossoms on one stem: lockspur, lily of the valley, dendrobium orchid, etc.) are used more often to achieve a light, airy effect.
- The availability of what once were considered exotic flowers (orchids and tulips) from many sources almost all year long has made their prices less prohibitive and their use more prevalent.
- Fragrance and freshness combined in a softer look is what most brides want, even for formal weddings.

Tips on Choosing and Using Flowers

Select flowers in season; not only will they be the most economical choice, they will also perform in harmony with nature (particularly important for weddings held in impressive natural surroundings).

Capitalize on the abundance and sentiments of the holiday periods: roses and carnations around Valentine's Day, tulips and hyacinths around Easter, poinsettias and holly at Christmas. You may be able to take advantage of decorations already in place at ceremony and reception sites.

Rent, rather than buy, large potted plants, shrubs, or topiary trees for spatial decoration. Check with a local florist or nursery, or with a plant service that supplies local businesses or corporations.

Buy potted plants (geraniums, azaleas, mums, etc.) at a nursery or garden center and put them into decorative containers to enhance a garden or patio setting.

Consider lighting and contrast when choosing flowers, especially for wedding photography. Pastel colors against pastel grounds will look washed out; candlelight, stained-glass windows, or diffused daylight at dusk can affect the appearance of color.

Evaluate the mood and tone of your overall celebration, and make your floral selections accordingly. Formal weddings demand more traditional bouquets and arrangements of sophisticated flowers: roses, orchids, calla lilies, carnations, or stephanotis; informal or garden weddings may employ sprays, pots, or baskets of wildflowers, lilies, daisies, or mums.

A Checklist for Flowers

	Description	Number	Approx. Cost
Rehearsal Dinner			
Bride's corsage			
Mothers' corsages			
Table centerpiece			
Ceremony			
Bridal bouquet			
Headpiece(s)			
Maid or matron's bouquet			
Bridesmaids' bouquets			
Groom's boutonniere			
Ushers' boutonnieres			
Fathers' boutonnieres			
Mothers' corsages			
Other men (relatives, readers, etc.)			
Other women (relatives, houseparty, etc.)			
Flower girl (petals, basket, etc.)			
Ceremonial arrangements			
Pew markers			
Aisle runner			
Other			
Reception			
Centerpiece—main table			
Centerpieces—other tables			
Drapes, garlands, decorations (buffet tables, bride's book, etc.)			
Stationary—stanchions, topiary, potted plants, etc.			
Flowers for guests (optional)			
Flower petals for tossing			
Bride's corsage (if not part of bouquet)			
Other (ladies room, cake knife, etc.)			

If you're having difficulty locating a florist with whom you can work, call Telaflora (310-826-5253) and ask for Customer Service. They will help you find a reputable florist in your area.

A Floral Dictionary

Here is a reference for the most popular wedding flowers, with comments on their uses, costs, and meanings. Air shipping, greenhouse cultivation, and import agreements have made many varieties available even when not in season anywhere in the United States. Even so, expect costs and availability to vary from region to region at any time of year.

★The most popular wedding choices.

Variety	Description and Use
Alstroemeria	A variety of the lily family; available in many colors: purple, yellow, pink, white, red; useful as a filler in corsages and arrangements; hardy Available: year round Cost: inexpensive Smbolizes: devotion
Anemone	Large single or double blossoms in pink, red, or white; useful in bouquets and arrangements; hardy Available: winter Cost: moderate Symbolizes: expectation
Aster	A large filler flower; available in purple, lavender, pink, and white; useful in bouquets and arrangements; hardy Available: summer and fall Cost: inexpensive in season Symbolizes: elegance, love
Azalea	Multiblossomed decorative flower; available in pink, deep pink, and white; best used potted; hardy Available: late spring and summer Cost: moderate Symbolizes: temperance
Baby's Breath	A light filler flower; available in pink or white; useful in bouquets, corsages, and boutonnieres; hardy Available: year round

	Cost: inexpensive Symbolizes: innocence
Calla Lily★	Not really a lily; large white, yellow, or pink tropical flower; high-style best used in bouquets or arrangements; hardy Available: spring and summer Cost: expensive Symbolizes: magnificent beauty
Camellia	Large fluffy blooms with shiny foliage; available in pink or white; useful in bouquets and arrangements; delicate Available: spring Cost: moderate in season Symbolizes: perfection, loveliness
Carnation★	Popular, versatile, full-sized or miniature blooms; available in pink, red, or white, but may be dyed other colors; useful in bouquets, boutonnieres, and arrangements; very hardy Available: year round Cost: inexpensive Symbolizes: love, devotion
Chrysanthemum★	Several varieties: pom-pom, spider, miniature buttons; in many colors; useful in bouquets and arrangements; very hardy Available: year round Cost: inexpensive Symbolizes: wealth, abundance, truth
Daffodil	Miniature or full size trumpet-shaped flower; in orange, yellow, white, or exotic varieties; often potted for garden settings; hardy Available: spring Cost: inexpensive in season Symbolizes: regard
Dahlia	Large, multipetaled, daisy-like flower; available in many vivid colors; used in bouquets and arrangements; hardy Available: summer Cost: moderate Symbolizes: dignity, elegance
Daisy	Wildflower in yellow or white; best used in casual bouquets and arrangements; fairly hardy Available: spring and summer Cost: inexpensive in season Symbolizes: innocence, romance

Delphinium★   Large, multiblossomed flower; in white or shades of blue; a traditional wedding flower best used in arrangements; hardy

Available:	summer
Cost:	moderate
Symbolizes:	swiftness, lightness

Freesia   Fragrant, seasonal flower available in many colors, including mixed; used in bouquets; sometimes imported; delicate

Available:	spring and summer
Cost:	inexpensive in season
Symbolizes:	innocence

Gardenia   Fragrant white flower; used in bouquets and boutonnieres; fragile

Available:	year round
Cost:	expensive
Symbolizes:	purity, secret love

Geranium   A favorite potted flower with bright green leaves and compact white, pink, red, or rose blossoms; best used in containers; very hardy

Available:	summer
Cost:	inexpensive
Symbolizes:	home, hospitality

Gerbera Daisy★   Large, daisy-like flower; available in many vivid colors; used for bouquets and arrangements; fairly hardy

Available:	year round
Cost:	moderate
Symbolizes:	beauty

Gladiola   Tall, stately, multiblossomed stems; available in many colors; best in arrangements; very hardy; "glamillia" blooms plucked and wired together for corsages

Available:	year round
Cost:	inexpensive in summer
Symbolizes:	generosity

Hyacinth   Multiblossomed bulb flowers; in white, pink, purple, and blue; best used in pots for garden setting; very hardy

Available:	spring
Cost:	moderate
Symbolizes:	joy, play

Iris   Small Dutch iris or large, bearded iris; available in blue, white, and exotic varieties; used in arrangements or potted; hardy

Available:	spring
Cost:	moderate to expensive
Symbolizes:	a message of faith, wisdom

Ivy★   Green filler, English or petit point; lovely in cascade bouquets; hardy

Available:	year round
Cost:	inexpensive
Symbolizes:	fidelity, friendship, marriage

Lily★   Large, star-shaped flowers; available in orange, yellow, pink, white, and exotic varieties; used in bouquets and arrangements; hardy

Available:	year round
Cost:	moderate (in summer) to expensive (when imported)
Symbolizes:	majesty, truth, honor

Lily of the Valley   Traditional marriage flower; fragrant, small, bell-shaped flowers; always white; used in combination with other flowers; fragile

Available:	spring and summer
Cost:	expensive
Symbolizes:	happiness

Marigold   Small to medium blossoms; available in a range of fall colors; called the Virgin Mary's flower in the Middle Ages; best used in casual bouquets and arrangements; very hardy

Available:	late summer and fall
Cost:	moderate
Symbolizes:	good luck, magic, vision

Nerine Lily   Tall, multiple trumpet-shaped blossoms; exotic look in pale or hot pink; used in bouquets or arrangements; hardy

Available:	imported, year round
Cost:	expensive
Symbolizes:	majesty, power

Orange Blossom   A traditional wedding flower from ancient times; very delicate and difficult to obtain; stephanotis is now used in its place

Available: rarely; sometimes
               found dried or
               preserved
Cost: expensive
Symbolizes: purity, chastity, love

Orchid★   Large and small, in many exotic colors
               and varieties including white; used in
               bouquets, corsages, and boutonnieres;
               hardy
               Available: year round, imported
               Cost: expensive
               Symbolizes: love, beauty

Peony   Large, fluffy pink or white flowers;
               best used in arrangements; fragile
               Available: late spring
               Cost: expensive
               Symbolizes: bashfulness, also
                              the American spirit
                              of ambition and deter-
                              mination

Queen Anne's Lace   A lacy white filler; used in corsages,
               wreaths, bouquets, and arrangements;
               delicate
               Available: summer
               Cost: inexpensive
               Symbolizes: magic, trust, healing

Rose★   A fragrant, traditional bridal flower;
               full bloom or buds, available in many
               colors and varieties; used in bouquets,
               corsages, boutonnieres, and arrange-
               ments; very hardy
               Available: year round
               Cost: moderate to expensive
               Symbolizes: love, joy, beauty

Statice   A filler flower; available in yellow,
               white, and purple; used in arrange-
               ments; very hardy
               Available: year round
               Cost: inexpensive
               Symbolizes: none recorded

Stephanotis★   A traditional bridal flower; fragrant,
               white or pink trumpet-shaped blos-
               soms; used in bouquets and arrange-
               ments; hardy
               Available: year round
               Cost: moderate
               Symbolizes: marital happiness

Stock★   Large, multiblossomed; available in
               many colors; used as a filler in arrange-
               ments; hardy
               Available: year round
               Cost: inexpensive
               Symbolizes: lasting beauty

Tulip   Stately imported flower; in many col-
               ors and varieties; used in arrangements
               and bouquets; fragile
               Available: late spring
               Cost: expensive
               Symbolizes: love, passion

Zinnia   Small to large mum-like garden flow-
               ers; available in many bright colors;
               best in casual bouquets and arrange-
               ments; hardy
               Available: summer
               Cost: inexpensive
               Symbolizes: friendship, affection

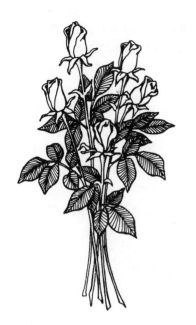

CHAPTER 14
Music: The Sound of Love

"That which comes nearest to expressing the inexpressible is music," said the writer Aldous Huxley. It is particularly so with wedding music. Aside from the ceremony itself, no other single element of your celebration has the power to move your guests and engage the emotions of all in attendance the way beautiful music does. And the music is an important part of your celebration that can be recorded and enjoyed forever!

You don't have to be an expert in the classics or a devotee of the opera or the symphony to select wonderful music that will set the mood for your ceremony and reception, but you do have to give this choice at least as much time and attention as you have each of the other elements of your wedding. Fortunately, there are many resources available to help you, and professional musicians are always eager to talk about the art they love.

Music for the Ceremony

The first thing you must do before planning the music for your ceremony is to be clear on whatever restric-

tions may prevail where your wedding takes place. More and more houses of worship are adopting policies on what they feel are, and are not, appropriate wedding selections, and it is wise to know what that policy is before getting your heart set on music you cannot have. Some consider such well-known pieces as the "Bridal Chorus" from Wagner's *Lohengrin* (the "Here Comes the Bride" melody) and Mendelssohn's "Wedding March" (the theme song of "The Newlywed Game") as secular, nonsacred selections, and thus will not allow them.

Therefore, you need to meet with the musical director of your house of worship to learn about the parameters for your selections. Even if you are not being married in a religious setting, you will still want one or more musicians, who may or may not be liturgically trained, to provide ceremonial music.

Those who do weddings regularly will have a repertoire of appropriate music and will be happy to play samples of their usual selections for you. Chances are you'll recognize many of the melodies once you hear them. You can also buy tapes or CDs of popular wedding music to familiarize yourself with traditional selections.

Determining the music will be easier if your house of worship has an accomplished music director, an experienced choir, and/or an impressive organ or piano in place, because you'll have all of these resources, and more, at your disposal. Choral directors will have access to, and recommendations for, other vocalists and musicians in the area who can enhance your wedding ensemble. Be prepared to pay their standard performance fees, however, and maybe even a bit more if several rehearsals are required.

You should also know that, if you decide *not* to use the services of the organist or choral director at your house of worship, you will still probably have to pay his or her standard fee. This practice is considered professional courtesy, and it is endorsed by The American Guild of Organists.

If your house of worship has no music director, or if you're being married at another location, you may find musicians for your ceremony through the music departments of colleges and universities, your local musicians' union, or area orchestra and symphony groups. Don't hire any vocalist or musicians you haven't actually heard, though; your wedding music is too important to be left to chance—or to neophytes.

Once you have arranged for a professional to work with you in determining music for the service, you'll have to consider the four distinct parts of the wedding ceremony for which appropriate selections must be made.

The Prelude

Your wedding music actually begins 20 to 30 minutes before the ceremony. Called the prelude, this short program sets the mood and provides listening enjoyment for your guests as they arrive and take their seats.

The prelude program may contain any kind of music, vocal or instrumental, that you feel is appropriate to your celebration and that your guests will enjoy. Often, the repertoire is a medley of classical and contemporary pieces, from Bach to Broadway to the Beatles. Bear in mind, though, that if your ceremony is being held in a church or synagogue, liturgical restrictions may also apply to the musical selections for the prelude.

The organist or musicians who will be performing for the ceremony may begin with the prelude, or you may engage other musicians for this part of the program: a string or brass quartet, harp, flute, piano, harpsichord, etc. You might even want to coordinate the musical selections of the prelude to the ethnic, thematic, or holiday motif of your wedding celebration: classical jazz, Baroque, Spanish guitar, or Christmas carols. Remember, you're trying to set a mood, and music is one of the most effective ways of doing that.

The musicians you engage for the prelude will no doubt have some suggestions to help you achieve the proper atmosphere and variety. If you plan on having a printed program, it's a nice idea to include the prelude selections along with the names of the composers and the performing artists, so that your guests will know what they're enjoying.

Fees for each musician to play a half-hour prelude will probably start at around $50.

The Processional

The processional begins as the mother of the bride is seated, the groom appears, and a breathless hush of anticipation comes over the crowd. Organ accompaniment is, of course, traditional for wedding processionals, but if you can afford to engage just one other musician, professionals agree that it should be a trumpeter. The trumpet adds a royal touch, and there are many beautiful arrangements written especially for an organ and trumpet combination.

Processional music is generally joyous and majestic and builds to a crescendo for the entry of the bride. (You may use one selection for the attendants' processional and another for yourself, or you may use the same selection for all with increased volume and intensity for the bridal march.) Whatever you choose should have a clearly audible cadence so that it's easy for you and your attendants to keep time while walking.

Some popular processional selections are:

"Bridal Chorus" from *Lohengrin* by Richard Wagner
"Wedding March" from *A Midsummer Night's Dream* by Felix Mendelssohn
"Canon in D Major" by Johann Pachelbel
"Coronation March" by William Walton
"Prince of Denmark's March" by Jeremiah Clarke
"The Rondeau" by Jean Joseph Mouret

The Ceremony

Soloists, vocalists, and choirs have their special places in the music that accompanies the ceremony itself. Depending on how the ceremony is structured, those gathered are likely to hear Schubert's "Ave Maria" (or the Bach-Gounod arrangement of it), "Oh Promise Me," "Sunrise, Sunset," or any of the other popular ballads or biblical psalms set to music.

You'll want to work with your music director to choose a combination of vocal and instrumental selections to enhance your ceremony and make it distinctive. If appropriate, you might even choose songs that are particular favorites of yours or ones that have special meaning to the two of you and your relationship. Ceremonial music is also helpful in extending an otherwise very brief ceremony and making it seem like more of a service.

If your ceremony is being held within the context of a religious service, then some musical selections will necessarily have to be hymns that are a part of that service, such as the "Alleluia" or "Holy, Holy, Holy" in a Catholic Nuptial Mass. Depending on your wishes and the custom in your congregation, you may or may not invite those gathered to participate in song. Many couples do feel, however, that the joined voices of their guests in the singing of favorite hymns adds to the communal spirit and joy of their celebration.

The Recessional

Of all your musical selections, that for the recessional should be the most jubilant. Now you are husband and wife, and you, your wedding party, and guests will naturally exit the ceremony with a skip in your step prompted by a lively melody.

Some of the most popular recessional selections are:

"Ode to Joy" from the Ninth Symphony by Ludwig van Beethoven
"Pomp and Circumstance No. 4" by Edward Elgar
"The Rondeau" by Jean Joseph Mouret
"Trumpet Fanfare" by Jean Joseph Mouret
"The Four Seasons," first movement by Antonio Vivaldi
Selections from "The Water Music Suite" by George Friedrich Handel

Music for the Reception

A diverse selection of music is the key to a fun-filled reception. The possibilities are literally as endless as your tastes: classical, romantic, rock, pop, jazz, big band, ethnic, etc. The music you choose will include your personal favorites, as well as renditions that guests will find pleasant for listening and/or dancing.

Dance Bands and Orchestras

For a large dinner and dance reception, most couples choose a proportionately large band or orchestra. The size of the crowd determines the size of the reception location; that, in turn, requires a musical group appropriate to the space.

The general rule is that you will need an ensemble of at least five pieces to keep 150 guests dancing, six or seven pieces for a wedding of 200, and the full sound of a full orchestra for 300 guests or more. Of course, the common sense rule of sound in space

Getting in the Mood

Music should match the mood, setting, and degree of formality of the wedding, and be conducive to the activities you expect your guests to enjoy at the reception. Here are some possibilities:

Type of Reception	Mood	Suggested Music
dignified brunch, lunch, or afternoon tea	subdued to allow for conversation	instrumental: piano, harp, violin, string quartet, taped background music
garden parties, lunch, afternoon cocktails	lively, but not obtrusive	instrumental, some vocal; strolling musicians, combos & quartets, guitar ensembles
cocktail party/cocktail buffet	sophisticated & contemporary; limited dancing	instrumental & vocal; jazz combo, soft rock, lively piano, DJ
dinner & dancing	varied for different activities	vocal/instrumental; dance bands, combos, full orchestra, DJ

works the other way, too; that is, too much orchestra for too few people in too small an area can be deafening and can send your guests fleeing in all directions in search of places where they can talk.

Start researching reception bands early, especially if you have a popular one in mind and if your celebration is to be held during a peak wedding and party season. It's not unusual for well-known groups to be booked as far as 18 months in advance, and you'll want to allow yourself time to interview those you're interested in, to hear them play, and to compare costs and packages.

There are two absolute *musts* in your search for a dance band:

(1) *Never hire a band you haven't heard.* If you can't sneak in to listen at a local engagement or hear them during a rehearsal, then you should at least be able to get a demo tape and/or video. And, once you have heard them, make sure that the group you've decided on is the group you're going to get (same bandleader, same vocalist[s], same combination of musicians).

(2) *Insist on a varied program* and make sure the group is able to play—or is willing to learn—any special requests you have. The guests at most large weddings range in age from 18 to 80. To keep everyone in the party spirit, there simply has to be something for everyone to dance to. That means the tempo must run the gamut, from the foxtrot to the frug. Without this broad-based appeal, the whole purpose of engaging a dance band for your reception is defeated.

Those who are experienced performers at weddings generally have a good sense of audience and know how to pace their selections and vary their repertoire, so you need not specify every single number to be played all night long. But you probably will want to make specific requests to accompany certain reception activities: the couple's first dance, the bride dancing with her father, cutting the cake, etc.

Also, if your relatives and friends will expect particular ethnic selections to be played, don't disappoint them. Make sure the band knows those numbers and has some idea of when, and how often, they should be played.

CONTEMPORARY SOLUTIONS

PERSONAL

❦ *If your ceremony and reception are informal, or if they are both being held in the same place (at home, or in a hotel or club), then consider having the same musician(s) play for both.* This is not only a sensible choice in terms of cost and convenience, but it will also allow you to coordinate all the music for your celebration through one professional.

Most accomplished musicians play more than one instrument, so that even if you have your heart set on organ music for the ceremony, the organist may very well become a pianist at the reception. Furthermore, you can usually count on a professional to have a wide range of musical selections appropriate for many moods and occasions in his or her repertoire.

PERSONAL,
SOCIOECONOMIC

❦ *If your reception is to be large and long (5 hours or more), consider different types of music for the different stages of the celebration.* You might have a soloist or a small combo during cocktails, for instance, followed by a large dance band after dinner.

This kind of variety doesn't have to be a bother to arrange. Sometimes a few musicians, all part of a larger orchestra, also play together as a duo, trio, or quartet. You can hire them separately for an extended period of time.

SOCIOECONOMIC

❦ *If your budget for reception music is tight, look for those instrumentalists who can give you a wealth of sound for one small price, those with electric organs or pianos, accordions, or synthesizers.*

By the same token, if you don't want "Daddy's Little Girl," "The Bunny Hop," or other selections that have become fairly routine at receptions, make sure the band director knows that. If the bandleader is also acting as your announcer/master of ceremonies, then he or she will also need a list of names (to introduce attendants, family members) and a schedule of activities, as well as a song list of specific requests.

Disc Jockeys

An increasingly popular, and usually less expensive, alternative to live music is hiring a disc jockey (DJ). Some of them are shows in themselves, with the lights, bubbles, and other special effects they bring along. A good DJ will get people moving and will definitely promote a party atmosphere.

A two-person team is preferred to keep things running smoothly and prevent lapses: one acts as music mixer (plays the discs) and the other as the announcer. Even though the music is taped, you will need the same kind of planning for selections and scheduled activities with a DJ as you would with any bandleader.

QUESTIONS TO ASK

1. Will the musicians/vocalists I've heard and seen be the ones actually playing at my wedding?
2. How will the musicians be dressed for the occasion?
3. How many breaks will you take, how often, and for how long? (One an hour, of five to ten minutes, is standard.)
4. Are you able to provide continuous music or taped music for the interludes?
5. Will the band take requests from guests?
6. Do you have, or require, a special sound system? Is the one you have compatible with my reception site? What is the cost of obtaining what you need?

7. Are there any extra costs not included in your quoted fee? (Often there are charges for travel, set-up time, continuous music, cocktail hours, and overtime.)

8. What is your payment schedule and cancellation policy?

What Will It Cost?

When it comes to music, you're paying for more than the sound; you're paying for experience, reliability, and professionalism. Unless you decide to entrust your ceremony and reception to students or talented amateurs, that means you're going to pay at least minimum union-scale wages to musicians and vocalists. Popular, well-known artists (even if only well known locally) will charge more than the minimum.

In major urban areas, you can expect to pay anywhere from $1,000 to $3,500 for a five-piece band for four hours. A larger orchestra can run from $5,000 to $7,000, or more, depending on demand and reputation. A single musician may charge only $200 for four hours; some DJs start at around $300 for the same amount of time.

The price you are quoted will be for a set number of hours with a set number of breaks. Anything over that will be charged at hourly overtime rates; sometimes even partial hours will be billed as a full hour of overtime. Be sure you know what those overtime rates are, and try to avoid them. Make your initial booking for as long as you think you'll want to celebrate.

You do not tip band directors, nor should you be expected to pay any so-called union tax. (Any manager claiming otherwise is probably dishonest.) Some states do include musicians under service taxes, however. Your contract should specify all charges, and any legitimate extras, in writing.

Most bands require a 25 to 50 percent deposit at the time of booking, with the balance due either at the reception itself or shortly before at the final reconfirmation. Usually, the deposit is fully refundable up to 60 days before the event, and partially refundable with up to 30 days notice.

You are expected to provide refreshments for musicians working at your reception, perhaps even a light supper if their employ extends over mealtime from early evening to late at night. But you do not have to offer them the same meal your guests are receiving, nor are you obligated to provide alcoholic beverages. Make arrangements with your caterer to have a table set aside just for the musicians and specify, in advance, what they are to be served.

Finally, be sure to check with your reception site before you book the band. Find out when the orchestra can get set up, what kind of equipment and facilities they have for musicians, and what is the outside time limit by which you and your party must vacate the premises. Also, be extra sure that there are no fees or restrictions on bringing in your own musicians. (Some establishments have their own bands, which they require you to use, and/or other "entertainment" policies.)

Know Your Contract

Expect to sign a written contract with reception musicians that specifies the following:

- The date, time, and location of your party
- The name of the bandleader and any lead vocalist
- The exact number and instrumentation of the band
- Hourly fees and overtime rates
- Any legitimate additional charges (continuous music, technicians, equipment, taxes, etc.)
- The number and length of breaks
- Payment terms and cancellation policy
- Attire that will be worn

CHAPTER 15

Capturing the Moments:
Photography and Videography

When the day is done and all has become a memory, the one thing you can count on to help you relive your wedding is the pictures. You'll find yourselves returning to your wedding album or videotape time and time again over the years, on anniversaries, on visits with friends and relatives, or during those special moments when your children beg to see them.

That's why it is so important to enlist the services of an experienced wedding photographer and/or videographer to be sure that this family rite of passage is preserved. Sure, your friends and relatives can bring their cameras and camcorders to the wedding, and yes, one of them may even capture some memorable moments, but you don't want to leave the record of events that will only happen once in a lifetime to chance, or to the luck of an amateur.

Wedding photography isn't what it used to be. In addition to constantly improving equipment, technology, and printing techniques, the photographers, themselves, are emerging as artists in their own right, with some of the best devoting their talents almost exclusively to the wonder and magic of weddings.

Gone are the days when you would have to settle for the same frozen images and requisite poses in a wedding collection that looked like every other bridal album on the coffee table. Now, you have real choices—and plenty of them.

After generations of sameness, wedding photography has finally come into its own. In fact, it may be the most exciting and dynamic sector of today's wedding-services industry. Whether you choose to work with an established studio or you contract an innovative independent, you will find that personalities, of both the professionals and their subjects, have become the driving force of artistic success and customer satisfaction in this field.

Of course, in order to "capture the moments" of your wedding in a way that will last and remain true over the years, you will have to educate yourselves and learn to appreciate the nuances of each photographer's style and vision. Look at other couples' wedding albums and ask for word-of-mouth recommendations in your area. Then, plan to spend some time interviewing prospective photographers, examining their portfolios, and questioning them about their particular wedding philosophies. Ultimately, you want to choose someone whose attitudes and printed images match your own ideas of what wedding photographs should represent. And you want to choose a person with whom you feel some rapport. After all, a wedding is a very personal affair.

Photographic Style

Trends in wedding photography today go in two very distinct directions, both equally valid: one is the "portrait" or "studio" style, in which the events of the day are interpreted through the eye of an artist. Here the photographer uses his or her knowledge, skill, and technique (lighting, special filters, photo retouching, etc.) to interpret the mood and capture the fantasy of a wedding. Even candid shots are, in effect, perfect. Often, the photographs will require planned time before the ceremony and reception. While the sample albums of classic stylists will reflect some "prompted" candid moments, overall the percentage of posed photographs will dominate. This is the dignified, more romantic approach to wedding photography.

At the other end of the spectrum are the photojournalists. These professionals see themselves as recorders of events, not orchestrators of them. Fewer than 5 percent of the photos in the album will be staged; the intent is to capture the realities of the day, and the thrust of the collection is to tell the true story of the wedding and of the people in it. The philosophy is that people photograph best when they are unaware of the camera.

So much has happened in the field of wedding photography in recent years that shopping for these services has become almost as personal as buying a dress. The "style and fit" has to be just right. These days, most studios employ a number of photographers whose attitudes run the gamut of styles. The trick to ensuring satisfaction with the end result is to examine the work of the various photographers, and to pick the artist for your wedding whose style and philosophy seem most in line with your expectations.

The Classic Approach

Make no mistake, being of the traditional portrait or studio school doesn't mean that the photographer is staid, stodgy, or dated. Far from it. The classicist eschews the trite and artificial as much as the photojournalist and, in doing so, achieves a very contemporary, yet still classic, look.

David Ziser, a photographer in the Cincinnati area, has been interpreting weddings to his customers' satisfaction since 1978. In the tradition of great portrait painters from decades past, Ziser attempts to develop a rapport with his clients. His collections tell a traditional wedding story, with some interesting subplots along the way, but the whole is presented with taste, dignity, and artistic sensitivity.

"I want my clients to know that I'm honestly concerned about the beauty, the mood, and the excitement of their day," Ziser says, "but I also want the photographic record of that day to exceed their photographic expectations, not only for the moment, but for a lifetime. I do that by bringing to bear everything I know as an experienced professional to produce a wonderful, exciting study of their extra-special occasion."

The Photojournalist

Denis Reggie, the Atlanta photographer who has done every Kennedy wedding since 1980, has become synonymous with the "natural" or photojournalistic style of wedding photography. "My job is to follow the day, to capture accurate, sensitive, believable impressions of the wedding," he says, "not to lead the day, to concoct a version of my own or to impose my vision on the people and events involved."

While Reggie admits that there is a place for the three or four requisite, portrait-type photographs, his wedding albums are magazine-like in format and the truly candid shots constitute the bulk of the whole. He attempts to present the sequenced, unique, and true story of each individual couple, as well as the unrehearsed emotions and reactions of all those valued family and friends.

"The way I see it, the classic photographer's style is to mine as fiction is to nonfiction," Reggie says. "Ultimately, the couple has to decide which version of the truth will best suit their memories and expectations."

Choosing a Photographer

According to the Professional Photographers of America (PPA), the world's largest and oldest association of professional photographers/videographers with 17,000 members, most brides-to-be consult at least two and as many as nine prospective photographers before making a wedding commitment. That's a good idea. The best way to make a preliminary list, of course, is to ask for recommendations from people you know. Other wedding professionals (caterers, florists, etc.) might also have some suggestions. You can even contact the PPA directly for a list of member photographers in your area (see Appendix for the address). Membership in the Professional Photographers of America indicates that the photographer subscribes to the organization's Code of Ethics for Wedding Photography and satisfies federal, state, and local requirements for doing business.

Start early, at least four months in advance. Well-known photographers, many of whom limit their bookings, could be committed up to a year in advance, especially during peak wedding seasons. Once you have a list of prospects, call and set up an appointment for a personal visit with each one. Certainly, you and your fiancé should go together, but you might also take along anyone close to you who has a special interest in, or knowledge of, photography.

Making the Decision

Bachrach Photographers, famous for their portraits of American presidents, has been in business since 1868. Their West Coast director offers these pointers for conducting successful interviews with prospective photographers:

- Take the time you need to really talk to the photographers so you can compare styles and services, as well as price.
- Look for sharp, clear images that are technically good, that show real emotion, and that indicate the relationship between the subjects.
- Ask if the photographer is familiar with the locations of your ceremony and reception; if not, will he or she become so?
- Compare the percentage of candid to posed shots in any given collection; that's one way to identify the photographer's style.
- Ask about the photographer's wedding philosophy; try to ascertain whether he or she is dedicated and enthusiastic about weddings, or if this is just a sideline business.
- If there are several photographers in the studio, make sure that the one whose work you like will be the actual photographer doing your wedding day.
- Find out how long negatives are kept on file; you may want to place additional orders at a future date.
- Realize that you are being shown the artist's or studio's best work; it won't get any better than this, so if you don't like what you see, go elsewhere.
- Check the availability of your wedding date and ask for a brochure outlining wedding packages and services to take with you.
- Take notes during, or immediately after, your visit to help you remember the details and distinctions later.
- After you've completed all interviews, sit down, review what you've learned, and make your decision.

Engagement Pictures

It used to be that when a bride scheduled a session for engagement photographs, it was with only a black-and-white, head-and-shoulders newspaper photo in mind. But not anymore! Today, couples, and their families, often want these informals as part of their permanent collection of memories. Furthermore, they think it's high time that the groom be as much a part of all the prewedding publicity and activity as the bride.

Many newspapers print engagement photos of the bride, or the couple, along with the engagement announcement. Some studios even include a prewedding shoot of informals in black and white as part of their wedding packages—wisely so, since that gives the photographer a chance to get to know the couple and to see how best to photograph them.

But, even when not included in the package, an informal engagement session can be a good idea, and a cost-effective one, too. Not only does the photographer "get a jump" on how photogenic you will be on your wedding day, but framed informals or small folio sets make lovely prewedding gifts for those you love.

If you plan to send an engagement photograph to the newspaper, be sure it is a black-and-white, 5 × 7 or 8 × 10 glossy print. Tape, or lightly write in pencil, a photo identification on the back (engagement photo, name, address), and mail it with a protective piece of cardboard and your engagement information to the society editor.

The Bridal Portrait

Typically, the formal bridal portrait is taken of the bride alone about a month before the wedding. But again, more and more grooms are being included, and more and more published wedding announcements in newspapers feature pictures of the couple together. You two, and your families, will have to decide how you want to define "the bridal portrait."

Formal, prewedding portrait sittings are often included as part of the photographer's wedding package, but not always. Even when they are, variations, such as portraits of each of you alone and together, and black-and-white prints (for newspapers) as well as color (for framing and keeping) may incur charges beyond the basic price. Check to see.

Photographers often shoot the formal portrait in their studio, or they may shoot it in your home or even at your bridal salon on the day of your final fitting. The important thing to remember is that this portrait should look as if it were taken on the day of the wedding. That means every aspect of your appearance—hair, makeup, gown, headpiece, accessories, and undergarments—has to be exactly as it will be on the wedding day.

Even the most dedicated photojournalists do formal wedding portraits because they recognize the traditional sentiment associated with them. Most parents frame and display an 8 × 10 or larger formal print in their homes, and most newspapers (except those in large, urban areas) still run formal wedding portraits along with wedding announcements (and want those photos about ten days in advance so that the story will be timely). In some areas, though, where newspaper timeliness is not an issue, the formal portrait is done on the day of the wedding itself.

Again, from the Professional Photographers of America, here are some tips for beautiful bridal portraits:

• Schedule your formal portrait as early as possible; your schedule will be less hectic and you will be more able to look your best.

• Your hairstyle should complement your gown and headpiece and not be too fussy; consult your hairdresser well in advance, and make sure you can replicate the style in your portrait sitting on your wedding day.

• Makeup should be natural and not overdone for photography; the one exception may be eye makeup, if you're not accustomed to wearing any at all. Get professional consultation well in advance of both your portrait sitting and your wedding day if you need it.

• Make sure your gown is pressed and perfectly complete, with all accessories, for your portrait; if need be, bring someone with you to help you change into your bridal attire at the studio.

• Be well rested; no amount of makeup can improve a fatigued, frazzled look.

The Wedding Album

Beyond the regrettable error of entrusting wedding photography to an amateur or to some fly-by-night wonder who promises the world and delivers nothing, the next biggest mistake couples make is assuming that they can save big bucks, or that the photographer makes big bucks, on the wedding albums that preserve and contain the photographs. So prevalent is this misconception that we feel it is important to explain why photographers offer the albums/cases/folios they do, and why this part of the wedding package can't be matched at your local discount store.

Art Leather of Elmhurst, New York, is the world's largest album/folio manufacturer, and they have been in business for over 40 years. They supply the majority of professional photographers/studios/videographers across the country, and their products are not available directly to the consumer. They offer literally thousands of cover choices, spine sizes, and mat configurations that enable photographers to construct each wedding collection in their, and your, individual way. Once your proofs are ordered, the photographer "designs" the album to tell your wedding story, and the specifications of that design are custom-made for you by Art Leather.

Each wedding album or parent's album or folio or video case is made by a combination process of modern manufacturing methods and hand craftsmanship. The padding, hand-turned corners, special mats, gold-embossed edges and finishes, masonite supports, and characteristic silk-moire linings guarantee these albums for life. The quality and durability are there to protect, and enhance, the photographic record of your day. The customized lettering of names and wedding date on the cover means that this album has been especially created for you.

Reputable photographers consider presentation as a cost of doing business and, while most will have several styles and price ranges of albums from Art Leather or other manufacturers available to fit your budget, they are not relying on album sales as profit centers. Rather, they are selling the quality and the service of their art, and seeking to present that art in the most appropriate, pleasing way possible.

Mark H. Roberts, president of Art Leather, is committed to quality, aware of photographers' creativity, and ever-mindful of the consumer's needs. "We listen," he says, "and we respond. We are constantly adapting our products and our services to meet both the creative requirements of the artists and the practical considerations of the customers."

QUESTIONS TO ASK

1. What, exactly, does the package price include (engagement shoot, bridal portrait, number of wedding prints, etc.)?
2. How many rolls of film will be shot for engagement informals and formal portraits?
3. How many hours of coverage are included for the wedding?
4. Are there any additional charges for overtime, site visitation, photographic assistants, travel time, etc.?
5. How many proofs will there be? Will there be an extra charge if I want all the proofs?
6. How long do you keep the negatives, and for how long can I order additional prints at the same price being quoted now?
7. What is your payment schedule? (Generally, 30 to 50 percent is required at time of booking, the balance at time of proof selection.)
8. How long after the wedding can I expect to be called for proof selection?
9. How long after the wedding can I expect my albums to be delivered? (Three to four months is average, provided proofs have been selected promptly.)

10. What presentation (quality, types, numbers, and sizes of albums and folios) is included in the price package?
11. How will the photographer be dressed at my wedding?

Picture Specifications

We are not including what professionals call "the punch list" (list of requisite photos) under the assumption that experienced, reputable wedding photographers should know what they're doing and should know enough to get the basic shots: the bride and groom, the couple with their families, and the couple with their attendants. Beyond that, you will have to discuss with your photographer exactly how many and what kind of traditional shots you definitely want taken.

It is helpful to provide the photographer with a general schedule of events (arrival at the church, receiving line, first dance, cutting the cake, etc.) and with the names of the not-to-be-missed subjects (grandparents, godparents, childhood friends, etc.). It is also wise to make someone among your family or guests, who knows all these people, the designated liaison to help the photographer identify those VIPs and make sure they are all on film.

In spite of the old wives' tale about the groom not seeing the bride before the wedding, most photographers today ask that the couple, their families, and their attendants arrive for photography before the ceremony. That way, guests are not kept waiting outside reception doors during a lengthy photography session. It makes sense, and it poses less of an interruption to your own enjoyment of the day.

Meet with your photographer about a month before the wedding to finalize all arrangements. Then, just relax and trust him or her to do the job.

What Will It Cost?

Standard price packages from wedding specialists we've talked to around the country run anywhere from $1,700 to $2,500. Generally, this includes the formal bridal portrait, coverage of the wedding for a specified number of hours, a standard number of proofs from which to select, and a finished wedding collection of approximately 50 pages or photographs professionally bound in a durable, attractive leather album. Some studios include an additional, informal prewedding shoot, smaller albums for the parents, or all the proofs they take as part of the package; others charge separately for every additional print, album, or proof. A good photographer should keep your negatives on file for three to five years (many file them for even longer) in case you decide to order additional prints later.

Price, however, is not the only consideration in choosing a photographer, and what initially seems "too good to be true" usually is. Some less than reputable businesses may quote you a very low price initially (usually for a very limited number of prints), only to hit you with the "hard sell" later on, after you've seen the proofs and decided that you want more than the original package offered. In interviewing reputable photographers in your area, you will find that those with established reputations tend to be fairly uniform in price.

There may be legitimate additional hourly fees charged for overtime, billed travel expenses (if you are bringing a photographer in from somewhere else), costs for additional assistants (to cover very large weddings), and separate charges for separate albums (for parents).

About Videography

"The problem with wedding videography," says Richard Rader, chairman of the Electronic Imaging Group of the Professional Photographers of America and a pioneer in the wedding video industry, "is that it's an afterthought with most couples, an extra. People have the idea that anyone who owns a camcorder, Uncle John or the next-door neighbor, can satisfactorily videotape a wedding. So, they hire a professional only if their budgets will allow, and usually that allowance is found at a very late stage of wedding planning."

Rader and his videographer son, Vic, have been in the wedding video business for over ten years in the Omaha area. They have won awards, instructed other professionals, and been through, in just one decade, three entirely different levels of technology in the equipment they use. "The capability and technology of video recording changes so rapidly," Rader says, "that a professional has to spend almost as much time educating himself as practicing his art."

While the rapid increase in technology may have presented a challenge to the videographer, it has meant a boon for the consumer. More high-tech equipment and more competition in the industry have meant that prices for wedding videography have actually come down. The average package price for a videotaped wedding story of five to eight hours coverage is now anywhere from $400 to $1,000, depending on editing sophistication and special effects.

Today's videography team is composed of two, or maybe three, people at most. Wireless microphones, unmanned automatic cameras, and low-light or "bounce light" equipment minimize movement and distraction, especially during the wedding ceremony. Lightweight cameras and increased mobility allow the videographer to be on the scene wherever events are happening, inside or outside.

Most videographers work with super VHS tape. Your copy is edited down from this master. (Often, you can arrange to purchase the unedited master at a nominal price and store it for the future.) A tape made from such a master is of superior quality, and a studio-edited tape is preferable to a camera-edited one (meaning the camera operator edits events while shooting).

Some photography studios have videography as part of their total service, but many do not. Some photographers may recommend videographers with whom they've worked compatibly before. In any case, you should interview prospective videographers in the same way as you would photographers, by looking for a special rapport with the professional and by comparing samples of the work and assessing the appropriateness of the artistic style.

Standard video packages include the full wedding story, from the time the bride and groom and their families arrive at the wedding site until the time of the couple's departure from the reception. A finished, edited tape of the day's events will run 1 1/2 to 2 hours. Special effects, prewedding stories, interview segments, voiceovers, and superimposed music and titles will all add to the cost, as will multiple copies. Many videographers also produce a wedding highlights tape, about 15 minutes in length, and some will offer that as part of their package.

Rader, while employing state-of-the-art equipment himself, emphasizes that this is not the most important criteria for hiring a videographer. "The most important consideration," he says, "is the audial and visual quality of the taped samples you see, and the depth of emotion captured. Video should be living and real. After all, it's that living, moving, sounding dimension of videotape that makes it so special and so very different from what print photography has to offer."

QUESTIONS TO ASK

1. How unobtrusive will you be?
2. How familiar are you with the locations of my ceremony and reception?
3. How will you capture close-up shots (stationary cameras, wireless microphones, etc.)?
4. What is your editing process? Is the unedited master tape available for purchase?
5. How many hours of coverage does your package include?
6. What end product(s) does the price include (length of tape, number of copies, special cases, etc.)?
7. What are the extra options?
8. How long after the wedding will my tape be ready for preliminary viewing? (Generally, couples are well advised to leave the editing to the professionals, but some videographers do allow for a preliminary viewing.)

9. How long after the wedding will my final tape be delivered?
10. How will the videographer(s) be dressed at my wedding?
11. What is your payment policy?
12. What are your guarantees and liabilities?

Taking Care of Your Videotape

You'll want to be able to enjoy your wedding video for years to come. A little extra care can extend its life. Here are some tips from the Professional Photographers of America:

• Always rewind the tape after viewing; uneven "packing" of the tape in the cassette can cause it to stretch.
• Avoid accidental erasure by breaking off the black tab on the back; this protects the tape.
• Store the tape vertically in a cool, dry place; a case or sleeve will keep it dust free.
• Store the tape away from magnetic sources, such as VCRs and TVs.
• Mark the master tape and store it away separately, perhaps in a safety deposit box.

Know Your Contract

Be prepared to sign a written agreement with both your photographer and your videographer, and make sure that every element of coverage is specified: number of hours, staff, delivery and payment schedules, and final products.

Even though there are thousands of reputable, talented, experienced photographers and videographers across the country, the truth is that complaints about these services continue to be common. We think it has much to do with couples' unrealistic expectations of such services and/or their failure to devote the time to adequately interview and select the professionals who are right for them.

You should expect any professional photographer or videographer to:

• Be as unobtrusive and congenial as possible during the wedding day activities.
• Be sensitive to you and your families' special needs and requests.
• Use their expertise to help you, and all their subjects, look great and appear natural.
• Dress and behave appropriately.
• Stand behind their products and services and guarantee your satisfaction (within reason, of course).
• Clearly specify their terms, services, and products up front, and commit themselves in writing at the time of contract.

In return, you need to help this professional do the job by being honest and specific about what you want and need. Your ability to communicate your expectations is integral to his or her success, to your satisfaction with the finished product, and to the preservation of your memories forever.

Spotlight on Wedding Photography and Videography Trends

• A return to black-and-white photography and hand-tinted black-and-white prints.
• On-location/environmental engagement photos.
• Engagement pictures of both the bride and the groom.
• Display "folios" of from five to seven engagement or wedding prints as keepsakes for yourselves, families, and friends.
• Studio backgrounds for formal portraits.
• Double-page "bleed" photos in wedding albums.
• Specially mounted (matted) photos of various sizes in albums, making more of a storybook.
• Live music and sound recordings on video.
• Still photos combined with live footage on video.
• Minimal special effects (photo optics, borders, etc.) in favor of a more natural looking video story.
• Personalized leather cases for the videocassette.

CONTEMPORARY SOLUTIONS

FAMILY

❦ *There's been an acrimonious divorce in the family and one set of parents, bride's and/or groom's, do not want to be seen together in the pictures. How can you keep hostilities from erupting?*

You'll have to level with the photographer and make arrangements in advance. Either have one set of photos taken with one side of the family before the ceremony and the other taken after the ceremony, or plan two separate photography sessions at the reception.

SOCIOECONOMIC

❦ *You live in a medium-sized town, and one photographer is head-and-shoulders above the rest. But so are his prices. After interviewing several others, you still like his work the best, but you can't see how you can afford him.*

Talk to the photographer again. Explain that you really like his work, but that your budget is very limited. Most photographers are eager to work with couples who really want to work with them, so he may have some cost-cutting suggestions. If not, take the most basic package you can afford, be sure he keeps the negatives on file, and plan to order more prints or albums at a later date when you can better afford it.

PERSONAL

❦ *You live in a small town. There is only one photographer, who does everything from school yearbook pictures to anniversary parties, and his style is very traditional. You had hoped for a more contemporary, candid record of your wedding day. What choice do you have?*

Assuming that there aren't other photographers within 50 miles or so who might be willing to make the trip to cover your wedding, contact your local newspaper. Staff photographers there are likely to be more of the photojournalist school, and one of them might welcome the opportunity to photograph your wedding. To be sure you get the must-have moments on film, consider hiring the one professional in town for formal portraits and maybe for "limited" wedding coverage.

❦ *A friend from college was a film major, and he's been "dabbling" in video ever since. He's offered to videotape your wedding as his gift to the two of you. While you imagine he's more than just a rank amateur, you know nothing about this work and have no idea how this will turn out. What can you say?*

First, be sure you have a good print photographer. If you had not otherwise planned to contract a videographer, then you have nothing to lose and everything to gain by letting your friend do the honors. Just be sure to meet with him in advance, and express your expectations for your wedding. You don't want an overly enthusiastic video buff jamming a camcorder in everyone's face all day long.

On the other hand, if you were planning on obtaining the services of a professional, then you might explain to your friend that you have already made those plans and tell him that, while you appreciate his offer, you would much prefer that he enjoy your wedding as a valued guest rather than as a "working professional."

CHAPTER 16
Romantic Roots:
Ethnic and Theme Weddings

Traditions are the ties that bind, across continents and across generations. So diverse are the 280 million Americans that difference is about the only thing we have in common. We are "a nation of nations," a land of many customs and cultures, habits and tastes. And, whenever traditions have died out or have been misplaced, we're not above resurrecting them or creating new ones to take their place and fill the need for continuity.

Weddings are about continuity, about the ties that transcend time and the symbols that have universal meaning. Two different people from two very different backgrounds find the common ground between them and call it love. They marry, and in doing so, they merge their families, their histories, and their identities.

Acknowledgment of each other's personal heritage in a wedding celebration has a way of emphasizing the common bonds between the partners and easing the transition from one generation to the next, especially when backgrounds are disparate. Some couples show respect and continuity by integrating elements of their ethnic traditions into the wedding; others do it by incorporating a thematic motif that has special significance for them both. Either way, it is the intention that counts, the quest for the unity and harmony that a meaningful celebration is supposed to represent.

Ethnic Weddings

So varied are Americans that even anthropologists and sociologists can't agree upon an exact definition of ethnicity. Language, race, religion, food, folklore, and national origin are aspects of it, but so are regional customs and group identification. Consequently, any listing of ethnic groups in America is as likely to include "Southerners" and "Yankees" as it is those identified by national origin.

For most of us, ethnicity becomes as much a matter of choice and community affiliation as it does birthright. Only that can explain why a bride in southwest Texas might, quite appropriately, choose a lace mantilla, Mexican food, and mariachi music as components of her wedding celebration even though she, herself, is not of Mexican descent.

To equate ethnic with foreign in the United States is a mistake; to align it with regional customs and family values is perhaps closer to the mark. Ironically, even the so-called typically American, nonethnic wedding is actually a composite of traditions that come from somewhere else: the ring, the white gown, the veil, the attendants, the toasting, the cake—all of these are legacies from other places, other cultures, other times. All have evolved out of generations of immigrants adapting, blending, and amending the ways of the "old country" to the conditions that existed in the "New World." As more and more couples realize that, more and more of them have the desire to reclaim the traditions that are a part of their heritage.

Wedding Traditions of Ethnic Groups in America

If you have maintained a strong identification with a distinct ethnic community, then you and your family will no doubt know what the traditional wedding customs are and how to honor them in an authentic way. But, if you have lost sight of your traditions, or if you are marrying someone whose heritage is very different from your own, you might find that your wedding presents the ideal opportunity to rediscover your roots and to revive some of the signs and symbols that have special meaning for you, your families, and your community.

Here, gathered from numerous interviews with individuals still connected to their roots and preserving their traditions, are identifiable, easily integrated customs from major ethnic groups in America. Special thanks for this section goes to The Balch Institute of Ethnic Studies in Philadelphia and their traveling exhibition, "Something Old, Something New: Ethnic Weddings in America," with photographs by Katrina Thomas; to The Polynesian Cultural Center on Oahu, Hawaii; and to The Navajo Nation, Navajoland, Window Rock, Arizona.

If any of these ethnic customs belong to you, use them; if you want to find out more, check the Appendix and do some research. If you simply want to gain an appreciation for the tremendous diversity of wedding celebrations in America, or to get a sense of the customs held in common by so many different peoples from around the world (crowns, capping ceremonies, money dances, binding of couples, or the universal symbols of food, flowers, and colors), you'll enjoy reading through all of them.

African
- Bride wears veil of braided hair over her face as a symbol of modesty
- Guests, officiant, members of the wedding party may wear traditional African robes
- Drums and Congo music
- Wine is poured on the ground as a libation to the gods
- "Jumpin' the Broom": the couple jumps over a floral-covered broom as a symbol of jumping over the threshold into domestic life; seems to have originated as an old Gypsy custom in the American South

American Indian (Navajo, the largest nation in existence)
- Traditional bridal dress woven in symbolic colors: white for the east; blue for the south; yellow (orange) for the west; and black for the north
- White corn meal symbolizes the male; yellow corn meal symbolizes the female; before the traditional ceremony, the meals are combined into a corn mush and put into a Navajo wedding basket; the couple will share this during the ceremony to symbolize the bonding in marriage
- Water as a symbol of purification and cleansing; the bride and groom have a ceremonial washing of hands, to wash away past evils and memories of past loves

- Silver concho belt and turquoise and silver jewelry are worn by both the bride and groom; jewelry is a shield against hunger, fatigue, illness, bad fortune, etc.
- Traditional time of day for a wedding: the evening
- Ceremonies take place facing east, the direction of the future

Amish
- Bride wears new, but ordinary, Sunday clothing
- Weddings are held exclusively after the harvest, usually midweek
- Wedding invitations are delivered by hand through personal visits

Arabic
- Bride's hands and feet are decorated with henna in a lattice pattern
- Wedding wail; women mourn the loss of the bride
- Bride wears an ornate caftan
- Arabic *oud* music, pigskin drums, singers, and rhythmic dancing
- Receptions are segregated by sex
- Middle Eastern foods are served

Armenian
- Elaborate, prewedding dressing ceremony for both the bride and the groom

Cajun (Louisiana Creole and Acadian)
- Traditional foods: boudin sausage, cracklins, jambalaya, spicy peppers
- Guests may bring hundreds of homemade cakes to the reception; there might be a "cake room" in the bride's home
- Jazzy wedding march in which everyone falls in line behind the bride and groom, dancing and waving handkerchiefs (napkins)
- Single women dance on overturned washtubs

Caribbean (English speaking)
- Traditional wedding cake is a dark fruitcake made with candied lime, orange, and citron, heavily steeped in rum; cake may take various shapes, such as gardens, houses, etc.
- Calypso music, steel drums, guitars
- In Bermuda, the couple plants a tree for posterity

Chinese
- Ceremony of obligation, in which parents and elders are honored
- "Lucky money" is presented in red envelopes
- Red and gold are traditional colors of happiness and wealth; invitations, decorations, gift wrap may all be in red
- Firecrackers are set off in the couple's path to ward off evil spirits
- Bride typically changes outfits three times over the course of the celebration

Croatian
- Capping ceremony, in which the mother of the bride replaces the bridal headpiece with the kerchief of the married woman

Cuban
- Spanish-Cuban music
- Couple gives gifts to every guest
- Guests throw rice as symbol of fertility
- Guests bring gifts to the wedding, and a very large table is set up for them

Czech
- Male sponsor (*starosta*) presents the bride to the groom outside of the church and admonishes the couple to fulfill their duties to each other
- After the ceremony, ribbon is stretched across the road in the way of the couple; money must be paid (by friends and family) for the couple to pass
- Bridesmaids pin a spring of rosemary on each guest as a symbol of fertility and constancy
- Bride's veil is removed and replaced by a matron's bonnet and a housewife's apron while the guests sing the wedding song, *"Pisen Svatebni"*

- Traditional foods: sauerkraut, klobase (sausage), apple strudel, kolaches (fruit-filled rolls)
- A baby is put on the marriage bed as a symbol of fertility

Dutch
- Hope chest for the trousseau
- Couple plants pips of lily of the valley in their garden after the wedding; when they come up each year, the couple is supposed to renew their love

East Indian
- Red (or vivid pink) is the traditional color of celebration and happiness
- Bride's hands and feet are painted in an elaborate henna pattern
- Groom may wear white silk brocade suit, sword, and turban
- Bride's face is decorated with jewels (now that she is about to be a married woman)
- Garlands of white flowers are used to welcome and honor family members
- Groom may wear veil of flowers over his face and turban (*sekera*) on the way to the ceremony
- Wedding procession of family and guests from the groom's home to the bride's home to the ceremony
- Money is presented in baskets by the family (brothers, cousins, etc.)

English
- Couples in the countryside traditionally walk to church with their wedding party on a path strewn with orange blossoms
- Bride carries a ribbon-bedecked horseshoe on her arm for good luck
- Bridesmaids are young girls, not women; there are no groomsmen
- Weddings are traditionally held at noon; afterward, there is a sit-down luncheon, called a "wedding breakfast"
- Wedding cake is a rich fruitcake topped with marzipan; the top tier is called a "christening cake" to be saved for the birth of the first child

Filipino
- Men and women dancing with the bride and groom respectively will pin money to their clothes; often there is a competition between the family and friends of the bride and those of the groom to see which group can give the most
- Giant bell made of flowers containing two doves is hung high above; at the end of the reception, the couple pulls ribbon streamers and releases the birds as symbols of everlasting love
- Traditional foods include roast pig
- Rice is thrown at the departing couple as a symbol of fertility and prosperity

Finnish
- Capping ceremony, in which the bridal headpiece is replaced by the matron's linen cap

French
- "Wedding armoire" (hope chest) hand-carved with symbols of wealth and prosperity, for the bride's trousseau
- *Coup de mariage,* or wedding cup from which the couple drinks
- Laurel leaves are strewn outside of the church for the couple's departure
- *Chiverie*—the wedding-night prank of clanging pots to interrupt the nuptial couple; the groom must invite the mischief makers in for refreshments
- Everything is white: flowers, dresses, decorations, etc.

German
- *Polterabend* (wedding eve party), in which the couple is teased and dishes are broken
- *Fraktur* (wedding contract)
- Traditional foods: a sumptuous feast including spiced wine and beer, and marzipan confections
- Horse-drawn carriage, with black horses, for the bride/couple to and from the church
- "Roping the couple" with red ribbons and garlands of flowers across their exit; the bridegroom must

buy their ransom with money or with the promise of a party
- During the wedding day, or immediately thereafter, guests are invited to the couple's home to inspect the gifts and furnishings; the groom offers guests schnapps

Greek
- Candy-coated almonds wrapped in tulle (symbols of fertility) are given as favors to guests
- Traditional circle dance with handkerchiefs at the reception (called *Kalamantiano*)
- *Koumbari* (wedding sponsor) selects and pays for the favors for guests
- During the ceremony, the chanter admonishes the groom to honor the bride, and she lightly taps the groom on the foot for emphasis
- Traditional foods: stuffed grape leaves, lamb kabobs, Greek wine

Haitian
- Guests bring gifts (not money) to the wedding
- Wedding cake is not cut at the reception, but later at the bride's home
- Ceremony is in French (Creole)
- Traditional foods: *griots* (fried pork), *lambi* (conch), and black rice

Irish
- Couple is showered with flower petals for good luck
- *Claddagh* (wedding ring) fashioned with two hands holding a heart with a crown above; when hands are worn facing in, the bride is married
- Dances at the reception include lifting the groom in a "jaunting car" (chair) to present him as a married man
- Traditional foods: ham and cabbage

Italian
- Candy-covered almonds to symbolize the bitter and the sweet of marriage are presented to guests; sometimes, sugared almonds, called *confetti,* are tossed at the couple

- *Busta* or wedding bag is used by the bride for gifts of money
- *Tarantella*, a traditional wedding circle dance, is done at the reception
- Bridal parties are large and wedding feasts are sumptuous

Japanese
- Bride wears an elaborate wedding costume of a white silk jacquard kimono woven with the groom's family crest, a special wedding wig, and ornaments
- Reception includes toasts, speeches, and stories about the couple told by older honored guests
- *Kyogashi*, colorful candies made in the shapes of flowers or themes, are signs of celebration
- Red is the joyous, lucky color
- Traditional foods: *sekihan* (red rice), *kombu* (kelp), *tai* (sea bream—the ceremonial fish of happiness), and *sake* (rice wine)
- Bride changes out of her wedding costume for the banquet

Jewish
- Bride attends the *mikva*, or traditional ritual bath, to mark the transition from single to married life
- *Ketubah*, or marriage contract, often artistically rendered and preserved in the couple's home
- *Chuppah*, or wedding canopy, under which the couple is married
- Stomping of the glass by the groom at the end of the ceremony
- *Hora*, or traditional dance of celebration at the wedding reception
- "Kosher" or "kosher-style" foods: no pork or shellfish; meat and dairy products cannot be served at the same meal

Korean
- *P'yeback* ceremony, an intimate family ritual in which the bride is welcomed into the groom's family

- Bridal makeup includes a red spot on each cheek (to ward off evil spirits)
- Bride wears a multicolored silk gown with white sleeves and a black silk crown; groom wears "court" dress
- Dates, *ju jibes* (red dates), and chestnuts are symbols of fertility and happiness
- Bride may change out of her wedding costume one or more times during the celebration

Laotian

- Couple's wrists are bound with string during the ceremony (*Siquan*)
- Bride has a special wedding hairstyle
- Groom wears a blue-and-white prayer stole (for praying to Buddha)

Latin American

- Father of the bride holds a covered dish of coins, a symbol of the dowry
- Flower girl and ring bearer are dressed as miniature versions of the bride and groom
- Wedding sponsors (*padrinos* and *madrinos*) have a part in the ceremony

Lithuanian

- Couple passes under a bridge of embroidered sashes on the way to the church
- After the ceremony, the couple receives bread, salt, wine, and honey from their parents; this symbolizes the elements of their lives together

Mexican

- *Lasso*, a figure-eight rope that symbolically ties the couple together during the ceremony
- Blessing of the *arras*, a small chest of gold coins symbolizing wealth and strength; groom may present 13 gold coins to the bride as a symbol of his commitment to support her
- Parents bless their children in the home before the ceremony
- Ceremony conducted in Spanish
- *Padrinos* (godparents) have a special role in the ceremony
- Couple has a special kneeling pillow

- *Mariachi* (guitar/vocal) music
- Traditional foods: rice, beans, tortilla dishes, chicken, and beef

Pakistani

- Bride arrives in a bridal tent
- Couple uses a mirror to reflect upon each other for the first time

Polish

- *Rospleciny*, the prewedding undoing of the bride's maidenly braids by the bridesmaids
- Children put ropes or chain across the couple's way; the best man pays them off
- Bride wears a laurel wreath
- Couple is welcomed by their parents with bread and salt, symbols of prosperity and bitterness
- Guests give the couple money; the bride gives guests gifts in return
- Traditional music are polkas and mazurkas
- Make-believe kidnapping (bridal capture) is acted out at the reception
- Traditional foods: veal roasts, pickled herring, noodles, and the wedding bread (*szsyzka*) in the shape of pine cones, animals, or flowers

Polynesian (Fijian and Samoan)

- Traditional bridal dress of tapa cloth (made of paper mulberry bark)
- Fresh flower leis are worn by the bride and groom
- Samoan bride wears a *Palefuiono*, a crown made of mother-of-pearl shells
- Fijian bride carries a *Tabua* (whale's tooth), the highest gift a Fijian can have or give
- After the ceremony, both families gather to display and exchange gifts
- Traditional foods for feasting: yams, roast pig, fish

Puerto Rican

- Money dance in which money is pinned to the bride's dress by each man she dances with
- Doll dressed like the bride is covered with *capias* (pins with the couple's names and wedding date); the pins are distributed to guests as favors
- Rice is thrown as a symbol of fertility

Russian

- Champagne glasses are thrown to the floor after toasting; if they break, the couple can expect future happiness
- Nuptial couples may tie a doll on their wedding car to indicate they want their firstborn to be a girl, or a bear if they want it to be a boy

Scandinavian

- Bride wears an elaborate, jeweled wedding crown (Vasa crown) as a symbol of innocence
- Traditional wedding toast, *skoal,* with a specially brewed beer
- Fiddlers and horns accompany the wedding procession to the church
- Birch boughs are traditionally used for decoration
- "Care cloths" are held over the couple as they receive their final blessings (to protect from evil influences)
- *Brundlaupskling,* the traditional Swedish bread-like wedding cake
- Traditional foods: a *smorgasbord* of artfully arranged hot and cold foods

Scottish

- Groom wears a traditional kilt
- Bagpipe music accompanies the procession and recession

Slavic (Bulgarian, Albanian, Yugoslavian)

- Mother of the bride pours water over the steps before the bride leaves home to symbolize the washing away of her old life
- Traditional circle dance, the *horo,* is done at the reception
- *Koluk* is the traditional, bread-like wedding cake

Slovak

- Capping ceremony, when the bride's wedding headpiece is replaced by the *cepec* (a crocheted cap)
- Guests wear bits of live green rosemary pinned to their lapels
- Bride wears (and keeps) an elaborately embroidered wedding shawl

- Guests dance the *csardas* at the reception
- Music includes polkas and waltzes
- Foods include poppyseed pastries

Ukrainian

- Parents present the couple with religious icons before the ceremony
- *Korovai,* the traditional wedding bread, is decorated with symbols
- Part of the celebration is hanging the matchmaker in effigy
- *Umykannia,* or mock capture of the bride, is reenacted at the reception

Vietnamese

- Wedding celebration consists of two parties: one given by the groom's parents and one by the bride's
- Groom's family makes an offering of clothes, money, and jewelry to the bride
- Bride wears red or pink, colors of happiness
- Flowers and decorations are also red
- During the preparation, serving, and enjoyment of wedding foods, families and guests must be very careful not to break a dish or glass; to do so is a bad omen indicating a breakup of the marriage

Theme Weddings

The couple arrives in a horse-drawn carriage to trumpet fanfare. The colors are green and gold; the symbols are pineapples for hospitality. Attendants carry circular brass hunting horns adorned with garden flowers; the wedding feast consists of grilled fowl and Virginia baked hams. The scene is Colonial Williamsburg, but the wedding is being held 1,500 miles away.

Why? Because the bride went to school in Virginia and worked in the White House.

The couple arrives by boat; the colors are blue and white. Male attendants wear navy blazers and white slacks, and the women wear white linen afternoon dresses with sailor collars. The wedding fare is seafood, and the reception site is a yacht club with a view of the bay. Compasses, sextants, and flags are worked into nautical arrangements.

Why? Because the couple met through sailing and will honeymoon on a yacht.

The couple arrives on a tractor; the setting is a ranch and the fare is barbeque and beer. Colors are red and white plaid, and the music is country. It's an old-fashioned, down-home celebration for several hundred of the couple's nearest and dearest.

Why? Because the families are ranchers who also own farm equipment franchises. The couple's lives will be built on the family businesses.

Bridal consultants around the country report the increasing popularity of theme weddings. No doubt part of this trend is because couples are older and more sophisticated, and have a more refined sense of entertaining style. But, part of the trend may also be attributed to the desire for unity and commonality, the need to emphasize the interests, occupations, or occasions that have brought a couple together.

Those who choose a theme wedding want it to be distinctive and memorable, and they will go to great lengths—and expense—to ensure that the affair is authentic in every way. Jo Anne Gregoli, a New Jersey wedding consultant, has become known for doing theme weddings. She admits that she spends "hours in the library" researching periods, details, and accoutrements. "Couples who want a theme wedding don't want a carbon copy of other celebrations," she says. "They want to be different, they want to be original, and they want everything just right."

The only limitation to a theme wedding is your own imagination, and the resources you have to devote to it. The only consideration is that you be consistent without going too far; it is not the number of thematic details you employ to establish a motif, but the distinctiveness of those you choose. Here are some ideas.

Seasonal/Holiday Themes

A candlelight ceremony is followed by an evening reception in the great hall of a European-style castle. Attendants are all in formal black; the bridesmaids carry an assortment of vivid fall mums trailing sequined ribbons. Wrought-iron hurricane lamps line the entry to the mansion.

Inside, more dramatic sophistication. Tables are covered with ecru lace over orange liners and set with shimmering black china. Centerpieces feature sequined masks and satin pumpkins amid a profusion of mums; chocolates boxed in gold and black mark each place. This Halloween wedding is being held on October 30.

You don't need a special excuse to take advantage of the spirit of the holiday or season that surrounds your wedding date, nor will it be especially difficult to establish the motif. Flowers, colors, and symbols of major holidays are universally recognized, so a few touches here and there are all you need. For those celebrated when Mother Nature dons her own best dress for the occasion, such as seasons of fall foliage or spring profusion, don't forget to choose spectacular locations that will show off nature's attire and underscore your theme.

Autumn Harvest/Halloween/Thanksgiving
Winter Wonderland/ Christmas
New Year's/Mardi Gras/Carnivale
Valentine's Day
St. Patrick's Day
Spring Garden/Easter
Summer Seashore
4th of July

Period Themes

The scene is the historic Deco District of Miami Beach. The couple pulls up in front of one of the hotels in a 1933 Stutz Super Bearcat replicar, and the bride emerges looking "Vogue-ish" in a classic, fitted charmeuse gown. She carries a cascade of white calla lilies.

Inside, wedding colors harmonize with the muted mauve and grey decor. Tables are done in pink and silver, and floral arrangements, also featuring calla lilies, stretch upward out of sleek ceramic vases. A jazz combo provides mellow background music. The bride and groom, and their guests, have been transported back to a different time.

Sometimes couples choose an historic period theme for their weddings because the era is one for which they both share a special interest or affection. Sometimes, a ceremony or reception site cries out for the complement of period detail that could enhance it, such as a Medieval castle or a Victorian mansion. Just as often, though, the idea of a period wedding comes about because the bride finds a gown in a retro look that she simply can't resist.

Susan Lane, a West Coast bridal designer whose signature has become the recreation and restoration of authentic period gowns, says she "can't think of anything worse than walking down the aisle in an ordinary wedding dress, in an ordinary location, accompanied by ordinary music and ordinary fare." Lane has done her share of studio work for wedding sequences on several major television shows, but the popularity of her dress designs among a growing number of "ordinary brides" proves that many women share her philosophy about the fantasy of this once-in-a-lifetime event.

Go with it. If you feel you were born too late, or if you simply want to capture the romance of a bygone era on your very real and present day, combine a little research with some creative imagination to recreate your dream.

Medieval
Elizabethan
Revolutionary or Federal (American)
Victorian
The Roaring Twenties
Art Deco
The Sixties

Occupational Themes

The wedding couple are both professors in the Boston area. For their reception, they choose an historic townhouse restaurant on Beacon Hill. The high ceilings, book-lined walls, and library paneling reflect the atmosphere in which the couple spend their lives. Books provide a thematic motif, as a matter of fact, and each guest receives one as a favor—a miniature volume of famous love poems with the couple's names and wedding date embossed in gold on the cover. Wedding colors are white and gold, in contrast to the dark woods of the interior; floral arrangements are traditional white roses; tables are set with stately crystal and gold-edged plates.

Formal or informal, serious or light, shared occupations make a wonderful wedding theme because you can count on recognized symbols to carry it: the gavels and scales for lawyers, instruments for musicians, easels and palettes for artists, etc. When you can't rely on symbols, rely on talent and creativity instead: architects, for instance, might design beautiful graphics for their invitations and placecards, and integrate repeating angles and curves in imaginative floral arrangements; real estate brokers might have a cottage wedding cake and issue "deeds of happiness" to their guests.

It may take some thought to come up with appropriate motifs and symbols of your profession to use at your wedding, but when you share a love of the same work, the challenge of finding them will be fun.

Location Themes

The wedding and reception are held at a winery in the Sonoma Valley in northern California. Rustic surroundings are accented with natural "wine" colors: deep purple, burgundy red, and light green. Flowers and ribbon garlands drape the rails of outdoor terraces, and table arrangements incorporate clusters of sugared grapes and miniature casks. Every guest takes home a split of wine, custom-labeled with the couple's names and wedding date.

Where you live or where you choose to be married can create its own natural theme. So can a honeymoon destination. Take advantage of the ambiance of the location to provide distinction and originality for your wedding celebration.

Kentucky Bluegrass
Southern Plantation
Western Ranch
French Quarter
Country Farm
New England/Cape Cod
Mountain Lodge
Island/Tropical
World Capitals — Paris, London, New York, etc.

Other Themes

Almost anything the two of you enjoy and know something about can become a theme for your wedding. Consider special interests or hobbies: photography; skiing; sailing and boating; golfing or tennis; racing (horses, cars, etc.); scuba diving or swimming; fishing, hunting, camping, or mountain climbing; flying, skydiving, or gliding; and collecting, just to name a few.

Remember, too, that an ethnic wedding is, in its way, also a theme wedding, especially if the ethnic culture is not your own. Weddings held in a Spanish mission, for instance, will assume an ethnic character even though the couple may not share that particular heritage.

The best thing about a theme wedding is that it makes for a great and memorable party, something many modern couples want their wedding celebration to be. As long as you don't altogether lose sight of the reason the party is being held, there is nothing wrong with wanting your event to be remembered in a special way.

A Theme Wedding How-To

There are several books available devoted exclusively to the subject of theme weddings (see Appendix), and many others on general entertaining that will give you holiday and seasonal suggestions for menus, flowers, and decorations. You might also look to the write-ups of society weddings and gala community or charity functions in large city newspapers for ideas. Once you have a theme in mind, do some research in your library. Histories of costume and fashion, art and architecture, and furniture and decorative design will be especially helpful. Of course, you can also enlist the help of a professional consultant or party planner.

Finally, beyond the colors, flowers, symbols, locations, guest favors, and attire that can enhance your theme, don't overlook the following areas for possibilities:

• Menus—period, ethnic, or regional foods, service, and beverages;

• Music—period pieces and types of instruments;

• Entertainment—hired sketch artists, magicians, singers, etc.;

• Invitations, wedding programs, and placecards—all thematically designed;

• Costumes—for waiters, valets, even hired performers;

• Wedding transportation—unique conveyances.

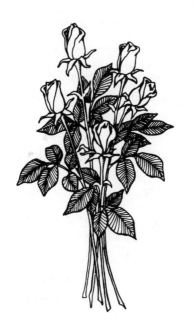

CHAPTER 17
Honeymoons and Honeymoon Weddings

The honeymoon is the trip of a lifetime that is not to be missed, even if only a few days are spent a few miles away from home.

Modern Bride research reveals that 98 percent of all couples take a honeymoon, the average length of which is eight days. And, while most modern couples do enjoy making their honeymoon plans together, most grooms still feel that it is their primary responsibility to take charge of details and finances. Call it romance, call it chivalry, call it love.

Planning Your Honeymoon

You need to start discussing honeymoon plans as soon as you've set the date, time, and location of your ceremony and reception. Depending on the time of the year you're getting married, and the popularity of the getaway spots you're considering, you could find some destinations booked up months in advance. Furthermore, peak travel periods (summer, Thanksgiv-ing, Christmas holidays, spring breaks, etc.) will affect airline costs and availability, as well as prices of accommodations.

Generally, ski resorts, both here and abroad, and sunshine spots (south Florida and the Caribbean) will be in high season during winter or early spring. Accommodations will have to be secured well in advance, and you are likely to pay peak season rates. During the summer, northern beaches and resort areas and most European countries are in peak season, affecting their availability and prices.

Obviously, if you can choose an off-season destination, you may be able to save some money or to upgrade your accommodations to a level of luxury that you might not otherwise be able to afford. Off-season rates at some Caribbean resorts, for instance, are as much as 50 percent less in the summer. In addition, stores, restaurants, hotels, and places of interest will be less crowded, and tickets for air and rail, rental cars, sight-seeing trips, and special excursions will all involve less hassle and be easier to book.

As you discuss your wedding date and your budget, it's worthwhile considering the advantages of off-season travel among your list of honeymoon possibilities.

Determining Your Honeymoon Style

There's something magical about the phrase "going away," and people do change when they get away from their usual routines and environment. The workaholic suddenly becomes a beach blob, barely able to sit up long enough to eat a sandwich; the laid-back, easygoing type turns into an inveterate sightseer, feverishly marking off every visited site in the guidebook as if making notches in the handle of a sixgun.

The point is, if the two of you haven't traveled together before, you could be in for some surprises, not only about what each considers an ideal destination, but also about how each would choose to spend the time there. True, the honeymoon is not an ordinary vacation and, true, the two of you will probably want to spend more time and do more things together than you would, say, if one of you were simply accompanying the other on a business trip. But you don't have to spend every waking moment together on your honeymoon, nor do you have to participate in every single activity the other enjoys just because it's there. Then again, to book a golfing package at a world-class resort when only one of you plays the game would hardly be a choice conducive to a memorable honeymoon for you both.

There will be plenty of years and plenty of trips ahead when each of you will compromise your own vacation choice for the sake of the other's enjoyment, but this trip has to be planned with an eye toward the interests, activities, and atmospheres that will help you both relax and feel your best. So you need to be completely honest with each other about what kind of traveler you are and what expectations each of you has for this all-important, once-in-a-lifetime getaway.

QUESTIONS TO ASK

1. How well do we travel? Does one of us suffer from motion sickness, airplane anxiety, undue stress over changes and delays? Do we easily adapt to new surroundings, or does it take several days to feel comfortable? Do we enjoy new cultures or find them stressful? Does either of us have any special dietary or medical needs that must be considered?

2. What is the perfect setting? Do we like warm climates, cool climates? What do we find romantic: snow-covered mountains, fields of wildflowers, swaying palms, or bustling cities? Do we like big hotels, small hideaways, or unusual lodgings with a distinctive character and charm?

3. How do we like to spend our days: golfing, tennis, sailing, scuba diving, skiing, biking, hiking? Are we avid sightseers, enthusiastic shoppers, lazy beach bums?

4. How do we like to spend our nights: dining in gourmet restaurants, dancing in discos, gazing at the stars, or eating take-out food in front of the TV? Do we expect to "dress for dinner," or are we only planning to pack jeans and T-shirts?

5. How secluded do we want to be from others and the world? Do we want a choice of organized sports and sight-seeing activities and a chance to meet other people through them, or are we just as content to take off and explore on our own? Do we want to really rough it, or would we be lost without a television, telephone, radio, and air-conditioning?

6. Are we looking for a one-place, one-price, all-inclusive, something-for-everybody destination, or do we want to customize our own itinerary and leave room for serendipity? Do we want to go to a place and stay put for the duration, or do we want to travel around from place to place in a general area?

7. How much can we afford to spend on this trip, and what financial priorities can we give our travel agent to help us plan within our budget?

About Honeymoon Packages

The world is a big place and, unless you're seasoned travelers, honeymoon choices can seem overwhelming. Plus, if you've never taken a trip together before, how can you be sure of what will please you both?

It was just that quandary and just that need that led to the origination of the "all-inclusive" honeymoon resort in the Pocono Mountains as far back as the 1940s, and the idea has been going strong ever since. In fact, the Poconos, the 2,400 square miles of northeastern Pennsylvania, identifies itself as "The Honeymoon Capital of the World" and still draws over 200,000 honeymooners each year. In more recent years, all-inclusive resorts—where one price covers meals, entertainment, sports, and accommodations—have become increasingly popular in Jamaica and around the Caribbean.

Honeymoon packages are another popular option. They offer an economical way to travel to the most romantic destinations worldwide. Packages typically include airport transfers (transportation to and from the hotel), a selection of romantic room accommodations, all or most meals, use of sports and recreational facilities and equipment (sometimes even instruction), evening entertainment, and complimentary gifts, parties, and/or other special events that appeal to newlyweds. There also may be available options, such as sight-seeing tours and day trips, rental cars, bikes, or mopeds, or even "exchange dining" privileges with other nearby restaurants and hotels.

Although not billed specifically for honeymooners, most airlines, major hotels, and tour companies (such as American Express) also offer their versions of "packages" that are marketed to a broader segment of the traveling public. Thus, you will find golf packages, ski packages, and all sorts of other special-interest categories, as well as fully escorted and semi-escorted tours. Accommodations, transfers, some meals, and some special events/facilities/equiment are usually covered in a basic price, and air and rail transportation, motorcoach, and/or car rentals are often included, as well.

The advantage to booking any sort of a travel package, honeymoon or otherwise, is that most of your major expenses are locked in and paid for before your departure. It is easier to budget for your actual trip then because you know exactly what additional expenses (those items not included in the package) to plan for. Most of the time, you will get more for your money in a package because tour operators have purchased airline seats, hotel rooms, etc., in bulk and can pass those savings on to you.

Packages are not a value, however, when they don't meet your basic needs or when they include many amenities you don't want or aren't likely to use. Once you start paying additional fees to upgrade rooms or meals, to book optional tours or additional cities, or to extend your stay beyond the designated length, you may easily negate any advantage the package offered. Likewise, if the plan includes all meals but you end up eating out at a different restaurant every night, or if it provides diving lessons and expensive equipment but you never quite seem to be able to make it to the instruction sessions, then you have clearly wasted money.

The best advice is to talk to your travel agent and to thoroughly investigate any package, and read the fine print, *before* putting down the deposit. Note the following when discussing any travel package:

- Air carriers: not all package transportation is provided by regularly scheduled airlines; this can prove an inconvenience, especially when they reserve the right to cancel at any time. Some charter airlines are respectable and reliable; others are literally "fly-by-night." Check into it.
- Upgrades: most packages assume standard rooms and standard meals; ocean views, suites, gourmet entrees, etc., may be obtained at a surcharge, but surcharges can add up. Investigate.
- Additional charges: usually, the following are not included in packages: liquor and wines, gratuities, government taxes and hotel surcharges/service charges, room service, valet and laundry service, telephone calls, airport departure taxes.

• Cancellations and restrictions: There can be stiff penalties if your plans change. Know what the terms are before you sign, and ask your travel agent about trip cancellation insurance.

About Cruises

A cruise is truly a hassle-free way to travel, which is a good reason for its popularity. Cruise ships are the floating equivalent of full-service, self-contained resorts. Everything you could possibly want, and more, is on board: fabulous restaurants and nightclubs, movie theaters, beauty salons, shops and stores, saunas and fitness centers, swimming pools, game rooms, casinos, sun decks, libraries, hospital facilities, on-board telephones, radios, business centers, and VCRs. You'll find everything you could possibly want to do on the larger ships: recreation and sports, including fishing, diving, and water activities; dining, dancing, and entertainment; sight-seeing, on-shore excursions, and other organized activities. And everything is just a short walk from your cabin door!

Ship sizes, facilities, and destinations vary, of course, along with the cost of passage. Some cruises are geared to special interest groups or organized around a theme. You can take a cruise for as little as three days, or you can sail around the world for months. It's all up to you.

As with a resort package, the biggest advantage to booking a cruise is that you know exactly how much it's going to cost and you pay for it in advance. The only additional costs are tips, drinks, and shore excursions.

If you think a shipboard romance is just the way to get your marriage started, then ask your travel agent to fill you in on the wide variety of cruise packages and destinations. You may also write to Cruise Lines International Association for more information (see Appendix).

Choosing a Destination

Forty-six percent of all honeymooners choose destinations on the mainland United States, and when they do, Florida is the most popular choice. Little wonder: beautiful beaches, hot Miami nightlife, Disney World and Epcot Center, the Florida Keys, Kennedy Space Center, the Everglades. And, as if that weren't enough to offer, it's just a hop, skip, and a jump—or a cruise—from there to the blue-green waters of the Bahamas and the Caribbean, to Puerto Rico, the U.S. Virgin Islands, and all the other wonderful, tropical fantasy islands. The Caribbean, in fact, is the most popular honeymoon destination outside of the continental United States.

Besides the natural beauty and honeymoon fun these destinations offer, they have another advantage, particularly for those who live in the eastern half of the country: they are easily accessible. Florida, the Caribbean, Bermuda, and cities in eastern Canada are all serviced by regularly scheduled flights and can be reached in a matter of hours. This is an important consideration for couples who don't want to spend a significant portion of their honeymoon time getting there and back. Many couples also go westward to California, the Rockies, and all points in between.

Couples in the central and western United States also choose Hawaii and Mexico for much the same reasons that Easterners choose the Caribbean. (Actually, Mexico gets her fair share of honeymooners from all over because of her "dead center" location.) Again, regularly scheduled flights make these romantic destinations attainable with a minimal amount of travel time and fatigue. And Hawaii and Alaska have the additional advantage of allowing you to be away from the continental United States in exotic locales while feeling comfortable with the same language and the same currency in your own country.

What Florida, the Caribbean, Hawaii, and Mexico all have in common are temperate climates and lush natural landscapes. There are many things to do and see, or not, as the mood strikes you, and plenty of opportunities to be alone or to be with others, as you wish. They are affordable destinations, with a wide variety of packages in all price ranges, because their popularity with travelers has made them so. They are romantic destinations because the tourist industries in these places have made it their business to see that honeymooners are treated as VIPs.

This is not to say that there aren't many, many other wonderful honeymoon destinations at home and abroad where you will find the utmost in accommodations and service, and from which the two of you will bring home blissful memories. You will have to talk about what you want, and how much time and money you have to spend, and you will have to research the possibilities.

Look through the travel pages of bridal magazines together, and order the wealth of free tourist information available there. Browse the travel section of your favorite bookstore, or go to the library. Many have travel videos you can check out so you can get a firsthand view of any destination you might be considering. You can also write the local tourist boards in those cities or countries you're considering.

When you've finally narrowed down your choices, probably six to eight months in advance of your wedding, you're ready to go to a travel agent and get all the facts and details.

Working with a Travel Agent

A travel agent's services are free of charge because they earn their income on commissions paid from airlines, cruise lines, and others. An experienced travel agent can save you time, money, and aggravation, because he or she knows what's available and has instant access, through computer, to every necessary bit of current information.

You'll want to find an agent who is experienced in personal and vacation travel planning (as opposed to business travel), who will take the time to meet with you and help you explore all the options, and who seems sensitive to your needs and wants. As always, the best recommendations are those obtained by word-of-mouth from satisfied customers. Look

for agents who are members of the American Society of Travel Agents (see Appendix).

The travel agent should be able to arrange it all, from airport transfers and sight-seeing tours, to rental cars and rail tickets. A good one will also be able to give you lots of advice regarding packing, currency exchanges, legal requirements, even a recommended list of things to see and do. The agent may charge you for long-distance telephone calls or telexes if your arrangements are very involved, and you may be asked for a deposit if your itinerary is complicated or unusual.

Be sure to reconfirm all your arrangements about a month before departure, and check and double-check all vouchers, passes, and tickets when you pick the packet up.

Legal Requirements of Travelers

For domestic destinations, a current driver's license and at least one other form of identification (usually a credit card, which you would hardly leave home without) are all you'll need. As a newlywed, your license, credit cards, traveler's checks, and any other legal documents you obtain before your marriage will carry your maiden name.

One caveat: note that in some locations you must be at least 25 years old to rent a car. Ask your travel agent.

Passports

A United States passport will be needed as proof of identity and citizenship in most foreign countries except Canada, Mexico, and some Caribbean countries. (Ask your travel agent to be sure.) If you are going abroad on your honeymoon and you don't already hold a valid U.S. passport, you'll need to apply for one at any of the 13 U.S. passport agencies around the country, at a county clerk's office, or at a major post office.

TRAVEL TERMS YOU SHOULD KNOW

Airlines

nonstop—a flight directly from one place to another with no stops in between.

direct—the plane may stop along the way, but you will not have to get off.

connecting—you will have to change planes somewhere along the way to reach your destination.

Car Rental

drop-off or intercity charge—a fee for returning the vehicle in a town or location other than the one in which it was rented.

unlimited mileage—you pay for the gas and are not charged per mile.

additional insurance—car rental agencies always offer optional collision and damage insurance, for which you pay an additional fee, but you may already be covered; some major credit card companies, such as American Express, provide that coverage automatically when their cards are used to pay for the rental. Check to see. You can also check with your personal insurance agent to see whether your own homeowner's policy includes liability coverage for car rentals.

Hotels

double-occupancy rate—a per person price based on two people sharing the room.

double-room rate—the quoted price of the room (to be occupied by two people).

guaranteed late arrival—confirms your reservation no matter what time you arrive; typically, the room must be paid for in advance, by either cash or credit card, to hold the room past 6 or 7 P.M. If you don't arrive, you will have paid for the room anyway.

standard—the basic accommodation.

first class—usually a notch above the basic.

superior—top accommodations.

suite—a bedroom with a separate sitting room.

(Note: Terminology for the levels of accommodations may vary from one hotel to another; sometimes, they are designated by bed configuration: twin, double, queen, king. In Europe and Asia, you may have to specify a "matrimonial bed"—they don't usually understand what we mean by double, queen, etc.).

oceanfront—directly facing the ocean, but not necessarily with direct beach access.

ocean view—you can see the water from somewhere in your room, but it probably won't be the panoramic view you expected.

Meal Plans

AP (American Plan)—includes breakfast, lunch, and dinner.

MAP (Modified American Plan)—includes two meals, usually breakfast and dinner.

EP (European Plan)—includes no meals.

BP (Bermuda Plan)—includes a full breakfast.

Continental breakfast—includes a light breakfast of rolls, jam, and coffee or tea.

Miscellaneous

vouchers—issued by the travel agent to be exchanged for meals, rooms, tours, etc.

duty free—means the items are sold free of that country's taxes; if you exceed your U.S. Customs limit, however, you will have to pay U.S. taxes upon return to this country.

options—those opportunities, like sight-seeing or sports activities, that are available at extra cost and not included in your package price.

rate of exchange—the current equivalent of foreign currency to U.S. dollars; generally, you get the best rate of exchange at a bank, the worst at a hotel.

traveler's checks—just like real money (which you have turned into the issuer) but safer than carrying cash because they carry your signature; the best known are American Express, but there are many others accepted worldwide. You should each have some of your own.

You'll need two duplicate, recent photographs of a specific size, an official birth certificate (obtained from the department of health where you were born), and an application (available at the post office). The fee for a new passport is $55, plus a $10 execution fee, and $55 for a renewal. Delivery will take about four weeks from date of application, so be sure to allow plenty of time.

Since your passport will be in your maiden name, avoid delay and confusion by ordering your plane tickets in your maiden name, as well. Once obtained, a U.S. passport is a vitally important, extremely valuable document. Carry it on your person, never in your luggage, and store it in the hotel safe when not needed during ordinary daily activities. Some countries have special rules about the handling of passports of foreign visitors. Ask your travel agent so you'll know what to expect. Also ask about immunizations, visas, or any other special requirements for your particular destination.

U.S. Customs

U.S. Customs' regulations are among the most stringent in the world, but getting home after a trip abroad doesn't have to be a hassle if you'll follow a few simple rules. On the flight home, you'll be given a custom's declaration form to fill out. Be honest! You don't want to start your married life as an amateur smuggler.

You are allowed up to $400 worth of purchases per person tax free returning from most parts of the world. If you return directly or indirectly from a U.S. insular possession, American Samoa, Guam, or the U.S. Virgin Islands, you are allowed a $1,200 exemption; from one of 24 beneficiary countries, including the Bahamas, Barbados, and the British Virgin Islands, you'll be allowed a $600 per person exemption.

You will have to make a written declaration of each item you've purchased and its value. If you are over your personal exemption, you will have to pay taxes on the goods over the limit upon re-entry. (If you're a big shopper, it's wise to keep a running list of your purchases and an envelope with sales receipts with you in your purse so that the task of customs declaration isn't overwhelming.) Purchases in duty-free shops and gifts (yes, even wedding gifts from friends abroad) are subject to tax when the total exceeds the personal allowance.

Whether or not you exceed the exemption, but especially if you do, it's a good idea to plan ahead for re-entry by packing all your purchases together in the same bag. That way, if a Custom's inspector asks to see the items on your list, you won't have to search through the contents of open bags to find them. And, officials may very well ask. If they do, don't be offended; just comply and try to keep a sense of humor about the whole re-entry procedure. After all, Customs inspectors are just doing their jobs.

In order to claim your exemption, you must have been out of the country for at least 48 hours (not so for the U.S. Virgin Islands and Mexico), and not have claimed an exemption from another trip abroad within the last 30 days. The goods must have been purchased for your own use; gifts may be shipped to family and friends, but only up to $100 per person per day. Anything shipped home to yourselves will fall under your personal exemption allowance.

If you are 21 or older, you will be allowed to bring in one liter of alcohol and one carton of cigarettes duty free (from the U.S. Virgin Islands, you're allowed one gallon of alcohol and 1,000 cigarettes; from Puerto Rico, you simply show receipts of the taxes you paid). The United States Department of Agriculture is very strict about the importation of plants and vegetables. If you purchase any to bring home, be sure that they have been sealed and approved for re-entry.

The U.S. Customs Service puts out a booklet, "Know Before You Go," that explains customs procedures and exemptions in more detail. Booklets are available at most passport offices and through travel agents.

Budgeting Your Honeymoon

The average couple spends between $3,000 and $4,500 for their honeymoon. Distance traveled and the duration of the stay are the biggest cost factors. Obviously, some couples spend a great deal more, while others spend a great deal less. What you choose to spend, and how you choose to spend it, will have much to do with the travel style to which each of you is accustomed.

But, even if your usual style is the economy motel just off the interstate, your honeymoon is the one time in your life when you ought to splurge for the best accommodations you can afford. Chances are you will be spending more time than ordinary travelers in your room, and a lovely decor with a beautiful view really does make a difference. There are, however, ways to cut costs without cutting niceties.

Ways to Save on Honeymoon Costs

- Take advantage of package deals.
- Travel off-peak and off-season.
- Steer clear of major cities; spend your time in the countryside and smaller towns.
- Consider a destination within driving distance.
- Look into condos/rentals where you can prepare some of your own meals instead of always eating out.
- Weigh the advantages and disadvantages of fewer days in a higher style to a longer stay in a more modest style.

If you're planning to pay for your honeymoon together, you'll be able to determine your priorities and establish your budget early on. Many couples open a joint bank account into which they contribute a few dollars each pay period for their trip. Remember that beyond the basic transportation, accommodations, meals, and sightseeing, you'll still need spending money for incidentals; ideally, each of you should have some discretionary funds of your own.

Travel Tips

Experienced travelers know that the secrets to "having a good trip" are to travel light, travel loose, and be prepared for the unexpected. Keep that advice in mind as you look over the following tips:

- Don't pack more than you need and leave some room in your luggage for purchases of keepsakes, a great way to relive honeymoon joy.
- Check with your travel agent to see if you need to bring a hairdryer or any other small appliances, or if you'll need adapters for them to work, before you drag them along; luxury accommodations and ship cabins often have everything you'll need there.
- Take one carry-on in addition to your handbag and keep all important and valuable items in it and with you: jewelry; passport, visa, or other documents; tickets and vouchers; list of all credit card and traveler's checks' numbers; list of major contents of luggage; important names, addresses, and phone numbers; prescription drugs (in their bottles with their labels); birth control items; camera; extra glasses or contacts and/or a prescription in case you lose your one pair; some makeup; a washcloth; fresh underwear (in case your luggage is lost); a small snack, crackers, or candy bar, to abate hunger.
- Store your valuables in the hotel safe.
- Pack a basic first-aid kit with essentials such as antacids, aspirin, antiseptic, Band-Aids, and suntan lotion.
- If you tend toward motion or air sickness, get a prescription from your doctor or use an over-the-counter remedy; take it 30 minutes *before* you get on the plane, ship, etc.
- If you're traveling abroad, watch what you eat; many travelers can be severely affected by changes in water and agricultural products. If sanitation in the country is questionable, avoid untreated water (even ice cubes), uncooked vegetables and unpeeled fruits, salad greens, and dairy products and foods that contain them. Don't eat rare or raw meat, or anything you can't identify.

The Honeymoon Budget Worksheet

Transportation

Major (air, rail, ship, car)	$_____
Airport limo	$_____
Tips	$_____
Gas	$_____
Tolls	$_____
Departure taxes	$_____
Rental cars	$_____
Taxis	$_____
Total Transportation	$_____

Accommodations

Daily rate x number of days	$_____
Daily taxes & surcharges x day	$_____
Tips and gratuities	$_____
Services (laundry, hairdresser, etc.)	$_____
Total Accommodations	$_____

Meals (per couple)

Breakfast at $_____ per day x number	$_____
Lunch at $_____ per day x number	$_____

Dinner at $_____ per day x number	$_____
Snacks and refreshments at $_____ per day	$_____
Total Meals	$_____

Entertainment

Sports/rentals	$_____
Theaters/concerts	$_____
Sight seeing/tours	$_____
Nightclubs/discos	$_____
Total Entertainment	$_____

Extras

Shopping/gifts/souvenirs	$_____
TOTAL	$_____

The Unexpected

Add 10 percent to the above for all the things you haven't thought of 10% =	$_____
GRAND TOTAL	$_____

• Limit exposure to the sun, especially in tropical areas or near water where the rays are exceptionally strong. Number 15 or higher sunscreen is a must.

• Relax and have a fabulous time!

Tips on Tipping

For those who haven't traveled a great deal, here are some guidelines on what is generally expected. It's a good idea to leave home with $10 to $20 in one-dollar bills, because you'll go through most of them in tipping on departure and arrival. Customs vary among countries and localities, so use your judgment to adjust these guidelines and, remember, tips should be based on the quality of service given.

• Taxi driver: 15 percent of the fare and 25 to 50 cents per bag.

• Limousine driver: 15 percent of fare (for complimentary service, 50 cents to $1 a bag).

• Porter: $1 a bag.

• Bellhop: 75 cents to $1 a bag.

• Doorman: 75 cents to $1 for hailing a taxi.

• Parking attendant: $1.

• Waiter/waitress: 15 to 20 percent of bill.

• Waiter on a meal plan: $5 a day.

• Wine steward: 5 percent of wine cost.

• Maitre d' or captain: $5 to $10, depending on special treatment.

CONTEMPORARY SOLUTIONS

SOCIOECONOMIC

❦ *You and your fiancé have planned a modest wedding, and no honeymoon, because you have invested everything you have in a new condo. But now, as the wedding draws closer and you feel more and more like you need a vacation, you've begun to regret your frugal decision. Would it be totally irresponsible to take some sort of honeymoon, what with so many other necessary expenses?*

It's never irresponsible to take care of yourselves. You deserve a honeymoon, and the one you take doesn't have to necessarily break the bank.

Ask your employers for a week off after the wedding for your "honeymoon," but don't tell anyone where you're going. Plan a two- or three-day stay in a nearby resort or elegant hotel, just far enough from home to give you that getaway feeling, but not far enough to incur big travel expenses. Then, spend the remainder of your honeymoon week in your condo, maybe just puttering around together or shopping for your new home. You'll be left alone, since no one will know you're home, and the few days of privacy will provide a relaxing, romantic transition to your married life.

PERSONAL

❦ *A classmate has found out about your wedding and, guess what? She's getting married the same weekend, and she and her fiancé are even planning a honeymoon to the Caribbean, just like you. She thinks it would be fun to honeymoon together, but you don't agree. In fact, she's bugging you so much about your plans that the two of you are considering changing destinations.*

It's hard enough to travel with other people when you're close and know each other well, never mind when you aren't especially friendly and your spouses haven't even met.

Don't let your classmate's intrusion make you change what you and your fiancé have already agreed upon. Firmly inform her that you and your fiancé are keeping your travel plans private because, after sharing the wedding with everyone else, the only togetherness you want is to be alone with each other. And don't worry about running into her; the Caribbean is a big place.

PERSONAL, CULTURAL

❦ *Your fiancé studied in Europe, and you've never been there. He can think of nothing more romantic than the pleasure of showing it to you. He is willing, able, and eager to pay for the whole grand tour for your honeymoon as his wedding gift. You know he means well, but the itinerary exhausts you. How can you tell him this without hurting his feelings?*

The two of you have to be honest about your visions of what a honeymoon ought to be. For openers, your approach might be to explain that, while you'd love nothing better than "the grand tour" with him as your personal guide, you'd prefer to make that trip when you're well rested and have had the time to properly prepare for it—neither of which is the case now. Suggest starting a "trip to Europe" fund and making plans to celebrate your first or second anniversary there.

In the meantime, if it's European history, tradition, culture, and language that have him so enthralled, consider going to just one place in Europe or look for a honeymoon destination with an unusual history and a distinctive culture of its own to explore. Mexico, Canada, certain islands in the Caribbean or the Pacific, and even Hawaii readily come to mind. Any one of these places would offer leisure and learning at the same time.

- Concierge: $2 to $5, depending on the special service he or she performs for you (obtaining tickets, tours, etc.).
- Coat check: $1.
- Beach/pool attendant: $1 per day.
- Tour guide: $2 to $4 for the day.
- Chambermaid: $2 to $4 a day, depending on what they do besides make up the room.
- Cruise personnel: check with the steward to see what's appropriate; some lines have specific policies.

Note: Always check your bill. Many restaurants and clubs add an automatic 15 to 20 percent gratuity, so that additional tipping is not necessary.

Honeymoon Weddings

Pat Gleason has a happy job. As Director of Romance at the Westin Maui Hotel in Hawaii—yes, that is her official title—she spends most of her days, and many of her nights, making nuptial arrangements for couples who want to start their honeymoon with their wedding in their ideal, dream location. Ninety percent of the weddings she plans are for couples from the mainland United States; many of them have never been to Hawaii before.

Honeymoon, or fly-away, weddings have become increasingly popular among marrying couples. For some, who have busy careers and sophisticated lives, the idea of getting away with a few close friends and family to an exotic location where they can celebrate their wedding and enjoy a wonderful vacation without months of planning time is the perfect solution. For others, who can't afford both the large wedding and the fantasy honeymoon they've always

dreamed about, combining the two makes economic sense.

Still others have more personal, private reasons. Sandy and Mike had been an "established couple" for six years. Both are career professionals who intended to get married some day, but never quite got around to it. Finally, they set a date, but soon after that Mike's father died and Sandy's mother became seriously ill.

"It would have killed my mother not to have been involved in gigantic wedding plans," Sandy explained on a beach on St. Croix the morning of her wedding. "I couldn't put that burden on her. Then too, Mike and I got to thinking that everyone considered us a couple already, that we already have a completely furnished home, and that we really didn't want all our friends and relatives to go to the expense of a wedding on our behalf."

So, Mike and Sandy flew to the Caribbean to be married. They were planning to give a party of their own, probably a "surprise" party to announce their marriage, when they got home.

Honeymoon weddings offer romantic, practical solutions for couples dealing with family difficulties, limited budgets, and unreconciled intermarriage situations. Many hotels and resorts in Hawaii, Jamaica, the U.S. Virgin Islands, and on other Caribbean islands now have staff experienced in making such arrangements via long distance. In addition to their already beautiful landscapes, many resorts have also constructed gazebos, glassed-in terraces, and other special environments for wedding ceremonies. The cost, for example at Jamaica's Sandals resorts, can be as low as $250 for a simple wedding ceremony, including the officiant, flowers, cake, and champagne.

Most, as at the Westin Maui, offer several "packages" for from two to ten people. Typically, the packages include the location, flowers, musicians, officiant, and photographer, and a champagne and wedding cake reception, along with suite accommodations for the wedding night. Arrangements are made with the wedding/catering coordinator, and long-distance conferencing assures that you get the colors, flowers, music, officiant, etc., that you prefer. If you come with a large group of friends, the resort will also give you group rates on rooms and services for your guests, as well as upgrading the ceremony and reception to meet your needs.

Gleason meets her couples at the airport, smooths the way for all licensing requirements (no waiting period in Hawaii), and finalizes all wedding choices with the couple the day they arrive. She shepherds her couples through every step of the process and begins to feel like they're family. "I want to be sure every couple has the wedding of their dreams," she says, "the wedding they deserve."

Contact major honeymoon resorts for more information on the fly-away wedding. Look for a director with whom you have an easy rapport to guide you through the local marriage requirements and make all the necessary legal, ceremonial, and reception arrangements for you. If your hearts are set on marrying in a locale with lots of red tape, such as some European countries or Mexico, be sure to hire a consultant who is experienced in dealing with complicated arrangements (see "Marrying Abroad" in Chapter 7).

Appendix: Helpful Sources

CHAPTER 2

Rings

American Gem Society
Dept. MB
5901 W. Third Street
Los Angeles, CA 90036

International Gemological Institute
580 Fifth Avenue, Suite 620
New York, NY 10036
(212) 398-1700

Engagement & Wedding Rings: The Definitive Buying Guide for People in Love, by Antoinette Matlins, Antonio Bonanno, and Jane Crystal. (S. Woodstock, VT: Gemstone Press, 1990).

CHAPTER 4

Planning

For a list of members in your area, write:
Association of Bridal Consultants
200 Chestnutland Road
New Milford, CT 06776

The Bride's Book of Beautiful Ideas, created and published by Hallmark Cards, Inc., (Kansas City, MO).

Limousines

For referrals of limousine companies in your area, call:
National Limousine Association
1-800-NLA-7007

CHAPTER 5

Receptions

Places: A Directory of Public Places for Private Events & Private Places for Public Functions, by Hannelore Hahn and Tatiana Stoumen. Available directly from:

Tenth House Enterprises, Inc.
Caller Box 810, Gracie Station
New York, NY 10028
(212) 737-7536

Can You Say A Few Words? How To Prepare & Deliver Wedding, Birthday, Anniversary Toasts, by Joan Detz. (New York: St. Martin's Press, 1991).

CHAPTER 6

Wedding Dressing

"Formalwear Guide" available for $1 and a SASE from:

International Formalwear Association
401 N. Michigan Avenue
Chicago, IL 60611

CHAPTER 7

Special Situations

For interracial couples:
New People Magazine
P.O. Box 47490
Oak Park, MI 48237

For referrals to rabbis who will marry interfaith couples, contact:
Rabbinic Center for Research & Counseling
128 East Dudley Avenue
Westfield, NJ 07090
(201) 233-0419

For officiants for interfaith couples from local societies, contact:
Clergy for Ethical Culture
(212) 873-6500

For interpreter service agencies in your area, write or call:

Registry for Interpreters for the Deaf
8719 Colesville Road, Suite 310
Silver Springs, MD 20910
(301) 608-0050

For help in marrying abroad, contact:
Weddings Around the World
5944 Luther Lane, Suite 302
Dallas, TX 75225
1-800-648-7000

CHAPTER 8

Preparation

For information on premarital enrichment programs:
Prepare/Enrich, Inc.
P.O. Box 190
Minneapolis, MN 55440
1-800-331-1661

For a booklet, "Guide to Finding a Personal Financial Planner," and for names of CPAs who are personal financial specialists in your area, contact:

American Institute of Certified Public
Accountants
Personal Financial Planning Division
1211 Avenue of the Americas
New York, NY 10036
1-800-966-7379

For a booklet, "How To Select a Qualified Financial Planning Professional," and for names of recommended CFAs in your area, call or write:

Institute of Certified Financial Planners
7600 E. Eastman Avenue, Suite 301
Denver, CO 80231
1-800-282-7526

For the location of a Consumer Credit Counseling Service office near you, call:

National Foundation for Consumer Credit, Inc.
8611 Second Avenue, Suite 100
Silver Springs, MD 20910
1-800-388-2227

For a booklet, "Your Legal Guide to Marriage & Other Relationships" (publication #235-0005; cost $2.50 plus $1 shipping and handling), call or write:

American Bar Association
Order Fulfillment
750 N. Lake Shore Drive
Chicago, IL 60611
(312) 988-5000

CHAPTER 9

Marrying Again

For premarital preparation programs, contact:
Prepare MC (married with children)
P.O. Box 190
Minneapolis, MN 55440
1-800-331-1661

For counseling, membership, newsletter, and resources in your area, contact:

The Stepfamily Foundation, Inc.
National Headquarters
333 West End Avenue
New York, NY 10023
(212) 877-3244

CHAPTER 10

Parties

Bridal Showers: 50 Great Ideas for a Perfect Shower, by Sharon E. Dlugosch and Florence E. Nelson. (New York: Putnam Publishing Group, 1984).

Wedding Occasions: 101 Party Themes for Wedding Showers, Rehearsal Dinners, Engagement Parties & More! by Cynthia Lueck Sowden. (Brighton, MN: Brighton Publications, Inc., 1990).

CHAPTER 12

Ceremonies and Protocol

Service Etiquette, 4th ed., by Oretha D. Swartz. (Annapolis: Naval Institute Press, 1988).

With These Words . . . I Thee Wed: Contemporary Wedding Vows for Today's Couples, by Barbara Eklof. (Holbrook, MA: Bob Adams, Inc., 1989).

CHAPTER 13

Flowers

Ask to see *Wedding Album* at Telaflora member florists, or for other brochures and information, contact:

Telaflora12233 West Olympic Blvd., Suite 140
Los Angeles, CA 90064
(213) 826-5253

CHAPTER 14

Music

For *The Bridal Guide*, 3rd ed., by Pamela Thomas (440 musical selections) available for $12.95 through:

The American Guild of Organists
475 Riverside Drive
New York, NY 10115
(212) 870-2310

For *Celebrating Marriage: Preparing the Wedding Liturgy*, by Paul Covino, Ed., avialable for $5.95 from:

National Association of Pastoral Musicians
Pastoral Press
225 Sheridan Street West
Washington, DC 20011
(202) 723-1254
(202) 723-2262 (fax)

"The Wedding Album," by RCA Victor, a collection of wedding music, available in music stores or by calling 1-800-221-8180

CHAPTER 15

Photography and Videography

For a brochure, "What Every Bride Should Know About Wedding Photography" and a list of professional photographers and videographers in your area, send a SASE to:

Professional Photographers of America
Membership Dept.
1090 Executive Way
Des Plaines, IL 60018

CHAPTER 16

Ethnic and Theme Weddings

For further research and information on their traveling exhibit, "Ethnic Weddings in America":

The Balch Institute for Ethnic Studies
18 S. 7th Street
Philadelphia, PA 19106
(215) 925-8090

Wedding Plans: 50 Unique Themes for the Wedding of Your Dreams, by Sharon Dlugosch. (New Brighton, MN: Brighton Publications, Inc., 1989).

CHAPTER 17

Honeymoons

For a variety of consumer pamphlets, including tips for packing and traveling abroad, send a SASE to:

American Society of Travel Agents
Dept. FC
1101 King Street
Alexandria, VA 22314
(703) 739-2782

For a brochure, "Answers to Most Asked Questions About Cruising," send a SASE to:

Cruise Lines International Association
500 Fifth Avenue, Suite 1407
New York, NY 10110
(212) 921-0066

About the Authors

Cele Goldsmith Lalli, Editor-in-Chief of *Modern Bride* magazine, is a nationally recognized authority on the American bridal market, wedding planning, and etiquette, and the changing needs of today's bride. She travels throughout the country speaking with brides and grooms about all aspects of wedding, honeymoon, and first-home planning. She writes a wedding etiquette column in *Modern Bride* and is a frequent guest on television and radio shows.

Mrs. Lalli, who began her publishing career in science fiction and then moved into the women's service field, has been an editor with *Modern Bride* since 1965. She was appointed editor-in-chief in 1980. A graduate of Vassar College, she lives in Stamford, Connecticut, with her husband, Michael. They are the parents of two daughters.

Stephanie H. Dahl is the author of one other bridal book and over 250 articles on marriage and family that have appeared in regional, national, and trade magazines. She has been a regular contributor to *Modern Bride* for the past 10 years. She holds an M.A. in English from the City University of New York, is a member of the Authors Guild and the National Federation of Press Women, and is a three-time winner of national writing awards.

Mrs. Dahl lives in Stamford, Connecticut, with her husband and son, where she also teaches writing.

Index

213

Notes

This section is for you to write down notes on places you visit, ideas you have, dresses you like, or anything else you need or want to remember. It is divided by chapter to help you keep it all organized. Some chapters are omitted from this list if there are no or few notes needed on the subject covered.

Chapter 2.   It's Official!

Newspaper Announcements

Wording of Announcement:

_____

_____

_____

_____

_____

_____

_____

Newspaper Name	Date Sent	Date Appeared

_____

_____

_____

_____

_____

_____

Chapter 3.   The Wedding Budget

Item	Approximate Amount	Who Will Pay

Chapter 4.   Developing a Wedding Plan

Ceremony Location

Site	Officiant	Notes

Wedding Consultants

Name	Phone	Fee	Recommended By

Setting the Date

Possible Dates	Available for Ceremony?	Available for Reception?

Wedding Transportation

Company	No. and Type of Vehicles	Price

Chapter 5.   Reception Options

Reception Location

Site	Contact	Est. Price	Notes

Wedding Cake

Baker	Description	Price

Seating

You can sketch your seating chart in this area, trying different arrangements.

Chapter 6. Wedding Dressing

Bride's Dress

Store and Contact	Description	Price

Bride's Veil

Store and Contact	Description	Price

Bride's Accessories

Store and Contact	Description	Price

Bridesmaids' Attire

Store and Contact	Description	Price

Groom's and Ushers' Attire

Store and Contact	Description	Price

Chapter 8. Preparing for Marriage

Religious Preparation

Requirements   *Date Completed*

_____

_____

_____

_____

_____

_____

_____

_____

_____

Legal Preparation

Requirements   *Date Completed*

_____

_____

_____

_____

_____

_____

_____

_____

_____

_____

Chapter 10.   People, Parties, and Things

Selecting Your Attendants

Name	Address	Phone	Clothing/Shoe Sizes

Gift Ideas for Attendants and Family

For Whom?	Description	Store	Price

Chapter 11.   The Honour of Your Presence

Invitations

Wording of Invitations

_____

_____

_____

_____

_____

_____

_____

_____

_____

Resource	*Description*	*Price*

Chapter 12.   Ceremonies and Protocol

Ceremony Ideas

_____

_____

_____

_____

_____

_____

_____

_____

Wording of Vows

_____

_____

_____

_____

_____

_____

_____

_____

_____

_____

Fees to Be Paid

Name	Function	Amount	Who to Handle

Readings, etc.

Reading	Speaker	Date Copy Given

Chapter 13.   Flowers: The Language of Love

Florist	Phone #	Est. Price	Notes

Chapter 14.   Music: The Sound of Love

Music for the Ceremony

Musical Piece	Vocalist	Musicians

Music for the Reception

Name and Phone #	Price	Notes

Song List for the Reception

Chapter 15. Capturing the Moments: Photography and Videography

Photographers

Name and Phone	Est. Price	Notes

Videographers

Name and Phone	Est. Price	Notes

Chapter 16. Romantic Roots: Ethnic and Theme Weddings

Ethnic/Theme Wedding Ideas

_____

_____

_____

_____

_____

_____

_____

_____

_____

_____

_____

_____

_____

_____

_____

_____

_____

_____

_____

_____

_____

Chapter 17.   Honeymoons and Honeymoon Weddings

Honeymoon Ideas

_____

_____

_____

_____

_____

_____

_____

_____

Travel Agency   *Contact/Phone*   *Notes*

_____

_____

_____

_____

Other Honeymoon Notes

_____

_____

_____

_____

_____

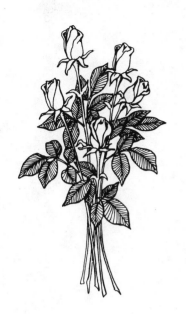

Your First Wedding Gift

On the following pages are special offers brought to you by:

Modern Bride

Marriott's Frenchman's Reef and Morning Star Beach Resorts

Islands in the Sun

American Express

Home Furnishings Council

We hope these offers and information make planning your wedding, honeymoon and new life together a little easier and much more pleasant! For your convenience, they can be photocopied.

Best wishes from us all.

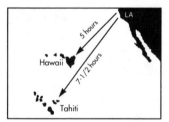

For your *FREE* copy of the HAVEN home decorating guide, visit your local home furnishings store that displays "heart and home," the sign of The Home Furnishings Council.

HOME
FURNISHINGS
COUNCIL

One of these gifts is worth more.

Personal Wedding Question For The Author?

Call 1-900-884-CELE

(95¢ per minute)

and leave your question. You will get a personal written response from Cele Lalli, Editor-in-Chief, Modern Bride magazine within four to six weeks. When you call, wait for operator instructions and then ask your question. You can also subscribe to Modern Bride.

Call 24 hours a day every day from any touch-tone phone on any long-distance carrier. If under 18, parental permission required. Call length is determined by topic discussed.

Modern Bride
M A G A Z I N E

MODERN BRIDE Magazine, Cahners Publishing Company, 249 West 17th Street, New York, NY 10011

For your *FREE* copy of the HAVEN
home decorating guide, visit your local
home furnishings store that displays
"heart and home," the sign of
The Home Furnishings Council.

HOME
FURNISHINGS
COUNCIL

The American Express® Gift Cheque—
The *more* thoughtful and elegant way to give the gift of money

The American Express Gift Cheque is like a universal gift certificate that can be used to buy anything, just about anywhere. With its own gold envelope and gift card for your personal message, a Gift Cheque is the perfect expression of how much you care.

A great gift for weddings, anniversaries or any other occasion. American Express Gift Cheques are available at most local banks, credit unions, American Express Travel Service Offices, and AAA Clubs.

AMERICAN EXPRESS Gift Cheques

If you love the book, don't miss the show!

"Getting Married - A Modern Bride TV Special"

This award-winning show looks at all aspects of everybody's favorite tradition — Getting Married! You'll be enchanted by the latest bridal fashions, romantic weddings and exotic honeymoons. You'll laugh and cry as other brides-to-be and their parents share their feelings and experiences. And you'll be captivated by host Debbye Turner (Miss America 1990) and co-host Cele Lalli, Modern Bride Editor-in-Chief and co-author of *Wedding Celebrations*.

**Watch for "Getting Married — A Modern Bride TV Special" around Valentine's Day, 1993.
Check local listings under FAM (Family Channel) and our ad in TV Guide.**